Business and Legal Forms
for
Theater

Business and Legal Forms

for

Theater

Charles Grippo

Allworth Press, New York

08   07   06   05   04   5   4   3   2   1

Published by Allworth Press
An imprint of Allworth Communications, Inc.
10 East 23rd Street, New York, NY 10010

Cover design by Derek Bacchus
Page composition/typography by SR Desktop Services, Ridge, NY

Library of Congress Cataloging-in-Publication Data
Grippo, Charles.
    Business and legal forms for theater / by Charles Grippo.
        p.   cm.
    ISBN 1-58115-323-6
    1. Theater—Law and legislation—United States—Forms.
  I. Title.

KF4296.A65G75   2004
344.73'097—dc22
                                                2003023471

Printed in Canada

For my brother Dean

Table of Contents

PREFACE

Shortly after the publication of my previous book *The Stage Producer's Business and Legal Guide*[1], a producer offered to present my play *A Wife's Tale*. After we negotiated mutually satisfactory terms, he asked me to prepare the production license between us. He said he wished he had a lawyer on retainer to prepare his contracts, but his company (a nonprofit) could not afford one.

With *The Stage Producer's Business and Legal Guide*, I set out to address the producer's need for legal advice in virtually everything he does. As an entertainment lawyer, playwright, and producer, I recognized, however, that few producers have the financial resources to keep legal counsel at hand.

The producer's request set me to thinking that, in addition to the material contained in *The Stage Producer's Business and Legal Guide*, theater people also need a ready source of legal forms. Most industry contracts contain fairly standardized terms and conditions. Often, only the specific items—like salaries and royalty rates—need to be negotiated between the parties. And these are based on the individual needs and facts of each particular situation. However, if producers and artists could have access to the essential agreements, well, at least half the work has already been done. Negotiations could be boiled down to the issues in the particular case. Both parties would save considerable time and money.

HANDY CHECKLISTS

Form agreements also serve as handy checklists, reducing the possibility that some particular issue might be overlooked. (As an attorney, I have found that those matters that the parties forget or fail to consider in negotiating their contracts are usually the ones that boomerang back later, to everyone's detriment.) Thus, by having the issues most common to each type of theatrical agreement codified in written form, both parties can make educated decisions before they enter into any contract. And any contract they sign is bound to be more comprehensive. Even if a dispute later arises, a court will better be able to decide what the parties intended to do.

EASILY UNDERSTOOD

However, I wanted to create agreements that would be readily understood by nonlawyers. I decided the language should be everyday English—colloquial, whenever possible. I wanted readers to be able to sit with the form in front of them and comprehend each term, as a theater person would, not as a graduate of Harvard Law School. The language and practices are those of the performing arts world.

THEATER

I define *theater* very broadly—in fact, perhaps *performing arts* is the better term. These forms are designed for anyone in the business of live stage shows—not just plays, but also music concerts, dance, stand up comedy, performance art, etc. Yes, some forms are particular to one type of theater or the other, but most, with a bit of modification, may be used in whatever area of the performing arts in which the reader participates.

For example, in chapter 3, Form 4, I have provided a standard booking agreement. This agreement is usable for producers of stage plays, stand up comedians, rock groups, symphony orchestras, dancers, ventriloquists, lecturers—well, you get the idea.

---

[1]Also published by Allworth Press.

EASILY ACCESSIBLE

I also wanted the forms to be handy and easily accessible. All of us are at a premium for time. It's not only that we want things quickly, but, in this busy world, we *need* things quickly. So, in addition to publishing the forms in printed text, we are also making them available on CD-ROM. You simply download the appropriate form, fill in the blanks, and, as fast as your printer can work, you have hard copies for each party to sign.

To make the book even more useful, I have provided a discussion of each agreement preceding the form. That will give you a clearer understanding of the legal ramifications of what you are doing.

HARD TO FIND

Producers and artists often need contracts that are hard to find. The truth is, you can't go into your local stationery store and purchase a form for a "Real Person Release," like you might buy an apartment lease. Yet many transactions in the theater cry out for readily accessible models theater people can use. Hence in this book you will find song licenses, stage combat contracts, nudity riders, and other difficult to find, yet practical agreements.

LEGAL DISCLAIMER

Okay, here's the disclaimer, folks.

Although these forms are useful in virtually every situation, no book of legal forms can—or should—take the place of an attorney's judgment, knowledge, and experience. I mean, let's face it. A dentist can write a book that tells you how to do a root canal. But would you really want to do your own?

Therefore, if, after reading the introductory material and the forms themselves, you still have questions, see an attorney. Just as I don't take responsibility for the do-it-yourself root canal, I also disclaim responsibility if you don't follow this advice and you lose your spouse, children, mother-in-law, and your great-aunt Gertrude in a legal dispute arising out of these forms. Use common sense.

One other suggestion: You will get a great deal more out of this book if you use it in conjunction with *The Stage Producer's Business and Legal Guide*. Yes, I admit to certain self-interest. However, the two books combined offer you a wealth of knowledge and understanding of performing arts law.

And that's why you're interested in the first place, isn't it?

HOW TO USE THIS BOOK

1. Read each paragraph of each form several times. Take your time. Make sure you understand each provision thoroughly. It may be easier to read the text version before you work with the electronic version of the form, so you can be sure you are using the right form.

2. All of the forms are fill-in-the-blanks.

3. The provisions in the forms are based on standard industry practice. However, standard industry practice varies according to the kind and level of production you are contemplating. For instance, standard industry practice for actor's contracts for Broadway shows are governed by extremely detailed contracts negotiated between Actors' Equity Association and the League of American Theatres and Producers. Since Broadway productions are capitalized in the millions of dollars, the standard Broadway actor's contract contains terms on a scale much greater than a non-Equity summer stock theater in Nebraska could possibly afford. Nonetheless, all producers and artists have many of the same concerns, regardless of their level of production.

Therefore, I have attempted to craft generic contracts that address those concerns, while still allowing the parties flexibility to negotiate their agreements within available resources.

4. Just as Broadway's union contracts represent the mere minimum terms which each party extracts from each other, the terms of the contracts in this book call for the mere minimums. Parties can—and should—always attempt to better the proffered terms.

5. Standard industry practice is not ironclad. One can always modify practice in contract negotiations.

6. Use these forms only as starting points for your discussions with the party with whom you hope to contract.

7. Wherever pronouns call for a particular gender—that is, "him" or "her"—it goes without saying you should simply pick the appropriate pronoun to describe the particular party to the contract.

8. For many terms, alternative possibilities are available. These alternatives are set off by brackets: [ ]. Consider each alternative carefully. Pick the one which best satisfies both parties.

GENERAL CONTRACT PREPARATION ADVICE

1. Contrary to popular opinion, most contracts do not need to be notarized to be enforceable. The confusion stems from the fact that some legal documents (such as deeds for the conveyance of title to land) do require notarization.

2. It is a good idea before you fill in the blanks to think carefully about what you want to say. Prepare several drafts of the information, using the principles enumerated in this section, until you have a draft that clearly states your agreement.

3. Be as specific as possible. Generalities lead to misunderstandings, disagreements, and eventually the need for a judge's intervention and interpretation. Specifics set forth exactly the agreement the parties have reached—or, elicit a response of "No, that's not what I meant." In the latter case, it is easier to redraft a provision until it says what each party really did intend. Be precise and concise.

4. Do not approach contract negotiations as an adversarial process. That is a sure way to create antagonism, which can lead to a disruption of the relationship. Whatever kind of performance or production you are contemplating, theater is a collaborative art. While a certain amount of disagreement is natural in any such process (and may sometimes even lead to better work), too much tension can destroy an otherwise promising project. It is not wise—and, depending on the circumstances, may even be downright stupid—to begin any theatrical enterprise with a civil war over the contract negotiations. You may think coming into the ring fighting will get you a better deal; in most cases, it will not. In fact, it may not get you a deal at all. If you really, absolutely, cannot negotiate without a chip on your shoulder, fire in your eyes, and a snarl on your lips, perhaps you'd better rethink whether you even want to enter into a deal

with the other party. Or it may be best that you turn the negotiations over to a lawyer or agent.

5. Although most terms in any kind of contract are negotiable, a number are not. For example, producers and publishers routinely expect even the biggest name playwrights to warrant (guarantee) that the work is original with them and does not infringe on copyrighted material owned by anyone else. This is reasonable. Producers and publishers do not want to leave themselves open to costly copyright infringement suits. In any event, it is foolish and a complete waste of everyone's time to haggle over the nonnegotiable terms.

If you are—or hope to be—a professional, learn what the industry standard is. Find out what the common, nonnegotiable terms are. Expect them. When you see them in your contracts, accept them, and instead focus negotiations on those terms that are flexible.

This is not to say, however, that even nonnegotiable terms can never be negotiated. Sometimes, while you must accept the basic concept, you can tweak the wording. In the above example, you may be able to limit your liability under the personal warranty. The producer may let you purchase an insurance policy that indemnifies him for any losses, if a court decides your work does violate someone else's copyright. Recognize also that many institutions, such as production companies and publishers, have terms in their contracts that are individual to them. Whether these terms are negotiable—and how far they may be negotiated—is usually a matter of policy within the house. I know of one play publisher, for instance, that will negotiate every term in its contracts, except royalty percentages. Yet I know other play publishers who will negotiate royalty percentages, yet little else.

In short, know your business. Then pick your battles wisely.

6. In connection with picking one's battles, know which battles are important and which are not. Prior to actually entering contract negotiations, regardless of which side of the table you are on, make a list of each point in the contemplated agreement. Think each point over carefully. Which points are important to you? Which are not? What do you hope to achieve out of the entire contract? What do you hope to achieve out of each specific point? What are your most important needs? Where can you give? If it is not important to you to change a particular point—that is, the term seems fair as it is—then it is not worth haggling over.

7. This raises another negotiating strategy. Always ask for more than what you really want. You might be surprised and actually get it. But by asking for more than what you want, you leave room to give a little here so you can get a little more there. If you immediately make your best offer, you are dead in the water if the other party says "No." Then, to save the deal, you have to adjust your best offer in the only direction it can go—which requires you to give up more. But by asking for more than what you want, you have flexibility to come back with a counter-offer if the other party says "No." Here's what I mean: You are negotiating for the production of a new play. If you are the producer, you first offer lower royalties than you really intend to pay. If the author says "No, I want more," you can raise your offer and go on raising it until you reach your limit. If you are the author, your first offer will be for higher royalties than you think you can get. If the producer says "No," you can go on lowering it until you reach the lowest royalty rate you will accept. At some point during these negotiations, both of you will reach a figure that is mutually acceptable.

8. Find out what terms are important to the other party. Usually you can do this by informal discussions. Learn as much as you can about the other party's situation. For instance, if you are about to negotiate with the bargaining agent for a union, it is helpful to understand the current concerns of his membership with your organization. Most likely he will bring them to the bargaining table. This advance knowledge gives you a feel for what demands you can expect and how far you can go with your own demands.

9. Except on very rare occasions, you need not commit to any terms or offers right away. Even a playwright negotiating her very first production has the right to "sleep" on any offer. And she should think over each term carefully. Simply tell the other party politely, "If you don't mind, I'd like to have a day or two to think about your offer." That gives you time to reflect, rather than act hastily and unwisely. It also gives you a chance to consult with colleagues, lawyers, agents, professional associations, and anyone else who might be able to help you reach an informed decision. Similarly, a producer may seek time to consult with his board, business affairs department, or other advisors.

Negotiations often take time. In Hollywood these days, it takes more time to negotiate the deal than it takes to make the picture. (Of course, neither side should take this as a license to unnecessarily prolong the process. No one wins by needlessly holding up a project.) Just take your time so you can make the appropriate decisions.

10. When one or more of the parties is a corporation, an authorized officer should sign all contracts on behalf of the corporation. First, you identify the corporation. Then the officer signs his name, preceded by the word "By," and his specific title. Here's an example:

"In Witness Whereof, the parties have hereunto set their hands and seals this day and date.

New Lincoln Theatre Corporation (Producer)
By: Charles Grippo (President)
William Shakespeare (Playwright)"

LEGAL BOILERPLATE

All contracts contain what lawyers call *boilerplate* clauses. These are fairly standard provisions, which cover what best may be described as generic issues, i.e., the kinds of matters which are usually more exciting to the lawyers than they are to the parties. This is because the lawyers see them as essential, while the parties view them as mundane.

You can have a perfectly enforceable contract without the boilerplate. However, if a dispute between the parties lands in court, the absence of these clauses may force the court to impose its own choices upon the parties—which may not be what they intended or wanted. In addition, in the event of a lawsuit, their absence may necessitate a great deal of legal wrangling over what they should be, which may drag out the case and increase its costs. Trust me. They are as essential to your contracts as any of the money issues.

That being said, not all of them need to appear in every contract. Where they are important, however, I have included them in the particular contract form. Except in the instances noted below, they should not be modified.

To simplify your understanding of these provisions—and because they are so standardized—I will discuss them all at once in this section.

JURISDICTION (LEGAL FORUM)

"This contract will be interpreted under the laws of the State of _____."

This is one of the few boilerplate clauses that the parties may need to negotiate and modify. They must decide whose state laws will govern their agreement. Obviously, this occurs most often when the parties are located in different states. Each party may want the laws of his own state to interpret the contract. This is because governing law usually only comes into play when one party sues the other over the contract.

Although many laws are similar from state to state, an equal number of laws differ greatly. And it is more than the statutory (the laws passed by the state legislature or local governments) laws on the books that differ. The common law (laws created by court decisions and local practice) also differs from state to state. Many courts (and juries) often look more favorably upon residents who are parties to a suit than nonresidents. In a lawsuit, one party may have a better chance of prevailing than the other, depending on which state's laws govern the agreement. These are the subtle, yet often essential, reasons each party has a vested interest in the jurisdiction (the state) under whose laws the contract will be interpreted.

AMENDMENTS

"This contract may not be amended, except by a writing signed by the parties."

This clause prevents either party from coming forward at a later date and claiming that the contract was changed orally. This does not, however, prevent the parties from agreeing, at a later time, to change one or more clauses in the contract. However, both parties must agree in writing to any changes.

This protects both parties from false claims or simple misunderstandings whether the contract was, in fact, changed. In the event of a dispute, the court may refuse to recognize any claimed modifications, unless the party who alleges that the contract was amended can provide proof in the form of a writing signed by both sides. If the parties do discuss amendments, just the fact that they both must sit down and reduce them to writing, which both parties have to sign, forces them to really think about what they are doing.

ARBITRATION

"In the event a claim or a dispute arises out of this contract, which the parties cannot resolve in face-to-face discussions, either party may bring the matter before a party may bring the matter before a member of, and under the commercial rules of, the American Arbitration Association. The arbitration will be binding on both parties. The arbitrator may require the losing party to pay the reasonable costs and attorney fees of the prevailing party. Judgment upon such arbitration award may be entered by any court of competent jurisdiction."

In recent years, arbitration and mediation, rather than the lawsuit, have become an increasingly popular way to settle contractual disputes. Litigation takes time and is costly. Mediation and arbitration are quicker. Expenses may be more easily controlled. Often the parties can resolve their disputes without even the need to call in lawyers, although, even in mediation and arbitration, one is still better served by obtaining legal advice.

In mediation, an impartial third person helps the parties devise their own settlement. The mediator can suggest and advise, but he cannot make a decision that binds the parties.

In arbitration, each side presents his case to a neutral third party—the arbitrator. The parties can submit any proof they believe bears on the issue, but the rules of evidence are not as formal or as technical as required by a court of law. The arbitrator hears both sides and attempts to reconcile the parties on the issues. In the end, the arbitrator decides for one party or the other. The arbitration may be binding, which means the parties have agreed in advance, in their contract, to abide by the arbitrator's decision, or it may be nonbinding or advisory. The contract may also empower the arbitrator to make the losing party pay the reasonable costs and attorney fees of the winner. The parties may also agree that any court may award judgment upon the arbitrator's award.

The forms in this book provide for binding arbitration, but you can modify them to nonbinding arbitration if you wish. And, if you would prefer taking your disputes to court instead of to arbitration, simply strike the clause altogether out of the form you are using.

EQUITABLE RELIEF

There is one other twist to settling disputes. As I indicate below under "Assignability," many contracts in the theater call for personal services. In a personal service agreement one party engages in a transaction with another party specifically because he wants to deal with that party and that party alone. A producer hires a star or a director because that person has a particular talent or celebrity. The same is true when a producer books an act for a particular engagement. If you want to present Elton John in concert, you want Elton John and, of course, so do the patrons who buy your tickets. If Elton John doesn't show up, his fans don't want to see rap star Ham 'N Eggs, no matter how talented he may be.

In such cases, you can sue or go to arbitration and maybe collect money damages. But sometimes money damages aren't enough. Sometimes you need *equitable relief*. This might be an injunction or a court order requiring the particular person with whom you have contracted to perform his obligations under your contract. You will see in Form 4, (Booking Agreement) which is a personal services contract, that in addition to arbitration I have provided the option of the producer seeking equitable relief. I have omitted it from the other forms, but you can modify any of them to include it, if you believe it is an option best for your circumstances.

ASSIGNABILITY

"This contract will not be assigned by either party."

Many business contracts allow one party to transfer his rights (and obligations) to a third party, usually in exchange for a monetary payment. The third party then steps into the assignor's shoes, receiving any benefits due under the contract and performing the assignor's obligations.

However, in the theater permitting assignability is not usually desirable. Theater people desire to do business with each other because the other party possesses capabilities, talents, or other characteristics unique to that person or business entity. Another party just won't do, as I indicated above under "Equitable Relief."

Every actor is a special individual, with her own capabilities, suitability for a role, or other attributes. A producer engages Mary Jones to play Aldonza in *Man of La Mancha* specifically because he believes she is right for his production, whether because of talent, box office draw, or a combination. He does not want Mary Jones to assign her contract to Elaine Smofulberger, who then appears at the half hour call to play the role.

A playwright contracting with Jed Harris to produce her play expects Jed Harris to produce her play. The playwright has determined that Harris shares her artistic vision for the script, as well as possesses the capabilities to actually get the show on, promote it, and otherwise give it every chance of success. She does not want Harris to assign his rights to Leonard Piffle, who may never have produced a show and knows nothing about theater. Therefore, the playwright will demand a "No Assignability" clause in her contract with Harris. (There is, however, an exception to the "No Assignability" clause in playwright/producer contracts, which we will treat separately in chapters 7 and 9, dealing with production contracts.)

Similarly, Harris has agreed to produce Charles Grippo's play because he likes my writing. My voice appeals to him. He does not want to discover on the first day of rehearsal that I have assigned my contract to Fred Hack, who will now do the rewrites.

Theatrical relationships are like marriages. They are very personal. If you promise to marry Fred Freeman, you don't want Boris Grant showing up at the church, because Fred assigned your marriage contract to Boris.

FORCES MAJEURE

Popularly known as the "act of God" clause, this provision was designed to protect each party when an unexpected circumstance occurs, which prevents the party from performing his end of the contract. The event must be something beyond the party's control, such as an act of nature like a tornado or hurricane (hence "act of God"). Other common *forces majeure* include labor strikes, fires, and government orders (such as a curfew during a riot). Such cases may excuse one party from performing without liability to the other.

It is wise to set a time limit as to how long the cause may legitimately prevent the party from performing without liability. During that time period, the agreement may be thought of as being placed on hold. Once that time expires, either the party must perform (if the cause no longer exists) or the other party may terminate the contract, if he so chooses.

The parties should also specify what happens to any advances, deposits, or other money previously exchanged. If the party has partially performed, should he be entitled to retain some or all of the money hitherto paid to him? Or must he refund all or part of it?

NOTICES

It is essential to detail the mechanics of giving notice to each party under the contract. The parties must know with certainty how to contact each other in a proper, lawful manner.

Many lawsuits have been lost because the plaintiff (the suing party) fails to prove he has given proper notice. Proving that one has, in fact, given proper notice, is often essential to pursuing a claim against the other party in court. One is entitled to be properly notified that the other party is making demands or claims against him.

Here's an example: Suppose Booth and Grippo are parties to a contract that requires Booth to notify me of the date I am to appear at his theater for the first day of rehearsal. My address has changed. Booth mails notice of the date of the first rehearsal by regular snail mail to my former address. I do not receive it. Therefore I do not know when rehearsals are to begin. I fail to appear on the designated day. Booth now claims that he sent me notice and since I missed the first day of rehearsal, I am in breach of contract and he does not have to pay me. By the same token, I can claim that I never received the notice. Booth has only his word that he mailed the notice to me at my last known address. Our contract is silent on these issues. Who wins?

These problems are obviated by a notice clause providing for the following:

1. Proper mailing addresses for each party, where notices are to be mailed.
2. All mailings must be done by certified mail, return receipt requested.
3. The effective date of the mailing—the date of mailing itself or the date when it is actually received by the other party. Both may be proved by the certified mail receipts.

Traditionally, certified mail with a return receipt was considered the most effective and easily provable means of giving notice. However, with the proliferation of private delivery services (such as Federal Express) and new technologies such as fax machines and e-mail, restrictions on delivery methods have loosened somewhat. Yet courts still wrestle with problems of whether proper notice has occurred when it is given by fax and by e-mail. With both of these technologies, correspondence can easily be delivered to the wrong parties. However, certified mail and Federal Express require signatures to show they were actually delivered to the intended recipient. Some contracts provide that facsimile transmission and e-mail are acceptable, as long as they are also accompanied by simultaneous ordinary (not certified) snail mail delivery with proof of fax or e-mail transmission. Personally, I believe that since you must also send the notice by snail mail, you might as well go one step further and require certified mail with a return receipt. Until the new technologies prove themselves more reliable, the traditional method seems the surest.

DEATH OR DISABILITY

Many agreements in the theater are personal services contracts. This means that at least one of the parties brings to the arrangement unique talents or abilities the other party desires. The most obvious example occurs when a producer contracts with a star to appear in his production. The star has certain specific abilities, as well as celebrity, no one else possesses. Similarly, a producer may commission a particular playwright to create a brand-new script for his theater. Only that playwright has the particular voice, point of view, writing abilities, and marquee name to serve the producer's purposes.

If the star dies or suffers a disabling illness (like a stroke), obviously the star can no longer perform (in both the theatrical and legal sense). The contract must terminate.

If one party has already paid money to the decedent, the question arises: what happens to that money? In the case of a star, if he has already substantially earned his advance, that is, appeared in the production long enough to use up the advance, the answer is obvious: he (or rather his estate) is entitled to keep the advance. But what happens if he dies or becomes disabled before he has completely used up the advance?

The same questions may be raised in the case of a playwright working under a commission. But we will deal with that issue in the section on commissions.

SUCCESSORS OR ASSIGNS

"This agreement will be binding upon each party's respective heirs, executors, administrators, trustees, successors, and/or assigns."

Despite the non-assignability provisions of the contract, its provisions must, out of necessity, bind anyone who may succeed the original parties. The most common instance occurs when one of the parties dies. His heirs, as well as the administrators of his estate, are bound to its terms. Likewise, they also receive its benefits.

Here's one example: David Belasco agrees to produce a play written by William Shakespeare Junior, called *Hamlet: The Prequel*. After the play is up and running, Junior passes away. The contract does not terminate. Belasco still retains his rights to play the show. Instead, Junior's grant of rights to the producer passes to his heirs, who are bound by them. By the same token, the heirs receive the royalties Junior would have received if he had lived.

Or suppose Belasco contracts with Ebenezer Scrooge to license Scrooge's theater—the Marley House—for his new musical *Belly Button*. During the run of the show, Scrooge passes away. Under the successors/assigns clause, Belasco's license continues under the terms of his contract with Scrooge, whose heirs are still bound.

TIME OF PERFORMANCE

"Time is of the essence."

This clause means that both parties must perform their obligations exactly according to the time constraints of the contract. If a party fails to do so, he will be in technical breach of the contract.

Pay very close attention to this innocuous sounding clause; it can be, in fact, harsh and unforgiving. It says, in effect, that the time limits as set forth in the contract are absolute, unwavering, and of such importance that missing them even by as little as one day causes the entire enterprise to fail. I call these the *sweat blood* clauses, because if one is committed to a particular deadline under the contract, one may sweat blood to meet it. No excuses will be tolerated.

To understand why this clause often carries great weight, one must put oneself in the other party's shoes. Both parties may make plans, commitments, expend money, and incur obligations of their own in expectation that the other party will perform within the time limit specified in the contract. For instance, in their production contract, producer Belasco and author Shakespeare may have agreed that Shakespeare will complete the new play *Romeo and Juliet* by October 1. While Shakespeare is busy at his word processor, Belasco is raising money from investors, contracting with actors and designers, as well as licensing a theater and hiring a director. In short, Belasco is putting himself under numerous obligations to many people and entities and promising them that rehearsals will start October 2. If Shakespeare does not complete his script sufficiently for rehearsals to begin on time, Belasco remains on the hook to all the persons with whom he has signed contracts. He must honor his own arrangements with them—which usually means substantial financial outlays by Belasco. Shakespeare's failure to finish the play on time imposes financial harm on Belasco. That is why courts take a strict view of "time is of the essence" clauses.

If such a clause appears in a contract offered to you, seek to strike it. Failing that, try to negotiate more time than you think you'll need to perform. Failing that, observe deadlines exactly. (I have deliberately left this clause out of the contracts in this book. I mention it, however, for those of you who wish to use it.)

WAIVERS

"If either party will, at any time, waive any term, provision, or condition of this contract, said waiver will be effective for the one time only, and will not be deemed or construed to waive that term, time, provision, or condition for any future or subsequent time, action, or breach. This will hold true, regardless of how many times or on how many occasions the party will waive said term, provision, or condition. Each said waiver must be in writing signed by both parties, to be effective."

Sometimes, in the course of doing business, the parties may desire to waive or give up a particular term or condition of the written contract. For instance, the playwright may have a right to hotel accommodations in the out-of-town tryout city equal to or better than the producer's hotel suite. On one occasion, the playwright may agree to waive that right and accept lesser accommodations. However, her one time waiver does not mean she forever gives up that right. In the very next city, she may very well insist upon equal accommodations. If the producer simply refuses to pay for the proper hotel suite in the next city, the playwright may sue or possibly even be excused from performing her obligations, because of the producer's breach of the contract.

It is not always practical to get every waiver in a signed writing, but I urge you to try. A signed writing, however crude in appearance, is always each party's best protection, in the event of a dispute.

ENTIRE UNDERSTANDING

"This Agreement constitutes the entire understanding between the parties. Unless contained herein, no representation, warranty, promise, covenant, or statement of any kind, whether oral or written, will be deemed or construed to be part of the agreement of the parties. The parties hereby acknowledge that only the provisions contained herein and no other induced them to enter into this contract."

This clause protects both parties from claims by the other party that their understanding encompasses other terms, promises, or provisions that are not part of the written instrument. In negotiating any contract, parties toss terms back and forth at each other before agreement is reached. This provision ensures that only those terms the parties intended, as they understood them, will prevail (as evidenced by the writing signed by both). It eliminates misunderstandings as well as downright fraudulent attempts to bring in obligations the parties didn't intend to undertake.

HOLD HARMLESS/INDEMNIFY

"_____ agrees to hold _____ harmless and indemnify _____ for all court ordered judgments, damages, attorney fees, and court costs which _____ may suffer and have to pay to a third party, as a result of any actions or failure to act by _____. _____ shall pay any settlements which _____ may enter into with a third party, only provided _____ has been consulted and approves of the settlement."

Each party should agree to hold the other party harmless and indemnify him because the first party has acted in such a way (or failed to act) that the second party incurs expenses.

Here are examples that call for this clause:

- A patron trips in the dark on worn carpeting and breaks her leg. As is common in these cases, she sues both the producer and the owner. The fault may ultimately lie with the owner, but the producer must pay attorney and court costs to defend himself. The court may even order the producer to pay the damages, even though the producer himself believes the owner is at fault. If, in fact, the producer can prove that the owner was responsible for the worn carpeting, then the owner must reimburse him, under the hold harmless and indemnity clause of their contract.
- A playwright warrants (guarantees) to her producer that her work does not infringe on anyone else's copyright. However, after the opening, another writer sues both the playwright and her producer, claiming she lifted major portions of her play from his copyrighted work. The court believes the other writer and orders both the playwright and the producer to pay damages. (In addition, the producer has incurred attorney fees and court costs of his own in defending the suit.) The playwright must reimburse the producer, that is, hold him harmless for his costs and the share of damages he has paid out.

It is a good idea to include in your hold harmless and indemnity clauses that the indemnifying party will pay all of the costs the other party incurs—court ordered damages, as well as his attorney fees and expenses.

A settlement is a different matter from a court judgment. Judgments are not made voluntarily; they are ordered by the court. However, sometimes to avoid the costs and publicity of a court case, a defendant (the person being sued) may settle a case with the plaintiff (the party suing) by agreeing to pay a certain amount of money to simply make the matter go away. This is all well and good, but the indemnifying party should be consulted and allowed to approve of the settlement, since, ultimately the indemnifying party will have to make good the defendant's payment.

For instance, the indemnifying party may very well have a defense to the plaintiff's claim, which, if she were allowed to present it, might persuade a court to deny the claim. In the case of the playwright being sued for copyright infringement, perhaps she can show the court that she did not, in fact, infringe on the other writer's copyright. In that case, no one would have to pay out any money. However, if her producer settles the case without her consent, he denies her the right to present her case and block the damages. Therefore, under the hold harmless and indemnity clause she would have to reimburse the producer for a settlement to which she did not approve and to which she has a defense. That is why she should insist in the hold harm-less and indemnity clause that the producer cannot settle the matter without her input and approval.

The quoted clause at the beginning of this topic is merely a generic example, for illustration purposes only, of the hold harmless and indemnity terms of a contract. Throughout this book, however, I have provided contract specific clauses.

THE FORMS

Not all boilerplates must appear in every contract. When a clause is necessary in a particular type of the-atrical arrangement, I have provided for it in the forms.

In the case of omitted clauses, there is nothing to prevent readers from adding them into a particular form, if its inclusion better codifies their agreement. (Remember that I created these forms for maximum flexibility.) Simply copy the appropriate boilerplate clause out of this chapter and insert it into your form.

part 1 **Production Management**

chapter **1** Rehearsal Rental

Commonly, shows do not conduct all of their rehearsals in the theater in which they actually give their performances. Another show may be playing at the theater, while the new show is rehearsing. Also it is much cheaper to conduct the early rehearsals in a space designed for that purpose than to rent an entire theater. Musicals frequently rehearse in different spaces—the orchestra in one place, singers in another, dancers in another, and the book scenes in still another location.

Whatever the circumstances, a license for mere rehearsal space is the simplest of all forms to negotiate. In fact, some rehearsal space owners simply operate on a handshake or letter agreement. I recommend a slightly more formal arrangement.

THE REHEARSAL SPACE

Rehearsals may be held in any room large enough to accommodate the cast. In New York's theater district, many rental spaces exist just for that purpose. Outside of Broadway, almost any space can be used for rehearsals—dance studios, park district activities rooms, public library meeting rooms, etc.

Because rehearsals are closed to the public, the space does not have to be licensed for public performances, and indeed few are.

Nevertheless, the producer must concern himself with the safety of the space. There should be proper fire exits. The room should be well maintained. In particular, the producer must inquire about the overall condition and cleaning of the floors. Even in the best of circumstances, dancers are prone to injury. A slick or poorly kept floor can increase the risk of harm.

THE REHEARSAL LICENSE

As I indicated, many rehearsal licenses are simple, even verbal arrangements. When reduced to writing, a good license can be no more than three pages long. It can even be in the form of a memorandum, as long as both parties sign it.

REHEARSAL LICENSE ESSENTIALS

1. *Occupancy dates.* The dates and times for which the production will occupy the space.
2. *Fee.* The fee may be hourly, daily, or weekly, depending upon the producer's needs.
3. *Purpose.* The purpose of the license.
4. *Producer representations.* The producer's representation and warranty that only persons connected with the production will occupy the space.
5. *Public not invited.* The general public will not be invited. In truth, no producer wants the public to view a show in rehearsal. However, it may be reasonable to invite members of the press into the rehearsal space to interview the cast and creative staff.

Form 1 Rehearsal Space License

THIS AGREEMENT dated this _____ day of _____, 20____, by and between _____, as Owner ("Licensor") of the rehearsal space located at _____ and _____, the Producer ("Licensee") of the production entitled _____ ("Production"), who desires to rehearse in the space.

1. Licensor hereby grants to Licensee the right to rehearse the production, at the times and dates specified on the following schedule:

   _____

   _____

   _____

2. (A) The license fee will be _____ per _____ [hour] [day] [week].

   [A day will consist of _____ hours.]

   [A week will consist of _____ days of _____ hours each.]

   (B) License fees will be paid _____ [daily] [weekly] in advance.

3. Approximately _____ people will occupy the space during said rehearsal time.

4. Only persons immediately connected with the production, and their invitees, will be permitted access to the space during the times and dates aforesaid. Members of the press may also, from time to time, be permitted for the purpose of publicizing the production.

5. The space is not licensed for public performance. The public will not, at any time, be invited or permitted entry to the space, whether or not admission is charged.

6. The Licensee will not bring into the premises flammables, explosives, chemicals, or other combustible or dangerous materials. The Licensee will not obstruct or block fire exits and will at all times comply with all building and fire codes.

7. No alcoholic beverages or illegal drugs of any kind may be used or consumed or sold on the premises.

8. The Licensee will be responsible for any breakage or damage to the space.

9. No props, costumes, or physical elements of the production may remain on the premises overnight, except _____. No personal property belonging to any personnel of the production will remain on the premises overnight.

10. The Licensor will provide reasonable security therefore. Upon vacating the premises at the end of this license the Licensee will remove all physical property belonging to the Licensee and/or its personnel, and the licensor will not be responsible for any property so left in violation of this agreement.

11. (A) The Licensee will indemnify and hold the Licensor harmless from and against all claims, actions, liability, judgments, or expenses of any kind (including court costs and attorney fees), which the Licensor may pay or incur by reason of injuries or loss occurring to people or property and resulting from any actions, or failure to act, by the Production and/or any of its personnel.

    (B) The Licensor will indemnify and hold the Licensee harmless from and against all claims, actions, liability, judgments, or expenses of any kind (including court costs and attorney fees), which the Licensor may pay or incur by reason of injuries or loss occurring to people or property and resulting from any actions, or failure to act, by the Licensor and/or any of its personnel.

12. The Licensor will clean and maintain the space during the term hereof and will use reasonable care in connection thereof.

13. The Licensor [will] [will not] provide a piano for use in rehearsals.

In Witness whereof, the parties have this day entered their names and signatures below.

_____ (Licensor)

_____ (Licensee)

By: _____ (Title)

2 Single Show Simple License

The owner of a theatrical facility may not be a producer herself. She may simply be in the business of owning a theater that she licenses out, on a consistent basis, in order to make a profit.

On the other hand, a theater company may own its space outright—or lease it on a long-term basis—for the purpose of presenting its own shows. Most companies, however, experience dark times, when, for whatever reason, they do not have a show of their own running. Nevertheless, during these "in between" periods the fixed costs of maintaining the facility go on. To help recover these expenses (and even to show a profit), the company may find it desirable to license its space to an outside producer.

A third possibility: Even if the company maintains a full schedule of programming, the space may be unused during the day, especially in the morning hours. It may be possible to squeeze some extra money out of the facility by licensing the space during those morning hours to a children's theater company. Businesses may also use the space for conferences and meetings.

Most often, the second and third possibilities described above represent opportunities to community, store front, and regional theaters. In most instances, all the theater company and the other producer need is a simple license agreement for a single show.

PRELIMINARY CONSIDERATIONS

Both the company (the "licensor") and the outside producer (the "licensee") must first ascertain that the licensor has the authority to rent out the space. If the licensor owns the facility, there won't be any restrictions as to what it may do.

However, if the licensor is, in turn, leasing the building from another party (the actual owner), it must make sure its lease permits it to make a second party license.

Often, leases prohibit "subletting," "subleasing," or "assigning" one's obligations without the owner's consent. Strictly speaking, the company is neither subletting, subleasing, nor assigning its obligations. In fact, it remains fully responsible for its promises under the lease.

This is because, when one permits another producer to use one's space, for consideration ("filthy lucre" in nonlegal terms), the "use" is structured as a license, not as a lease (see the next section). Nevertheless, many leases forbid the occupancy of the premises by anyone but the original lessee, i.e., the original theater company would be the licensor that entered into the lease with the owner. The mere use/occupancy by another producer—under license or otherwise—may violate these clauses.

If this all sounds like legal hair splitting, well, it's the kind of legal hair splitting that can land all of the parties in court and cost a great deal of money. It's much easier to ascertain that one is on solid legal ground from the first.

Okay, here's the problem laid out in simple terms: The New Lincoln Theater leases its space from Ebenezer Scrooge under an agreement that prohibits subleasing, assigning, or the occupancy of the space by anyone other than New Lincoln. However, New Lincoln licenses its morning dark time to Holiday Road for its production of *Santa's Children*. Ebenezer, never one to let Christmas go by without a chance to make a buck and throw someone out into the street, promptly files a forcible detainer (eviction) action against New Lincoln and Holiday Road. The court sides with Ebenezer—the lease did say no one may occupy the premises other than New Lincoln. Now both New Lincoln and Holiday Road are homeless. Holiday Road, in turn, sues New Lincoln for the losses it incurred because it had to shut down *Santa's Children*.

This whole problem would be obviated by making sure from the first that New Lincoln has the right under its lease to license Holiday Road to use its space.

The best solution? When New Lincoln entered into its lease with Scrooge, it should have asked for a clause specifically and expressly allowing it to license its space and permit others to occupy the facility, as it deems fit. This kind of clause can be structured in such a way—especially in a theatrical facility—so that it does not conflict with any desires by the landlord to prohibit subletting or assignment.

LICENSE OR LEASE

Regardless of how they come about, theater rentals for a single show are structured as licenses, rather than leases.

The reason? A lease creates a landlord-tenant relationship between the parties and imposes restrictions on what the lessee/lessor may do. For instance, if the landlord wishes to terminate a tenant's occupancy of the space before the time period specified in the lease, she must jump through a number of legal hoops, many of which are extremely technical. She must have cause, such as nonpayment of rent. She must give appropriate notices, during which the tenant may have rights to remedy his conduct—such as paying the rent owed—and defeat the landlord's attempts to recover possession of the property. Even if the tenant still does not correct the problem, the landlord must file suit and apply to the courts for help. This process is time-consuming and often expensive. Even if the court ultimately finds for the owner, it may give the tenant considerable time to move out. The entire process—before the landlord regains possession—may take months. During that time, the landlord cannot grant possession of the property to anyone else and restore her cash flow.

A license is a much simpler proposition. It is revocable upon minimal notice. It does not confer upon the licensee (producer) any long-term rights, even if the show settles in for a run of years. The owner can recover possession and re-license the facility to another production quickly. Unlike leases, licenses are not subject to landlord-tenant statutes and procedures.

A license also works to the producer's advantage. It is always difficult to foresee the duration of a show's life. Even a long-run hit can suddenly take, well, a *hit* at the box office. At that time it is simply prudent to close the show. No producer wants to continue to be obligated for space he can no longer use. He wants out quickly at the least possible cost.

Thus, it is industry practice to rent space under a license agreement.

THE SIMPLE LICENSE

The simple license is used more frequently in the situations I have described at the beginning of this chapter. A more complete license—what I call the *full license*—is appropriate for Broadway, touring companies, and larger, more expensive productions. (See Form 3, "The Full License")

SIMPLE LICENSE ESSENTIALS

1. *Rental fees.* Under a simple license, the licensee pays a flat fee rental to the licensor for the use of the space. The licensee, in turn, keeps all of the proceeds from the box office. The fee is due and payable, in full, regardless of the box office results. The licensee sets the ticket prices and maintains complete control over admissions—including the doling out of any complimentary or press tickets.

   Rental fees should be paid weekly, in advance, especially in small operations, that is, if the licensor wants to be sure of getting paid.

2. *Content.* One doesn't want to pass judgment upon another producer's choice of show. However, the licensor should inquire into the production the licensee wants to run in her facility. There can be valid reasons underlying this issue. For instance, a church would not want to rent its hall to a producer who intends to present content at odds with the beliefs of its congregation. A producer should be frank and willing to disclose his intentions and even provide a perusal copy of the script.

3. *Production.* The only obligation the licensor undertakes is to provide the space and basic utilities. The licensee provides the production itself—the play, scenery, costumes, etc.—and the personnel needed to run the show, such as the actors, stage, crew, etc. The licensee is responsible for all advertising, promotion, and security. Either the licensor or the licensee may provide the personnel to actually staff the box office and sell the tickets. In Form 2, paragraph 4, which follows, the parties can choose either the licensor or licensee as ticket seller. This is frequently called a *four wall* deal.

   Although the presenting producer will bring in his own staff to run lights and sound, he will use equipment belonging to the licensor. Therefore the licensor must insist upon having her own crew supervise its use.

4. *Take in/Take out.* The date when the licensee will be given first access to the premises to bring in his physical production is called the *take in*. This is negotiable, since it depends upon theater availability, as well as the amount of time the licensing producer needs to hang his scenery and lights. It is also likely the visiting production will need a few days for technical rehearsals in the space.

The parties must also agree upon *take out*. This is the date by which the producer must remove his physical production and restore the space to its original condition. Commonly, this time is measured in hours after the production plays its final performance. (On Broadway, this time is usually seventy-two hours after the last performance.) The licensor has a vested interest in regaining her space as soon as possible—either to rent out to another producer or to bring in one of her own shows.

(As a matter of course, road companies usually begin taking out their physical production immediately after the curtain falls on the last performance anyway. Road companies are on tight touring schedules. It is essential to get out of the current theater quickly and move the physical production to the facility in the next town in order to open there on time.)

The parties must also decide upon penalties if the licensee fails to remove his physical production on time. (Not every producer has another booking lined up for his show.) Commonly this may include forfeiture of the security deposit (see next paragraph). It may also mean the licensor may resort to self-help, that is, declare the equipment abandoned and dispose of it as she sees fit.

5. *Security deposit.* A licensor should always—always—insist upon a security deposit, especially in the small theater realm. I have seen too many situations in which theaters rent space to visiting producers without taking a security deposit, only to wind up bearing the trouble and expense themselves of disposing of the producer's physical production after the show closes. Producers of this kind often operate by the seat of their pants, with big dreams, but little money. When the show closes (usually because the box office take was poor), they disappear, leaving the licensor with all the headaches. In addition, the producer or his staff may be careless and damage the licensor's physical plant. A substantial security deposit discourages carelessness as well as outright abandonment. In the worse case scenario, at least it covers part, if not all, of the costs of disposal.

Incidentally, if a licensee tells a licensor he cannot afford a security deposit, I recommend very strongly turning down the rental. This is the classic producer operating on a shoestring. If he hasn't got the money at the outset, he's not likely to have the money to remove his production when the show closes.

6. *Security.* A licensor must insist the producer will provide adequate security, both to protect the public and the licensor's facilities and equipment. The kind of security needed obviously depends on the circumstances. It may range from locks all the way up to guards or bouncers. Below are some examples of what you should expect:

   a. Whatever you do, prohibit the use and sale of alcohol and illegal drugs.

   b. Forbid the use of chemical sprays. (Have you ever seen the effect pepper spray can have on a crowd? Panic, fear, stampede for the exits, injuries, and even death.)

   c. Prohibit smoking, flammable materials, chemicals, or other stage effects that could cause fires or explosions.

   d. Forbid the producer from locking or obstructing fire exits at any time when persons (crew or audience) may be on the premises. Do not permit the sale of standing room only tickets.

   e. Insist that the producer adhere to all fire and building codes.

   f. Security is another reason you should inquire into the nature of the show the producer intends to present. Let's face it. Some shows and performers attract controversy. And controversy can bring out rowdy crowds, as well as the nuts of the world. And do I even need remind you of the possibility of bomb threats?

   If the show is likely to stir up the community, make sure you and the producer are prepared to handle any fall out.

7. *Performance licenses.* The licensee must obtain any licenses required for the performance of copyrighted music, such as from the performing rights societies, like ASCAP or BMI.

8. *Insurance.* The producer, at his own expense, must purchase comprehensive general liability insurance for the production, naming the licensor as coinsured. The licensor should consult with her

own insurance agency to determine the appropriate limits of coverage and whether any extended riders may be needed.

9. *Indemnity.* Of course, our old friends, Mr. Hold Harmless and Ms. Indemnity should appear in your license. If the producer is operating by the seat of his pants, these clauses may not, as a practical matter, be worth anything. But the wise licensor makes them part of the agreement anyway.

10. *Taxes, permits.* The producer should be responsible for all amusement and other taxes that may be incurred as a result of the production. He should also obtain and pay for any special permits his show may require.

11. *Concessions/programs.* Whether the visiting producer or the theater company operates the concession stand during the production is negotiable. It may also depend upon the terms of the contract between the theater and the professional concessionaire and program supplier.

12. *Joint Venture/Lease.* Make sure the license agreement specifically disclaims the creation of any joint venture or landlord/tenant relationship between the parties.

Form 2 Single Show Rental License (Simple)

THIS AGREEMENT is entered into this _____ day of _____, 20___, by and between _____
_____ ("Owner"), as Owner of the _____
("Theater"), located at _____ and _____ ("Producer"). Whereas
the Owner wishes to license the Theater to the Producer and the Producer wishes to license the Theater for the presentation of the live stage event presently entitled _____ (the "Attraction"),
the parties, in consideration of the mutual promises, covenants, and conditions contained herein, hereby agree
as follows:

1. (A) The Owner grants to Producer the exclusive license to use and occupy the Theater, beginning _____
and ending _____, for rehearsals and presentation of the Attraction to the general public. The performance schedule shall be as follows:
(i) _____ evening performances, beginning at approximately ____ P.M. on the following days of the week:
_____; and
(ii) _____ matinee performances, beginning at approximately ____ P.M. on the following days of the week
_____.

    [*If the show is a children's theater company presenting morning performances, then the following should be used instead*:
_____ morning performances, beginning at approximately _____ on the following days of the week
_____.]
(iii) Producer shall also be entitled to utilize the space for rehearsals according to the following schedule:
_____.

    (B) The Producer and his personnel shall be permitted to enter the space _____ hours before each performance and
shall leave the space _____ after each performance, unless otherwise authorized by the Owner.
    (C) The Producer and his personnel shall also be entitled to enter the space for the purpose of adjustment and main-
tenance of the physical production of the Attraction.
    (D) The Owner represents and warrants to the Producer that the Theater is licensed by the appropriate govern-
mental authorities having jurisdiction thereof for live performances for a maximum seating capacity of
_____ persons. Sales of standing room admissions are unlawful and expressly prohibited under this
agreement.
2. The Producer shall pay to the theater the sum of _____ dollars ($_____), for the use of the space
according to the following schedule:
_____ dollars ($_____) upon the signing of this agreement, representing the license fee for the first
week's performance;
_____ dollars ($_____), for each week's performance, payable on the _____ day preceding the
week's performance.
All fees must be paid in advance.
Failure to pay any week's fee in advance as aforesaid, when due shall be cause for immediate revocation of this
license and restoration of the space to the licensor.
3. In addition to the weekly fees payable as aforesaid, the Producer shall also deposit with the Owner the sum of
_____ dollars ($_____) as security for his faithful and proper performance under the terms of this
agreement. Said deposit shall also be due and payable upon the signing of this agreement. No interest shall be
payable thereon. In the event the Producer performs his obligations faithfully under this agreement and is not otherwise in breach thereof, then within _____ days after the period for take out expires (as described below), the
Owner shall refund said deposit to the Producer. In the event the Producer fails to perform any obligation hereunder
or is otherwise in breach, Producer shall immediately forfeit deposit and Owner shall take as his sole property as liq-
uidated damages without any further claim thereon by the Producer. Nothing contained herein shall prevent the
Owner from pursuing any and all other remedies available to him in law or in equity.
4. The Producer shall solely determine all ticket prices for the production.

(A) The _____ [Owner] [Producer] shall engage in all ticket sales and provide the personnel to conduct same [according to policies established by the Producer]. [Said policies shall not be effective upon the theater or its personnel unless first conveyed to same in writing prior to the beginning of ticket sales by the owner and his personnel.]

(B) All disputes, questions, or other matters arising out of ticket sales with the general public shall be the responsibility of the Producer. The Producer shall hold the Owner harmless and indemnify him against any loss, damages, or costs incurred due any claims or disputes resulting from the sale of tickets, whether such sales are made by the Producer or by the Owner's personnel.

(C) All proceeds from ticket sales shall immediately become the sole property of the Producer.

(D) Producer shall be solely responsible for all taxes or other fees imposed on all sales of tickets, and shall hold the Owner harmless and indemnify him thereon.

5. The Producer, at his own expense, shall provide the cast, physical production, literary rights, publicity and advertising, and personnel necessary to operate the Attraction [except that the Owner may provide the following personnel _____, whose salaries and fees shall be paid for by the Producer at the rates that may, from time to time, be prevailing, during the term of this license.]

6. The owner shall permit the Producer to use his sound and lighting equipment, provided same are used only under supervision of the Owner's own crew. The Producer may, at his own expense, bring in additional equipment.

   [*If the performance is a morning show—say, a children's theater company—and the Owner is running its own or another producer's attraction in the evening, the following clause should be inserted*: "After each performance, the Owner shall refocus lights and readjust sound, as per the lighting and sound plots provided by the Owner or his evening licensee."]

7. After each performance the _____ [Owner] [Producer] shall be responsible for the cleaning of the Theater.

8. (A) Beginning on _____ [date], the Producer shall be permitted to bring in his physical production, including scenery, costumes, lights, etc., and to hang same according to the Hanging Plot, as described in section (B) below (the take in):

   (B) At least _____ days prior to the take in of the physical production, the Producer must furnish the Owner with the Hanging Plot of the show. The Producer may not begin take in until and unless he has first received Owner's written approval of the Hanging Plot. The Producer shall, at all times during the term of this license, comply with and follow the Hanging Plot, as so approved. No modifications may be made thereto without the written consent of the Owner.

9. Not later than _____ days after the last performance of the play, the Producer, at his own expense, must remove his entire physical production from the premises (the take out). If he fails to do so, as aforesaid, Owner may consider it a material breach of this contract. She may, at her option, and without further notice:

   (A) Declare the property abandoned and dispose of same as she sees fit, including sale of same. She will first apply proceeds of the sale to satisfy costs of removal and disposal; secondly, for any outstanding debts owed her by the Producer; and tender the balance, if any, to the Producer; or

   (B) Store any or all property in any facility of her choosing, without liability or obligation to safeguard same; and charge all costs of removal and storage to the Producer; or

   (C) A combination of (A) and (B) above.

   In addition to applying any proceeds of sale of said physical production, the Owner may deduct from the security deposit described in paragraph 3 above, the balance of costs of removal, storage, and disposal of said property, prior to refund of security deposit.

10. Producer, at his own expense, shall be solely responsible to provide adequate security to protect patrons, production personnel, and property.

   (A) Smoking is expressly prohibited anywhere on the premises, except that smoking which is part of the action of the Attraction.

   (B) The sale, consumption, use, or distribution of alcohol and/or illegal drugs on or about the premises is expressly forbidden, except that consumption or use which is part of the action of the Attraction.

   (C) Producer may not bring into the premises, or use, or store flammable or hazardous materials or chemicals of any kind.

(D) Producer shall eject rowdy or misbehaving patrons, whose conduct may cause injury to persons or damage to property.

(E) No chemical sprays of any kind shall be disbursed or directed at patrons or other persons on or about the premises.

(F) Producer shall keep all fire doors, exits, and staircases free of obstructions at all times, when persons are present on the premises.

(G) Producer shall obey all fire, building, and other safety ordinances which may be imposed upon or to which the theater or the Attraction may be subject, whether same are existing at the present time or created subsequent to the execution of this agreement.

(H) Producer shall take no action that may jeopardize or endanger the Owner's license or permits.

(I) Producer shall take no action that may jeopardize, endanger, or otherwise harm the Owner's Theater and equipment. Producer shall be responsible for any damage thereto, and Owner may deduct the reasonable cost of repair and/or replacement from the security herein deposited by the Producer. However, said deductions shall not release the Producer from any additional claims or rights which the Owner may have against him, nor bar any remedies which the Owner may have against the Producer, in law or equity.

11. Producer shall be solely responsible for all licenses from the performing rights societies, such as ASCAP, BMI, etc., and shall obtain, at his own expense, any licenses or agreements necessary to perform copyrighted material owned by persons or entities other than the Producer.

12. [Producer shall operate, staff, and maintain all concession stand sales. Revenue shall be divided _____% to the producer and _____% to the Owner.]

[*Alternate*]

12. [Owner shall operate, staff, and maintain all concession stand sales. All revenues shall belong solely to the Owner, except as follows: Producer may sell souvenir books and show related souvenir merchandise out of the concession stands, and revenue on same shall be divided _____% to the Producer and _____% to the Owner.]

For all purposes under this clause, each party shall have the right to inspect and audit each other's books for concession stand sales, to verify that all sales and revenues have been properly accounted for and divided.

13. [Owner shall pay the cost of all utilities and same shall be included in the license fee.]

[*Alternate*]

13. [Producer shall reimburse to the Owner the cost of all utilities used during the term of this license, in addition to all other fees due hereunder. Producer shall pay such costs immediately upon receipt of notice and demand for same from the Owner.]

14. [Producer shall, at its own expense, provide his own programs.]

[*Alternate*]

14. [Producer shall purchase programs from Owner's program supplier.]

15. This arrangement is for the mere use of the theater during the term stated herein above and is a license only. The parties hereby expressly disavow any intention or desire to create a partnership, joint venture, or a landlord/tenant relationship between themselves. This agreement shall not be construed or interpreted as forming a partnership, joint venture, or landlord/tenant relationship between the parties.

16. Producer shall, at all times, at his own expense, carry the following policies of insurance, for the designated limits of liability:

Type of Insurance   Limits of Liability

_____   _____

_____   _____

_____   _____

Producer shall name the Owner and the Theater as co-insureds, and deliver copies of the policies and proof of premium payments therefore to the Owner no later than ten days prior to Take-In. All insurance must remain in force for the term of this contract.

17. (A) Producer has inspected the Theater prior to entering into this agreement and has determined it is suitable and satisfactory for his needs and requirements. Producer further accepts Theater in "as is" condition.

(B) Producer has submitted to Owner a true and correct copy of the materials presently constituting the Attraction. Owner has deemed same suitable and appropriate for performance in her Theater.

18. Producer shall make no modifications, alterations, refurnishings, or other changes to the Theater, its structure, and equipment, without first (a) obtaining the written consent of the Owner; and (b) obtaining any approvals, licenses, or permits from the appropriate governmental authorities having jurisdiction thereof. Upon vacating the Premises, the Producer must restore the Theater to its original condition, unless otherwise notified by Owner. Any modifications, alterations, or refurnishings permitted by Owner will, at the Owner's option, belong to the Owner after the termination of this license.

19. The provisions of this agreement will survive the run of the Attraction and will be binding on both parties, their heirs, executors, trustees, and assigns.

20. Notwithstanding the provisions of paragraph 18, the producer may not assign this agreement without the consent of the Owner.

21. All claims, disputes, conflicts, and other disagreements concerning the provisions of this agreement will be submitted to binding arbitration conducted in the city of _____ under the rules of the American Arbitration Association, by an arbitrator selected by both parties. Any court of competent jurisdiction may enter judgment upon the award so granted. The arbitrator will require the losing party to pay the reasonable costs and attorney fees of the prevailing party.

22. This document constitutes the entire agreement between the parties. No modifications or consents will be valid or effective unless contained in a writing signed by both of the parties.

23. The Owner and/or the Theater shall not be at risk of loss from any action or failure to act by the Producer and/or persons in his employment or control which (a) cause harm, damage, or loss to third persons and/or property owned or possessed by third persons; (b) result in claims that a third person or corporation has been defamed; (c) result in claims that rights of privacy, publicity, copyright, and or trademarks owned or possessed by third persons or corporations have been violated or infringed upon; (d) result in any other claims that the rights of third persons or corporations, which exist or are granted under statutory or common law, have been violated. In the event the Owner and/or the Theater suffers loss or damages under any of the foregoing, the Producer shall hold the Owner and/or the Theater harmless and indemnify them for all costs, attorney fees, court ordered judgments or damages, or other expenses incurred by the Owner and/or the Theater, including the defense of claims made hereunder. The Producer shall hold the Owner and/or the Theater harmless and indemnify them for all moneys paid out in settlements to third parties, only provided the Producer has first approved and consented to such settlements.

In Witness Whereof, the parties have hereunto set their hands and seals this day and date.

_____ (Producer)

_____ (Owner)

Form 3 Single Show Theater Rental (Full License)

THIS AGREEMENT, entered into this _____ day of _____, 20___, by and between _____, ("Owner") as Owner of the _____ Theater, located at _____ ("Theater"); and _____ ("Producer"), as Producer of the Attraction presently entitled _____ ("Attraction"), which Producer desires to present in the Theater.

In consideration of the mutual covenants, agreements, and conditions hereby described and undertaken by the parties, it is hereby agreed as follows:

1. The Owner hereby licenses to the Producer the use and occupancy of the Theater for the purpose of rehearsing and presenting the public performances of the Attraction during the dates and upon the terms stated herein.

2. The Owner represents and warrants to the Producer that the Theater is properly licensed for performances to the public, and that _____ persons may be seated, at capacity, under all applicable codes and licenses. Sales of standing room only admissions are prohibited under law and expressly under the terms of this agreement.

3. A performance week shall consist of _____ evening performances, occurring on the following days of the week: _____; and _____ matinee performances occurring on the following days of the week: _____. Performance times shall begin, approximately, at the following times: _____ P.M. for evening performances occurring on _____; _____ P.M. for matinee performances occurring on _____.

4. The Producer's use of the Theater shall begin on _____, for the purpose of installing the physical production. His use of the Theater shall begin on _____ for the purpose of rehearsals. His use of the Theater for public performances shall begin on or about _____, regardless of whether the performances are labeled as previews.

5. Producer, at his own expense, shall furnish the full Attraction for the Theater, including (but not limited to) the cast, physical production, personnel to operate the show, literary and musical rights and licenses, publicity and advertising, and all other things necessary to present a proper and appropriate presentation, except those things which the Owner specifically agrees herein to furnish.

   Owner shall furnish full use of the Theater, including the auditorium, lobby, backstage areas, storage spaces, box office, dressing rooms (including showers), and washrooms. Owner shall be responsible for lighting, heating, air conditioning, cleaning, and otherwise maintaining said facilities and for ushers, ticket sellers, ticket takers, house managers, and for the minimal stage crew as required by applicable union agreements in effect during the term of this license.

6. (A) Producer shall, at all times, abide by and observe all rules and regulations of the Owner, as Owner shall promulgate, and Producer shall instruct his personnel to likewise obey same. Owner shall furnish to the Producer and Producer's personnel his written rules and regulations, upon the signing of this agreement. Owner reserves the right, however, to modify, change, delete, or add to his rules and regulations as he may, from time to time, deem appropriate. Owner shall notify Producer in writing of any such modifications and Producer and his personnel shall obey same.

   (B) Producer and his personnel shall, at all times, obey all building, fire, and other local codes and ordinances and shall do nothing to endanger Owner's license or cause Owner to lose same. In particular, Producer and his employees are specifically prohibited from blocking or otherwise obstructing any fire doors or exits. Producer hereby represents and warrants that all electrical equipment, scenery, and other property brought into the Theater conforms to all building, fire, and safety codes applicable to the Theater. In the event, at any time, the Producer shall receive notice by either the Owner or the applicable local authorities of any violations, Producer shall immediately take steps to cure such violations, and to pay any fines or charges imposed by local authorities for said violations. All scenery must remain currently fire proofed, and Producer must furnish certification of same to Owner, upon Owner's request. The Producer and his personnel may not, at any time, bring or cause to be brought unto the premises, any flammable or other hazardous materials or products.

(C) Producer shall comply with all governmental rules and regulations, including those related to nondiscrimination, which may be applicable or imposed upon the Theater by any governmental authority having jurisdiction thereof.

(D) Violation of any of the provisions of (A) through (C) above shall be grounds for immediate termination of this agreement. The Owner shall not be liable for any damages, including lost profits, which the Producer may suffer as a direct or indirect consequence of any such violations.

(E) The Owner reserves the right to correct any violation and/or to take any other actions as she may deem necessary and appropriate to bring the Producer's physical production into compliance with all applicable safety rules, regulations, and ordinances of the local governmental authorities, if the Producer fails to do so immediately upon receiving notice of same. All such corrections/actions undertaken by the Owner shall be at the Producer's expense.

7. Producer hereby represents and warrants that he has the legal authority to present all copyrighted materials owned by others and utilized within the Attraction. Producer agrees to hold harmless and indemnify the Owner from any liability, damages, cost, or claims (including attorney fees) resulting from any violations or infringements upon the copyrights, rights of publicity, rights of privacy, or defamation of other persons or entities occurring as a result of the Producer's presentation of the Attraction at the Theater.

8. (A) This license shall be exclusive for the run of the Attraction. The Producer may not present the Attraction at any other location within a radius of _____ miles of the Theater, for a period of at least:

   i) _____ days prior to the first performance of the Attraction at the Theater;

   ii) During the run of the Attraction at the Theater;

   iii) _____ days following the last performance of the Attraction at the Theater.

   Likewise, the Producer shall not permit or authorize any members of the company, any members of the cast, or any other party to perform any material contained in the Attraction at any other location for the same periods of time as stated above (except as specified below), whether or not for profit.

   (B) Producer may permit the presentation of an excerpt from the Attraction, not to exceed 300 seconds, on a radio or television news or commercial program broadcast, for the purpose of publicizing and promoting the Attraction. Producer may likewise present an excerpt of no more than the aforementioned length from the Attraction on any television or radio commercials, paid for by Producer, for the purpose of promoting the Attraction.

   (C) Producer may permit the presentation of an excerpt from the Attraction, not to exceed 300 seconds, on a radio or television awards production, in conjunction with the nomination of any person or part of the production, for the purpose of publicizing and promoting the Attraction.

   (D) Nothing contained herein shall prohibit the Producer from permitting the composer and lyricist, or any other persons or entities holding the copyright on the musical materials from commercially exploiting the small performing rights to the musical materials. [*See chapter 14, "Song Licensing," for an explanation of small performing rights.*]

   (E) Nothing contained herein shall prohibit the performance or broadcast of the cast album, or any portion thereof, on radio, television, or otherwise.

   (F) The foregoing provisions are of the essence of the contractual relationship between the parties. The Producer specifically understands, acknowledges, and agrees, in the event of any violation or attempted violation hereof, that financial damages shall not be sufficient to remedy Owner's loss therefrom. Therefore, in addition to, or in lieu of, financial compensation, the Owner may obtain injunctive relief, including prior restraint, in the event of any breach or attempted breach hereof. The Producer shall make no defense thereof.

9. At least _____ days prior to moving the physical production into the Theater, the Producer shall furnish the Owner with the Hanging Plot of the show, and Producer shall not move same in, without Owner's written approval. Further, Producer agrees to comply with and conform to the Hanging Plot at all times during the run of the Attraction and to immediately seek Owner's written consent, in the event modifications may be required or appropriate.

10. During the run of the show, the Owner shall have the exclusive right to operate (or to license others to operate) and maintain all concession stands and sales of refreshments, souvenirs, and other merchandise, as well as cloakroom facilities. All revenue earned from same shall belong to the Owner (and his licensees) as his sole property. Producer (or his licensee) shall have the right to sell souvenir books and other Attraction-related merchandise out of the Concession stands, provided the sales are supervised by the Owner (or his licensee) and that the Producer (or his licensee) pays the Owner (or his licensee) a royalty of _____% of the gross sales (less applicable taxes) of said

souvenir books and Attraction-related merchandise. Owner (and his licensee) shall have the right to inspect, inventory, and audit all sales of said books and merchandise and to examine the books of the Producer (or his licensee) for said purpose.

11. The Theater maintains a smoke-free environment. Therefore, smoking is forbidden to the Producer and all of his personnel, except that smoking shall be permitted as part of the action of the Attraction.

12. The Producer and his personnel are prohibited from bringing into the premises pets, animals, bicycles, or food, except that meals may be consumed on the premises between performances on matinee days. No alcohol or illegal drugs may be brought into, consumed, sold, or distributed on the premises at any time by any person, except as part of the action of the Attraction.

13. Producer has inspected the Theater prior to entering into this agreement and has found it satisfactory and suitable for his purposes and accepts same in "as is" condition. He shall not make any improvements, refurnishings, or modifications to the premises without (a) first obtaining the Owner's written consent; (b) obtaining all approvals, permits, and licenses, at his own expense, from the applicable governmental authorities having jurisdiction thereof; (c) receiving the approval of all fire authorities that all improvements and modifications comply with safety and fire codes. Owner shall not be responsible for the cost of same. All such improvements, alterations, or refurnishings shall belong to the Owner, at his option, upon the installation thereof. However, the Owner may, upon termination of the run of the Attraction, require the Producer to restore the Theater to its original condition, as stated further below.

14. Notwithstanding the provisions of paragraph 13 above, if the Producer has made any improvements, modifications, or alterations to the Theater, he must, upon termination of the run of the play, restore the Theater to its original condition, unless otherwise notified in writing by the Owner.

15. Producer has submitted to the Owner all of the performance materials, as presently exist, and Owner has approved of same as suitable and satisfactory for presentation in his Theater. [The Attraction is a "work-in-progress" and the Owner understands and agrees that the performance materials may be changed, modified, or otherwise rewritten during the course of the rehearsals and public performances, and therefore may, over time, evolve substantially from the content which Owner has reviewed and approved.]

16. (A) The Owner shall be entitled to reserve and purchase, at the full box office rate, for his own use House Seats according to the following formula:

    i)   For the opening night performance _____ orchestra seats and _____ mezzanine seats;

    ii) For all other performances _____ orchestra seats and _____ mezzanine seats.

House seats shall be in those locations that the Owner has customarily purchased for himself in the past.

All seats that Owner has not purchased for his own use by the following times shall be released for sale to the general public:

_____ on the day of each matinee performance;

_____ on the day of each evening performance.

(B) The parties shall jointly administer and control the distribution of free tickets to the press.

17. (A) The Producer shall pay to the Owner a fixed charge in the amount of _____ for each performance week, beginning with the week during which the First Preview or First Public Performance (as the case may be) occurs, pro rata, on the basis of a six day week. This fixed charge shall consist of the Owner's general and administrative costs (as defined below), depreciation, and interest amortization on mortgages. They have been calculated on the basis of the Owner's costs for same during the full fiscal year preceding this agreement. In the event the Owner's costs for these shall change, up or down, during the term of this license, that the Producer's fixed charge may increase or decrease by a like amount. Upon notification by the Owner, the Producer's fixed charge shall be adjusted immediately, to reflect the increase or decease in the aforesaid Owner's costs. All weekly payments for fixed charges shall be due and payable in advance on Monday of each performance week.

(B) The Owner's general and administrative costs shall include real estate taxes, general and liability insurance, cleaning, maintenance, refuse removal, utility charges, licenses, permits, supplies, and office payroll.

(C) In addition to the charges as set forth in (A) and (B) above, Producer shall pay all of the Owner's personnel costs, including wages and taxes, at the prevailing union rates as may, from time to time, be effective during the term of this agreement.

(D) In the event the Owner must pay any of the costs of the production on Producer's behalf, the Owner shall furnish Producer with an itemized written estimate of same. Producer shall, weekly, advance to the Owner sufficient amounts to cover all such estimates. On the _____ following each performance week, Owner shall provide Producer with written substantiation of the amounts actually paid. The parties shall make the appropriate adjustment between the amounts so advanced and amounts actually paid.

(E) In the event the Producer fails to make any advance payments required under sections (A) through (D) above, the Owner may, at his option:

i)   Deduct all sums due from any box office receipts due to the Producer;

ii) Declare this agreement terminated and recover possession of the premises;

iii) Both i) and ii).

19. (A) In addition to all payments required under paragraph 18 above, the Owner and Producer shall divide net weekly box office receipts (as defined below) according to the following formula:

_____

_____

_____

"Net weekly box office receipts" shall be determined as follows:

All revenue from all sources of ticket sales shall be added together to determine *gross weekly box office receipts*. From gross weekly box office receipts, there shall be the following deductions: sales taxes, sales commissions, credit card company charges, computer ticket charges, subscription fees, and discounts. The sum left over shall constitute net weekly box office receipts.

(B) Following each performance, the Treasurer of the Theater (the "Treasurer") shall prepare a certified statement of all ticket sales from all sources whatsoever, for that performance, and same shall be compared to the admission stubs collected at the door. Each Monday, the parties will settle and adjust receipts and payments accordingly.

(C) Each Monday the Owner will pay to the Producer his share of the net weekly box office receipts (as computed above and less any adjustments for monies due the Owner under paragraphs 18(A) through (E) for the previous performance week). Owner shall furnish to the Producer a statement certified by the Treasurer and the Owner of all box office receipts for the previous week and payments made thereunder.

(D) The Treasurer is authorized to accept in payment for tickets, personal checks, credit cards, money orders, and cashier's checks. Any losses resulting from the nonpayment or noncollection thereof shall reduce the gross receipts for that particular performance and shall be borne equally by the parties.

20. (A) The Owner shall have sole control and supervision of the box office. He shall furnish the Treasurer and Assistant Treasurer. The cost of a second assistant treasurer, if necessary, shall be borne by the parties according to their pro-rata share of the box office. The costs of additional personnel to handle box office, mail order, telephone and group sales, as well as any other expenses attendant thereto, shall be borne equally by the parties, according to their pro-rata share of the box office. All persons handling ticket sales and/or money shall be bonded.

(B) All ticket sales and distribution shall be under the sole control of the Owner. Producer shall not engage in any sales or distribution of tickets without the consent of the Owner. In particular, the Producer may not give or sell tickets to brokers or other parties engaged in the business of reselling same to the general public.

(C) Theater reserves the right to approve of the scale of ticket prices to be sold hereunder.

(D) All tickets must be sold at the full box office price, except group sales that shall be made according to the formula to which both parties agree. Both parties must consent to the sale and cost of any two for one or other discount ticket sales.

(E) The parties shall jointly negotiate any contracts with Group Sales and/or Theater Party Agents (including the Owner's Group Sales and Theater Party Department).

(F) The Treasurer is hereby authorized by both parties to endorse checks.

(G) Owner may contract with a credit card company of his own choosing in connection with the sale and distribution of tickets to the Attraction and may retain _____% of the receipts from such sales for his own account.

(H) Owner may sell gift certificates and retain _____% of the receipts therefrom to cover any sales commissions and costs of distribution and administration thereof.

(I) Producer understands and acknowledges that the Owner may offer and sell tickets to the Attraction as part of his season subscription program, at a discount of not more than _____% of the full box office equivalent price of tickets sold thereunder.

21. Either Owner or Producer may terminate this agreement upon the happening of the following event:

    [Gross ticket sales must be a minimum of _____ for at least two out of any four weeks period.]

    [*Alternate*]

    [Gross ticket sales fall below a minimum of _____ for any two consecutive weeks.]

    The party wishing to terminate this agreement under this paragraph must give the other party written notice not later than Monday night, at _____ P.M. following the aforesaid period. Provided such notice is timely made and delivered, the run of the Attraction shall terminate with the final performance on the following Sunday evening.

    In the event the Owner exercises his right under this paragraph to terminate the run of the Play, the Owner shall also forfeit all his "exclusivity" rights under paragraph 8 herein, and the Producer may contract to present the Attraction at another theater, in competition with Owner's Theater, at any time after the run of the play closes at the Owner's Theater.

    These provisions shall collectively be known as the "Stop" clause of the contract.

22. Regardless of whether the run of the Attraction terminates because the term of this license has expired, or because either party has exercised his rights under the "Stop" Clause above, the Producer must remove the physical production and all personal belongings from the Theater not more than _____ hours after the final curtain call of the closing performance. In the event Producer fails to remove any property from the Theater, the same shall be declared abandoned and the Owner may, at his option:

    (A) Dispose of same as he shall see fit, without liability or responsibility to the Producer whatsoever; in such event Owner may, but need not, deduct all costs of removal and disposal from any box office receipts and/or security deposits owed to the Producer;

    (B) Store all or any part of the property in any facility he chooses, and charge all costs thereof to the Producer; in such event, the Owner may, but need not, deduct all costs of storage from any box office receipts and/or security deposits owed to the Producer;

    (C) Sell all or any part of the property; in such event, the Owner may first deduct all costs of sale, and all charges owed to the Owner under this entire contract, from any proceeds of sale; after said deduction, the Owner shall pay all net proceeds to the Producer.

23. At the time of the signing of this Agreement, the Producer shall deposit with the Owner security, in the form of cash or a bond, in the amount of _____ dollars ($_____) to guarantee his performance hereunder. No interest shall be payable on same. In the event the Producer performs all of his obligations hereunder, then, within _____ days after the final curtain on the closing performance of the Attraction, the Owner shall refund in full the Security Deposit. In the event the Producer breaches any of the terms of this Agreement the Owner may deduct all sums owed to the Producer therefrom and shall then return the balance, if any, thereof, accompanied by a written statement of all deductions therefrom. Producer may not assign or otherwise encumber this Security Deposit. Owner shall not be bound to honor any purported assignment or encumbrance thereof.

24. In the event the Producer fails to present the Attraction at the time aforesaid, he shall forfeit the security deposit as described in paragraph 23 above, regardless of the reason for the nonpresentation. In addition, Producer shall also reimburse the Owner for any costs or expenses which the Owner has incurred in anticipation of the presentation of the Attraction.

25. Producer understands that the Theater has an exclusive contract to supply programs for its Attractions with _____ ("Program Supplier"). Under this contract, the Program Supplier has complete and total control over the content and format of the Programs, subject to the rules of all collective bargaining agreements. Producer agrees to use the Program Supplier and no other, for all programs distributed in connection with the Attraction (except souvenir books), and shall furnish to the Program Supplier all materials and information required in sufficient time to prepare the programs for the Attraction.

26. Producer acknowledges that the Owner is obligated under certain collective bargaining agreements with various unions whose members render services to the Owner and that the Producer is familiar with the terms of all such

agreements. Producer shall at all times adhere to said contracts and shall take no action which may impair or otherwise violate same. In particular, the Producer shall observe all safety rules and regulations required by the unions for the benefit of their members. In addition, the Producer shall not, without the consent of the Owner, seek any special rulings or determinations from any collective bargaining agents which may affect the interests of the Owner. Producer acknowledges, however, that the Owner may, without the consent of the Producer, during the term of this Agreement, enter into negotiations for the renewal or modification of existing collective bargaining agreements with the unions, and the outcome may affect the Owner's costs and the charges payable by the Producer under this agreement.

27. All sums due hereunder to the Owner shall be a first lien against any money due to and property owned by the Producer.

28. [Producer shall be solely responsible for the cost of advertising, publicity, and promotion for the Attraction.]
    [*Alternate*]

28. [The parties shall divide the cost of advertising, publicity, and promotion, according to the following formula: _____% paid by the Owner; and _____% paid by the Producer. It is estimated at this time that the total cost of advertising, publicity, and promotion for this engagement of the Attraction shall be _____, or as subsequently agreed upon by the parties.]

29. (A) At all times prior to, during, and thereafter the engagement of the Attraction, while any property, person, or thing of the Producer, his employees, agents, or assigns, and/or any property, persons, or thing of any person, firm, corporation, limited or general partnership, or any other person or entity for whom the Producer accepts or assumes liability is on or about the premises, the Producer shall carry insurance of the following types and minimal limitations of liability:

    (i) Worker's Compensation Insurance with statutory limits, including Employers Liability coverage with at least the following minimal limits:
    Bodily Injury by Accident: $_____ each accident
    Bodily Injury by Disease: $_____ policy limit
    Bodily Injury by Disease: $_____ each employee

    (ii) Comprehensive General Liability/Personal Injury/Bodily Injury:
    $_____ per occurrence
    Comprehensive General Liability/ Property Damage:
    $_____ per occurrence

    (iii) All Risks:
    $_____

    [*An amount sufficient to cover the full replacement cost of all property.*]
    "All Risks" must include, but shall not be limited to, damage and destruction to property caused by, or as a consequence of, the following perils: burglary, theft, riots, strikes, vandalism, malicious mischief, floods, aircraft or vehicles striking the building, fire, acts of nature, collapse, explosions, acts of terrorism. The Producer's insurance policies must waive subrogation against the Owner or any entity affiliated with the Owner.

    (iv) Umbrella Liability:
    $_____

    (B) All insurance coverage shall be at the Producer's sole expense.

    (C) All insurance policies shall name the Owner, and any corporation affiliated with Owner, as co-insured.

    (D) At least _____ days prior to Producer's first use of the Theater, Producer shall cause to be delivered to Owner a certificate of insurance, and proof of premium payment thereof, evidencing the above described coverages. Upon Owner's request, Producer shall, in addition thereto, furnish to Owner true and correct copies of the actual policies thereof. Until such evidence of insurance is delivered in a form satisfactory to the Owner, the Producer and his agents, employees, and other personnel under his control are prohibited from entering upon or using the premises of the Theater.

    (E) All insurance policies must contain an endorsement giving the Owner at least thirty days advance written notice of cancellation, nonrenewal, or any material change in the policy limits or coverage.

(F) All insurance policies must provide coverage over the persons and property of third parties entering upon the premises.

(G) For all purposes hereunder, particularly but not limited to Comprehensive General Liability and Umbrella Liability Insurance, required to be carried by the Producer as aforesaid, liability shall be apportioned as follows:

(i) Any acts, omissions, occurrences, or other incidents arising out of or relating to the operating of the Theater, the Owner shall accept primary responsibility;

(ii) Any acts, omissions, occurrences, or other incidents arising out of or relating to the presentation of the Attraction, the Producer shall accept primary responsibility.

(H) Notwithstanding any of the foregoing, the Producer shall hold the Owner and any corporation or entity controlled by him harmless and indemnify him for any claim, demand, judgment, costs, attorney fees, or losses incurred to any person, property, or thing brought into the Theater by the Producer.

(I) Notwithstanding any of the foregoing, the Owner shall hold the Producer and any corporation or entity controlled by him harmless and indemnify him for any claim, demand, judgment, costs, attorney fees, or losses incurred to any person, property, or thing brought into the Theater by the Owner.

30. The parties understand and agree that certain events beyond their individual control may affect the presentation of the Attraction (*forces majeure*). These events include, but are not limited to, any of the following: war, acts of terror, public emergency, strikes, fires, government restrictions, interference with or interruption of transportation, casualty, physical disturbance, acts of nature, calamity of any kind whatsoever, and the like. In such event:

(A) If the Owner may perform his obligations under this agreement, but a *force majeure* prevents the Producer from performance, then the Producer shall remain fully obligated to perform all of his duties under this agreement, including, but not limited to, making all payments required hereunder, as if the *force majeure* had not occurred;

(B) If *force majeure* otherwise prevents either or both parties from performance hereunder, all of the Producer's obligations hereunder shall be suspended or excused until such time as the circumstances causing *force majeure* shall have ended, except, however, the Producer shall remain obligated for all payments required hereunder. The Owner's obligations shall be excused or suspended until such time as the circumstances causing *force majeure* shall have ended.

(C) In any event causing *force majeure*, the Owner shall not be liable to the Producer for any expenses, costs, lost profits, or any other incidental or consequential damages, occurring because of *force majeure*.

(D) In the event the circumstances causing *force majeure* cannot be cured or resolved, in Owner's sole discretion, the Owner may terminate this agreement, without liability therefore, upon twenty-four (24) hours written notice to the Producer.

31. Producer is required to continue the run of the Attraction during all times in which the contract remains in force, until said agreement terminates under its terms or in accordance with any other provisions herein. Producer expressly may not close the play, even for brief periods of time, whether because of holidays, the vacation or illness of any star or other personnel, or for any other reason, except with the written consent of the Owner.

32. This agreement may not be assigned, transferred, or encumbered by either party, except:

(A) The Producer may assign this agreement to a corporation, which he controls, or to a limited partnership or joint venture organized by the Producer, of which he remains a general partner, which will produce the Attraction. In any such assignment, the Producer shall remain liable for all obligations hereunder. No such assignment shall become effective until (i) the assignee executes a written copy of same; and (ii) the assignee assumes, in writing, all of Producer's obligations hereunder; and (iii) said written assignment and assumption thereof are delivered to, and accepted by, the Owner.

(B) Owner may sell, transfer, or otherwise assign all of his rights and obligations under this agreement (including the title or leasehold to the Theater), without notice to or consent of the Producer. Provided the transferee assumes all of Owner's obligations hereunder, the Owner will be released from all responsibility, obligations, and liability herefrom. Owner may transfer any security deposits or other sums due and owing to the Producer to the transferee. Provided the transferee assumes all of Owner's obligations to hold such security deposit and other sums in conformance with the terms of this agreement, the Owner will be released from all liability therefore and will owe Producer no further responsibility therefore. The return of any security deposit or other sums due to the Producer will be the sole responsibility of the Owner's transferee.

33. Notwithstanding any other provision of this agreement, the parties expressly and specifically intend that this arrangement is a license for the mere use and occupancy of the Theater for the sole purpose of presenting the Attraction as aforesaid. Legal title to the Theater shall remain with the Owner at all times hereunder. The Producer may not operate or engage in any other business or activity therein, without an additional, written agreement signed by the Owner. This Agreement is not intended to create and should not be construed as creating a partnership, joint venture, or landlord-tenant relationship between the parties.

34. This Agreement shall constitute the whole contract between the parties. No amendment, modification, consents, or waivers of any of its provisions shall be effective unless contained in a writing attached hereto and signed by both of the parties.

35. In the event of dispute, claim, disagreement, or conflict arising out of this agreement, the parties agree to submit same to an arbitrator in the city of _____, under the Commercial Rules of the American Arbitration Association. The arbitrator is specifically permitted to award to the prevailing party, all costs, attorney fees, witnesses' fees, travel expenses, and all other charges incurred by reason of the hearing. Judgment upon any award so granted may be entered by any court of competent jurisdiction.

36. Notices required herein shall be directed to the parties at the following addresses:

_____ (Producer)

_____ (Owner)

All notices shall be sent by certified mail, return receipt requested, and shall be effective on the date of mailing.

In Witness Whereof, the parties have hereunto set their hands and seals this day and date.

_____ (Producer)

By: _____ (Title)

_____ (Owner)

By: _____ (Title)

chapter **3** Booking Agreements

A booking agreement codifies the arrangement between the owner of a particular venue and the act the owner wishes to present. Owners or landlords may negotiate the contract directly with the performer (or her agent) or with another producer who is packaging the show.

A booking agreement may be used by presenters of stage plays, stand up comedians, comedy clubs, pop or classical musical performers, touring theater companies, symphony orchestras, dance companies, lecturers, sketch comedy troupes, opera companies, performance artists—in short, just about everyone doing any kind of live stage performance. Even amateur and community theaters can use it if they wish to bring a special attraction into their facilities. That's why Form 4, which follows, may be the single most useful form you will find in this book.

That being the case, let's examine the essential terms every good booking agreement should contain.

BOOKING AGREEMENT ESSENTIALS

1. *The Act/Venue.* To simplify our discussion here, we will refer to the show as the "Act," regardless of the nature of the production or whether the contract is with the performer herself or an independent producer or promoter packaging the show.

   The agreement must first identify the performer and the venue. It should go on to describe the kind of show the parties are booking—stage play, musical group, dance company, etc.—in substantial detail.

2. *Specific description of the Act.* This should be self-explanatory.

3. *Fees.* The presenter may pay an act either a flat fee or a percentage of the gross box office ticket sales. Commonly, even for lesser known artists, the presenter pays a guarantee in advance against an agreed upon percentage of the gross box office. The latter

cannot be known in full until after the act completes its run. In that case, the presenter waits until the act has played its last performance, computes the box office sales from all sources for all performances, and, applying the gross percentage factor, compares that total with the guarantee he has already paid out.

If the result is more than the guarantee, he owes the act the difference. If it is less, he owes nothing. When he does owe additional money, he should pay it within an established time frame after the last performance. Guarantees are usually nonrefundable. The presenter assumes this risk, even if the act fails to generate enough box office sales to cover the presenter's costs.

4. *Self-contained productions.* Most acts booked in this way are self-contained productions. That is, the act itself furnishes the full attraction—i.e., performers, rights to copyrighted materials, scenery, costumes, etc. Musical acts—including touring musical plays—generally travel with a music director and the key musicians. When additional musicians are needed, the act, using a music contractor, hires out of the local branch of the American Federation of Musicians. All of the costs are figured into the amount of the guarantee the act requires. Sometimes, the guarantee will also include a reasonable profit. In other cases, the act hopes to make its profit out of its percentage of the box office.

   The local presenter rarely involves himself in the actual production or in engaging any of the needed local personnel, other than his own regular house crew.

5. *Transportation/Housing.* If the act is locally based, commuting and housing costs will not be a subject of negotiations.

   However, when the act is based out of another city, or is otherwise touring, and it has achieved a level of success, it may ask for, and receive, reasonable travel costs to and from its point of origin to the city in which it will now be performing. In addition, the act will negotiate in town housing accommodations. The kind and level of living quarters quite obviously depend upon the act. Paul McCartney can demand the moon and he will get it. An entry or mid-level act may have to settle for the Super 8 motel.

Major acts also negotiate accommodations for their entourage, which may include such necessary personnel as its road (stage) crew, and such unnecessary (from the producer's point of view) persons as the veterinarian to the star's pet poodle. Groupies are the performer's own responsibility, though I have seen demands for housing for "close friends."

Large touring shows, such as musicals, may require two hundred persons or more, all traveling as part of the company. Their producers may contract with major hotel chains to provide housing near the theater. These costs may be figured into the guarantee or they may be negotiated as separate terms.

6. *Special requirements.* Major acts may also have special requirements. For instance, a star may expect the producer to maintain fresh fruit and bottled water in her dressing room and hotel suite at all times. The producer may have to repaint dressing rooms to the star's favorite color.

All stars expect transportation between their hotel room and venue. For security reasons, some may actually prefer a modest vehicle with a bodyguard/chauffeur, while others may demand a stretch limousine.

Producers must be prepared to meet these requirements, whether they are part of the star's contract or not. It is a part of the cost of doing business. It always pays to keep the star happy.

7. *Exclusivity.* Producers must insist upon an exclusive booking with the act. No producer wants an act to play a competitor's venue the night before playing the producer's own booking. For that reason, producers justifiably demand an exclusive window for a certain, negotiated period of time before and after the booking, during which time the act may not play for anyone else in the producer's competitive geographic area. The size of the restricted area and the time windows are negotiable. This assures the producer that persons within his community who wish to see the show must buy tickets to his booking.

8. *Publicity/advertising.* National acts maintain their own countrywide publicity and marketing machines. In addition to press agents, they may also advise their fan base of their upcoming appearances through mailings, television appearances, and Web sites. These costs are borne by the acts themselves.

9. *Indemnification.* This is legal boilerplate that, in a booking agreement, is absolutely essential to protect the presenter. An act may not show up or be prepared to perform or may damage the presenter's facilities. Acts often bring with them baggage of all kinds. A wise presenter demands indemnification. (For further information, see "Legal Boilerplate," at the beginning of this book.)

Form 4   Booking Agreement

THIS AGREEMENT made this _____ day of _____, 20___, by and between _____
("Presenter") and _____ ("Act").

In consideration of the mutual covenants, terms, and conditions contained herein, the parties hereby agree as follows:
The Presenter hereby engages the Act to perform and the Act agrees to perform the Engagement ("Engagement")
upon the following terms and conditions:

1. The Act will commence performances beginning on _____ and ending on _____. The Act will
   present _____ performances upon the following schedule:
   _____ matinee performances on _____, curtain time at _____ [A.M.] [P.M.]
   _____ evening performances on _____, curtain time at _____ P.M.
   All shows will commence, more or less, at the scheduled curtain time.
2. The Act is more specifically described as follows: _____
   _____.

3. The Presenter will pay the Act the nonrefundable fee of _____ dollars ($_____), no later than
   _____ days prior to the first performance. Such fee will be a guarantee against the Act's percentage of the
   gross box office sales as described in paragraph 4 below.
4. After first deducting the guaranteed fee described in paragraph 3 above, the Act will also be entitled to _____%
   of the Gross Box Office Ticket Sales for each performance.
   Gross Box Office Ticket Sales will consist of ticket sales from all sources, including (but not limited to) box office, telephone, mail order, Ticketmaster, group, Internet, subscription, and ticket brokers, less sales commissions and taxes.
   Not later than five business days after the last performance, the Presenter will pay the Act its percentage of the gross
   box office ticket sales for the Engagement, accompanied by a detailed accounting statement signed by the
   Presenter and the box office Treasurer describing the disposition of all available tickets for each performance of the
   Engagement.
5. The Engagement will occur at _____ Theater, located at _____.
6. Ticket prices will range from _____ ($_____) to _____ ($_____) dollars.
7. The Act will be entitled to _____ pairs of house seats for each performance at the full box office price. House seats
   will be located in the section and rows customarily reserved for house seats in the particular theater. For matinee
   performances, the Act must purchase the seats not later than _____ hours before the performance; those house
   seats not purchased for that performance will be offered for sale to the general public. For evening performances,
   the Act must purchase the house seats not later than _____ hours before the performance; those house seats not
   purchased for that performance will be offered for sale to the general public. House seats may not be resold at a
   premium above the full box office price. The Act agrees to comply with all of the local laws, rules, and regulations
   pertaining to the use and disposition of house seats.
8. Presenter, at its own expense, will provide transportation to and from the Act's city of residence to the city of performance, upon the following terms: _____
   _____
9. Presenter, at its own expense, will provide housing accommodations for the Act in the city of performance, during
   the Engagement, upon the following terms: _____
   _____
   Said accommodations will be for all persons comprising the Act, as described in paragraph 17 below.
10. Presenter, at its own expense, will provide round trip transportation for the Act within the city of performance, from
    the Act's living quarters to the theater for rehearsals and performances, upon the following terms:
    _____
    Said transportation will be for all persons comprising the Act as described in paragraph 17 below.

11. In addition thereto, the Presenter, at its own expense, will provide the following special requirements of the Act:
_____.
Presenter understands the same are for the comfort and well being of the Act during its employment by the Presenter.

12. The Presenter, at its own expense, will provide security to the Act during its employment by the Presenter, as follows:
_____
_____.

13. Both parties understand and agree that publicity and promotion are essential to the successful marketing of the Act's engagement. Therefore the Act agrees to cooperate with all of the Presenter's reasonable publicity, promotional, and marketing efforts, including making itself available for interviews by the press in all media before and during the Engagement. The parties further agree to the following additional methods of publicity and promotion:
_____.
The parties will maintain joint control over the disposition of complementary tickets given to bona fide members of the press.

14. Both parties understand and agree that it is essential to the successful marketing of the Act's engagement and essential to secure the Presenter's investment that the Act's services will be exclusive to the Presenter. Accordingly, the Act hereby agrees that it will not perform for another Presenter within a _____-mile radius of the present engagement for a period of at least _____ days before its first performance and a period of at least _____ days after its last performance under this contract. Notwithstanding the foregoing, the Act may perform brief excerpts from its show, not to exceed _____ (seconds) on radio or television broadcasts before and during its engagement for the purpose of publicizing and promoting itself and the Engagement.

15. The Act represents and warrants that it either owns or has the license and permission to perform all material copyrighted by others in its show and that it will do nothing to infringe upon the copyrighted material of any persons or entities for which it does not have an appropriate license.

16. The Presenter, at its own expense, will provide front of the house management and personnel, and also a stage crew consisting of the following: _____.

17. The Act, at its own expense, will provide the elements necessary to provide a full and complete attraction, which will consist of _____.

18. In the event the Act requires on or off stage personnel, in addition to those persons provided by the Presenter, the Act, at its own expense, will provide same.

19. The Act will receive billing credits in all advertising, promotion, and publicity, as follows: _____
_____.

20. The Presenter will pay for all costs of theater rental and maintenance, publicity, advertising, and promotional materials, as follows: _____.

21. All publicity, advertising, and promotional materials issued by the Presenter are subject to the approval of the Act, which approval will not be unreasonably withheld. The parties will maintain joint control over the disposition of tickets to members of the press.

22. During this Engagement, the Act reserves the exclusive right to offer and sell to patrons merchandise, including wearing apparel, recordings, souvenir books, toys, games, jewelry, and other souvenirs containing its logo and/or trademarks. The Act agrees to offer and sell same only out of the concession stands located about the theater before, during, and after its performances. The Act further understands and agrees that the Producer and/or the Theater has a previously existing contractual arrangement with _____ [*the professional concessionaire*] for the exclusive right to sell concessions and souvenir merchandise during engagements at the Theater. Accordingly, the parties will split the proceeds (after deduction for sales taxes and the cost of refunds and returns) from the sale of merchandise, as follows:

_____% to the Act

_____% to _____ [*Professional Concessionaire*]

_____% to the Producer

_____% to the Theater

The Act will establish the gross sales prices for the merchandise so offered for sale, in consultation with _____ [*Professional Concessionaire*].

23. The Producer will provide rehearsal space to the Act, at his own expense, as follows: _____
_____
_____ upon the following schedule: _____
_____

24. No broadcasts or recordings, whether by film, video, audio, or other means may be made of the performances. Notwithstanding the foregoing, the Producer may present a brief excerpt from the performance, not to exceed _____ seconds, whether live, filmed, or on tape, on commercial radio or television broadcasts, including news programs, for the sole purpose of promoting and publicizing the producer's presentation of the Act, and provided the Producer does not receive any compensation or profits thereof, except for nominal out-of-pocket expenses connected thereto. The Producer will post notices in and about the theater, as well as publish same in the programs, that the recording of the performance by patrons or any others is strictly prohibited. Producer will use his best efforts to prevent same. The Producer will not use the Act's name and/or likeness or photographs or permit the use of same to expressly or imply any endorsement or tie in to any commercial product without the express written consent of the Act.

25. This contract is for the personal services of the Act and it may be not be assigned without the written consent of the Producer.

26. The Act will at all times comply with the rules and regulations of the Producer and the Theater, as well as with all applicable building and fire codes imposed by the local authorities having jurisdiction thereof.

27. All notices required hereunder shall be contained in writing and mailed to the parties by certified mail, return receipt requested, at the addresses following their signatures. The notices will be effective on the date of mailing hereof.

28. Except when the only remedy that will prevent irreparable harm is equitable relief, the parties agree to submit any disputes arising under this Agreement to arbitration conducted by a member of and under the commercial rules of the American Arbitration Association, in the city of _____. The Arbitrator will require the losing party to pay the reasonable costs and attorney fees of the prevailing party. Any court of competent jurisdiction may enter judgment upon the award so granted.

In Witness Whereof, the parties have hereunto set their hands and seals this day and date first above written.

_____ (Producer)

_____ (Address)

_____

_____ (Act)

By: _____ (Title)

_____ (Address)

_____

chapter **4** Joint Ventures

In a joint venture, two or more parties band together for the purpose of carrying out a single business enterprise, for a limited time, in the hope of making a profit. In the theater, joint ventures commonly occur in one of two ways:

1. Two or more producers create a joint venture for the purpose of raising funds in a theatrical limited partnership, to produce a show.
2. Two or more theater companies join together to produce a play, usually because for artistic or economic reasons the production is beyond the resources of each company individually.

Here's the way a joint venture works with two or more producers: Grippo options the rights to present a musical called *Diaper Rash*. But, to produce it properly I need ten million dollars, only I don't have the contacts with enough investors to raise that kind of money. So I join forces with Cash Callahan, whose Rolodex is jam packed with the private phone numbers of potential backers. We form a joint venture, which is a kind of partnership, in which we agree to use our best efforts to raise the money we need. Once we have the money, we will form a Limited Partnership with our investors, to produce the show.

In the commercial theater, the *limited partnership* is the way producers commonly finance a show. A limited partnership is a legal entity, organized by producers, in which investors purchase partnership shares at whatever price the producers establish. If the show is a success, the producer and the investors share the profits according to whatever formula to which they have agreed. If the show fails, the producer and the investors likewise share losses according to their predetermined formula. The investors may not take part in the managing of the partnership; the producers manage the partnership. In exchange, however, the investors cannot lose anything more than their original investments; their personal assets, like their homes and bank accounts, are protected from the claims of any creditors of the partnership. In addition, the investors may take any losses as deductions on their taxes against any other income they may have.

A limited partnership requires at least one general partner (one producer) and at least one limited partner (one investor). The joint venture arises when one producer joins forces with another—like I did with Cash Callahan—to raise the funds to produce the show. The joint venture terminates either because the funds are raised or the producers decide to abandon the project because they could not raise the funds or otherwise proceed with the project—for instance, if the star they hoped to sign decides not to do their show. Once the producers raise the funds, they create the limited partnership and proceed with the project.

Although the rest of this chapter details the mechanics of the joint venture, I have deliberately omitted the forms for creating the limited partnership. That is because a limited partnership is not do-it-yourself law. Creating a limited partnership requires substantial legal judgment and experience, particularly in securities and tax laws, both of which are highly technical. The penalties for failing to accurately comply with these complex regulations range from substantial money damages all the way to prison time. Besides, satisfying federal requirements, one must also comply with the requirements of the individual states in which one intends to solicit funds. A producer needs the help of both an attorney and a CPA who are also experienced in theater, securities, and tax laws.

I refer readers who are interested in learning more to see my book *The Stage Producers Business and Legal Guide*, in which I devote an entire chapter to a detailed discussion of the limited partnership.

Incidentally, while the example I used above for my joint venture for *Diaper Rash* relates to Broadway financing, joint ventures and limited partnerships are also the most common methods producers use to finance shows off Broadway and in large commercial regional productions. Obviously, the dollar amounts would be correspondingly different.

THE ELEMENTS

If you carefully break down my opening sentence, you will understand the basic requirements of a theatrical joint venture.

1. *Two or more parties.* Like a partnership, a joint venture is an association, which requires at least two parties. Theoretically, there is no limit as to the number of parties who may engage in a joint venture. Some big, expensive Broadway musicals have been joint ventures among ten or more producers. The associating parties may be natural persons, business entities (such as corporations), or a combination.
2. *Band together.* The parties agree to associate with each other, as opposed to acting independently as sole proprietors or sole business entities.
3. *Single business enterprise.* In a partnership, the parties engage in a complex pattern of many transactions, all of them flowing into or out of the partnership. In a joint venture, the parties intend to associate together only for one purpose—the production of a single show (as opposed to a series of shows). Once that purpose no longer exists—the show (and all its related touring, foreign, and other companies) closes—the enterprise dissolves.
4. *Limited time.* In a partnership, the parties usually intend their relationship to last for a long time—decades, often even for life. A joint venture exists for a fixed—though not necessarily specified—time period.
5. *Hope of making a profit.* The parties hope their show will make more money than it costs to produce, and they will each take some profits home during the life of the venture, even though in reality they may instead see losses. Even nonprofit theater companies hope to make some money out of their shows.

A joint venture agreement must be structured very carefully. Form 5 is an agreement that deals with producers forming a joint venture in the commercial theater to raise funds to present a single show. It may also be used by theater companies that desire to produce a play neither is capable of producing on its own. To keep the form manageable, I have drafted it for only two parties. However, by simply increasing the number of spaces for identifying the parties, you can accommodate as many joint venturers as you like.

For a more comprehensive discussion of joint ventures in the theater, see my book *The Stage Producers Business and Legal Guide,* chapter 8, "Joint Ventures."

JOINT VENTURES IN THE COMMERCIAL THEATER

Commonly in the commercial theater, one producer owns the option on the rights to a play he wants to present. Another may have access to the necessary financing. They may be joined by a third party who can bring a star into their production. The three producers decide to pool their resources to present the single show and its attendant additional companies in the territories for which the first producer owns the rights. This is the arrangement under which most Broadway shows come into being. However, this kind of venture works just as well in regional theater.

The purpose of the joint venture is to raise the money necessary to fund the commercial limited partnership, which is the entity that will actually produce the show.

For our purposes, we will assume both producers are natural persons, although Form 5 works just as well if the proposed joint venturers are business entities, or a combination of natural persons and entities.

JOINT VENTURE ESSENTIALS

1. *Identification.* Identify the parties, as well as the business name under which the parties will conduct the enterprise.
2. *Purpose.* Obviously, this will be to produce the particular play for which at least one of the parties holds the option.
3. *Territories.* Describe the geographic area in which the parties intend to present the show. As I indicated above, this is determined by the scope of rights that the playwright has granted under the option. It may be regional or broader in scope. For instance, under the standard option for First Class productions (Broadway) the playwright gives the producer the right to present the show on

Broadway itself, as well as throughout the United States, Puerto Rico, Canada, the British Isles, Australia, New Zealand, and in so-called Second Class productions.

4. *Agreement.* Agree to form the theatrical limited partnership that will actually produce the play.

5. *Individual resources.* Attorneys are divided whether to itemize the resources each party will bring to the joint venture. Obviously, it is crystal clear if one party owns the options on the rights to the play, while the other brings in all of the financing. However, from there, it can become murky—which is why specificity is often difficult. For instance, one party may have access to financing, but, in truth, all of the parties will (and should) use their best efforts to raise funds. Similarly, the party with access to a star cannot really guarantee she will appear in the show, until she has a signed contract. I prefer to leave this clause out altogether, but I mention it because its necessity invokes different opinions.

6. *Best efforts.* Despite the foregoing, joint venturers agree to use their best efforts to raise the necessary financing.

7. *Nonexclusive arrangement.* One of the fundamental differences between a partnership and a joint venture is the exclusivity of the former versus the nonexclusivity of the latter. In a partnership, the parties agree to devote all of their time to the enterprise. They also promise not to engage in other ventures, particularly competing ones.

Joint venturers make no such promises. In fact, the reverse is true. In a joint venture, each party only obligates himself to give as much time and effort as is necessary to the business. He reserves the right to participate in other businesses, either on his own or with completely different partners. He may even engage in competing businesses.

Thus a producer may participate in as many joint ventures as he wishes, even with competing shows.

8. *Capital requirements.* It is wise to set forth in the joint venture agreement the minimum and maximum amounts of capital the parties need to fund the limited partnership. Leaving this term open creates ambiguity. If you don't specify dollar amounts (in both directions), no one can determine whether and when the joint venture has fulfilled its function.

Of course, this means the producers must actually hammer out a proposed budget for their show before they sign any joint venture agreement. However, by this time, they should have an estimated budget in mind anyway, based on the needs of the show, and the proposed level of production. They most certainly will need one soon, since they must specify the budget in the offering circular (the prospectus), which they must give to potential investors.

9. *Profits.* Okay, here's the section you're really interested in—the money. The producers must negotiate the formula for splitting profits and losses within the limited partnership (between themselves and the investors) and also the manner in which they will split producers' fees, profits, and losses. Commonly, in a limited partnership, the producer/general partner receives 50 percent of any profits, and the investor/limited partners receive the rest. So now, as joint venturers, the producers must decide how they intend to split up their 50 percent. (Okay, the reality is that the show may tank and no one will see any profits. Producers are optimists. God knows they have to be in order to survive even twenty-four hours in this business. But, nevertheless, they must prepare for profits.) Sometimes producers split equally; other times, they divide the spoils based on the percentage of financing each producer raises.

Similarly, producers are entitled to a weekly fee for each company of the show they manage, as well as an office overhead charge (called the *cash office charge*). They divide these fees according to the same formula they used for profits, right?

Well, maybe.

Sometimes, in the course of events, since the parties do not make an exclusive commitment of their time to the enterprise, they chose to appoint one producer as day-to-day manager of the enterprise. The others participate in the broader, more substantial management issues. In such event, the weekly fee and cash office charge to the production remain the same. (It must or the investors would have the producers' heads on a silver platter.) But the administrating producer may ask for (and get) a larger piece of the action, since he is doing more work than the others. All is negotiable.

10. *Losses.* Okay, here's the part you don't want to know about, but you're going to hear it anyway. Losses, which in the theater, begin with a capital *L*. (Spoiled your day, didn't I?) Joint venturers usually share losses according to the same formula as profits.

11. *Front money.* This is money needed to pay expenses incurred before the producers may legally tap into limited partnership funds. Joint venturers who advance front money are entitled to reimbursement.

12. *Professional fundraiser.* Sometimes the parties are unable to raise all of the limited partnership funds themselves. They may need to bring in another party—a professional fundraiser—to supplement the work. Obviously, they must pay the professional for his services. In such event, it is fairest to share such expenses equally.

13. *Deadlocks.* It is crucial that all the producers share artistic and business decision making equally. Problems arise, however, when there is disagreement. The absolute worst situation that can befall a show is deadlock between the producers over a decision. In that event, a mechanism must be in place to resolve the matter quickly. Theatrical attorneys commonly recommend that the producers nominate a third, easily accessible, party to break the deadlock. They can nominate anyone they choose, although they would be wise to select a theatrical professional and foolhardy to pick a spouse or other closely related party whose decisions may be biased. Often, the producers select the production's attorney or accountant to decide business deadlocks, while they may choose a neutral, mutually respected artist—playwright, director, etc.—to resolve artistic deadlocks. A professional mediator usually decides any other deadlocks that may arise.

14. *Billing.* Producers like to see their names up in lights, just like everyone else in the theater, even though with rare exceptions, their names don't mean much to the ticket buying public. Oh, if they are lucky and their show wins the Tony for best play or musical, they get a fleeting moment on television. But the next day everyone remembers the star, playwright, or maybe the director. But the producer?

    (Don't believe me? Okay, here's a pop quiz: *The Producers* is one of the biggest and most honored musical successes ever. You can tell me Mel Brooks—and Thomas Meehan—wrote it. You can even tell me Nathan Lane and Matthew Broderick were the original stars. But can you name even so much as one of the show's fourteen producers without peeking at the cast album? Go ahead. I dare you.)

So the joint venturers establish a right to billing credit, usually on an equal basis, so they can get their measly shot at fame. And all of the producers should get the same billing credit whenever any of the others do.

15. *One member binds all.* Just as in a partnership, all of the members of the joint venture can individually bind the enterprise and each other to debts, regardless of whether the others know or consent to be so obligated. All of you must agree before any of the parties can enter into any contracts on behalf of the joint venture.

    Once all of the parties consent to the terms of a contract, any one of them should have authority to sign the contract on behalf of the joint venture. As a practical matter, each party should also have the right to sign routine checks individually.

16. *Termination.* A joint venture terminates:
    a. When the parties decide by mutual agreement, it just isn't working out.
    b. When the time arrives at last to create the limited partnership, i.e., when fund raising is complete.
    c. When one party dies, withdraws, or files for bankruptcy.

17. *Withdrawal of a party.* Suppose the show is up and running, but it is just plodding along. One of the joint venturers loses interest and decides it's time to post the closing notice. The other party disagrees. He thinks there's life in the old war-horse yet. Maybe it needs a little tweaking—a fresh star, a new publicity campaign—whatever. Provide a mechanism so the disinterested party can withdraw, taking with him only the profits, share of subsidiary rights, and obligations that have arisen during his time with the show. But let the still "believing in the show's chances" joint venturer take over the production—lock, stock, and headaches. From that day forward, he incurs the obligations, as well as enjoys any new profits, while the other walks off into the sunset.

18. *Agreement survives parties.* Even though the joint venture may terminate, the provisions of its agreement survive and continue to bind the parties, their heirs, representatives . . . well, by now, you know the drill.

19. *Selection of production professionals.* Pick the attorneys, accountants, and general manager for the show.

Form 5 Joint Ventures

THIS AGREEMENT entered into this _____ day of 20_____, by and between _____ ("_____") [*First Joint Venturer's last name*] and _____ ("_____") [*Second Joint Venturer's last name*], and hereinafter sometimes collectively referred to as the Joint Venturers and sometimes as the Parties, all of whom are of legal age and competent mental capacity, as of this date, time, and place.

Whereas _____ and _____ desire to associate together for the purpose of raising funds and creating a theatrical limited partnership for which they will act as the general partners, in order to jointly produce the play presently entitled _____ (the "Play"), written by _____, upon the terms hereinafter described.

It is hereby agreed as follows:

1. The undersigned do hereby create and form a Joint Venture, to do business under the name of _____ (the "Joint Venture"), for the purposes stated in introductory paragraph 2 above. The business address of the Joint Venture, for notices and all other purposes, shall be _____.

2. The parties intend to present the play in the following geographic environs _____ _____. The Joint Venturers contemplate presenting the play at the following level(s) of production _____.

3. (A) For the purpose thereof, the parties intend to raise money to create a Limited Partnership, which shall be known as the _____ Limited Partnership, and which shall be formed under the laws of the State of _____. The parties agree to form the Limited Partnership as soon as possible after sufficient funds (as defined in 3 (B) below) are raised therefore.

   (B) The minimum capital necessary to constitute "sufficient funds" to form the Limited Partnership is _____ dollars ($_____), while the maximum capital necessary is _____ dollars ($_____).

   (C) In the event that less than the minimum capital (as stated above) shall be raised, the parties may agree to either terminate this venture, or create the Limited Partnership nevertheless based upon the actual capital raised.

4. The Joint Venturers shall act as general partners of the Limited Partnership and shall assume all management responsibility and liability therefore, while the parties investing capital in the Limited Partnership shall be the limited partners, whose liability shall be limited, as provided by law. None of the Joint Venturers may also contribute capital as a limited partner.

5. The Joint Venturers shall use their best efforts, individually and collectively, to raise the funding described in paragraph 3(B) above.

6. The undersigned _____ presently owns the option to present the play at the aforesaid level of production and in the geographic environs so stated _____ hereby agrees to convey, at its original cost, said option to the Limited Partnership as soon as possible after its formation, as well as all other rights, interest, and agreements _____ may own that are necessary to, and appropriate, for the contemplated production.

7. In the event the parties are unable to raise all of the funds necessary to capitalize the limited partnership, the parties may agree to engage another party (the "fundraiser") to raise any part or all of the balance of the remaining funds. In such event, all fees and costs paid to said fundraiser, including any shares of the Producers' net profits, shall be borne equally by all of the Joint Venturers and shall first be deducted from any sums owed to the undersigned by the Limited Partnership.

8. Before any net profits are computed and distributed between the Limited Partners and General Partners, it will first be necessary to deduct any sums owed to gross and/or royalty participants in the play. Thereafter, net profits shall be computed and divided as follows:

(A) All limited partners shall first be repaid to the extent of their investments in the Limited Partnership, pro-rata.

(B) Net profits remaining thereafter shall be divided fifty percent (50%) to the limited partners and fifty percent (50%) to the Joint Venturers/General Partners. [*The standard split of net profits is on a fifty/fifty basis between limited partners and the joint venturers. However, this is negotiable depending on what investors might demand.*]

(C) Net losses remaining thereafter shall be divided fifty percent (50%) to the limited partners and fifty percent (50%) to the Joint Venturers/General Partners. [*See note B above, as losses are based on the same formula as profits.*]

9. Upon formation of the Limited Partnership, the Joint Venturers shall be entitled to recover from the capital thereof, all expenses and costs, as permitted by law, advanced by them on behalf of the Limited Partnership. Said costs shall be divided as were advanced by each Joint Venturer. [*Joint Venturers get their money back as soon as the Limited Partnership is formed, right off the top from the investors' funds—even if the show closes on the first day of rehearsal.*]

10. (A) The Joint Venturers shall divide the Producer's share of the net profits, or net losses, as the case may be, according to the following formula:

_____% to the undersigned _____

_____% to the undersigned _____

(B) The Joint Venturers shall divide the Producer's fee (as described in paragraph 11 below) according to the following formula:

_____% to the undersigned _____

_____% to the undersigned _____

(C) The Joint Venturers shall divide the weekly cash office charge (as described in paragraph 11 below) according to the following formula:

_____% to the undersigned _____

_____% to the undersigned _____

11. In their capacity as producers, the Joint Venturers shall be entitled to the following fees (in addition to net profits or net losses as described in paragraph 9 above), payable by the Limited Partnership in the following amounts:

(A) Producer's fee shall be _____% of the gross weekly box officer receipts of each company under the management of the Joint Venturers until the Limited Partnership recoups the production budget. Thereafter the Producer's fee shall be _____% of the gross weekly box office receipts of each company under the management of the Joint Venturers.

(B) The cash office charge shall be _____ dollars ($_____) for each company of the show under the Joint Venturers' management. Said fee shall begin _____ weeks prior to the first rehearsal of the particular company and shall end _____ weeks after each company plays its final performance.

(C) The Producer's fee and the cash office charge are payable by the Limited Partnership and are considered earned by the Joint Venturers, regardless of whether the production earns net profits or losses.

12. The Joint Venturers' shall share responsibilities as follows:

(A) All Joint Venturers must consent to all contracts, debts, or other obligations entered into on behalf of the Joint Venture, the Limited Partnership, or both.

(B) Subject to the provisions of paragraph 12 (A) above, any of the Joint Venturers shall have full power and authority to sign all contracts and checks on behalf of the Joint Venture and the Limited Partners and the same shall be binding thereon.

13. The Joint Venturers hereby select the following _____ [persons] [entities] to fulfill the following capacities on behalf of the Joint Venture and the Limited Partnership:

_____ General Manager

_____ Accountant

_____ Attorney

14. Whenever and wherever producer credits are given, credits shall be given in the following order and size and style of typeface:

_____ (Name) _____ (Typeface)

_____ (Name) _____ (Typeface)

Whenever and wherever billing credit is given to one producer, it shall also be given to the other producer.

15. It is agreed and understood that this arrangement between the parties shall be on a nonexclusive basis. Each party shall be free, during the duration hereof, to engage in other business ventures, either solely, or with other Joint Venturers, whether or not in competition with the subject enterprise and/or Limited Partnership. Notwithstanding the foregoing, however, each of the parties agrees to commit as much of his time as is appropriate and necessary to the management and operations of the Joint Venture, the Limited Partnership, and the production of the play.

16. All of the Joint Venturers shall contribute equally to the "front" or "preproduction" monies necessary and appropriate to fund the Joint Venture and undertake to create the Limited Partnership. Upon agreement of the parties, one party may advance funds to pay for budgeted expenses. Immediately upon creation of the Limited Partnership, all front monies so advanced shall be reimbursed to the appropriate parties out of the capitalization of the Limited Partnership.

   It is agreed and understood that it may become necessary or desirable to obtain some or all of any "front money" from a third party. In exchange therefore, the Venturers may have to assign a percentage of the producer's profits to said third party. In such event, the undersigned Joint Venturers hereby agree to share such assignment equally.

17. The parties shall make artistic, business, and all other decisions jointly. Each Joint Venturer shall have one vote in all such matters. In the event, however, it becomes apparent the parties cannot agree on a particular issue, they hereby appoint the following third parties to make decisions, and they further agree to be bound by said third party's judgment:
   Artistic Decisions by _____ (Third Party)
   Business Decisions by _____ (Third Party)
   The Joint Venturers agree to share any fees or costs charged by said third parties equally.
   The Joint Venturers agree to submit all other disputes and/or breaches of this agreement to arbitration conducted by a member of the American Association of Arbitrators in _____ (city), whose decision shall be final and binding. The arbitrator shall require the losing party to pay the reasonable costs and attorney fees of the prevailing party. Any court of competent jurisdiction may enter judgment upon the award so rendered.

18. In the event the parties cannot agree when it is appropriate to close the run of the play, then the party wishing to continue production (the "Persisting Party") shall have the right to assume total control and responsibility therefore. He shall give due written notice of his intentions to the other party, who shall then withdraw from the play, and all responsibility and control therefore (the "Withdrawing Party"). Transfer of control and responsibility shall be immediate. From that day forward the Persisting Party shall:
   (A) Bear all expenses and liabilities of the production;
   (B) Assume full management and decision-making authority;
   (C) Hold the Withdrawing Party harmless and indemnify him for all debts, obligations, and other liabilities occurring to the production beginning from the date of transfer of control;
   (D) Be entitled to all net profits and earnings of the play commencing on the date of transfer of ownership (except as provided otherwise below in section (G)).
   The Withdrawing Party shall:
   (E) Relinquish all rights to management and decision making authority;
   (F) Forfeit all rights, title, and other interest in the play (except as otherwise provided in section (G) below), including profits earned thereon;
   (G) Be entitled to his share of all of the producer's proceeds, profits, and losses of the play accrued or otherwise earned prior to transfer of control, even though same have not yet been distributed. This specifically includes producer's proceeds from the commercial exploitation of subsidiary rights.
   (H) Remain liable for all debts and obligations of the Joint Venture and/or Limited Partnership incurred prior to his withdrawal from the production.

19. All of the terms, provisions, and conditions herein shall survive once the Joint Venture, for any reason, shall terminate.

20. No party shall assign this agreement without the consent of the other, and no such purported assignment shall be valid unless accompanied by said consent.

21. The parties enter into this agreement on behalf of themselves, their heirs, and assigns (subject to paragraph 20 above) and same shall be binding thereon, now and forever.

22. This instrument contains the whole of the agreement between the parties. No purported amendment thereto shall be effective unless set forth in a written instrument signed by all of the parties.

23. The laws of the State of _____ shall govern this agreement.

24. Unless otherwise provided herein, the Joint Venture terminates upon the happening of one of the following:

    (A) The death, disability, incompetency, or bankruptcy of one of the parties;

    (B) Creation of the Limited Partnership, which is the purpose hereof;

    (C) Agreement of the parties;

    (D) Withdrawal of one of the parties.

25. Notices required hereunder to one of the Joint Venturers shall be mailed by certified mail, return receipt requested, to the address following the Joint Venturer's signature below and shall be effective upon the mailing thereof.

IN WITNESS WHEREOF, the parties have entered into this Agreement on this date hereinabove written by their hands and seals.

_____ (SEAL) _____

Name   Address

                                        _____

_____ (SEAL) _____

Name   Address

                                        _____

chapter **5** Concessions

In the very early days of motion pictures, the cost of the admission ticket was all the exhibitor expected to make off his business. However, independent entrepreneurs began setting up little stands outside the nickelodeons, out of which they sold candy, drinks, and other edibles to the theater owner's patrons, who would then bring them inside to munch during the show. As movies grew longer, from short subjects lasting only a few minutes to full length features lasting as long as an hour, audiences bought more munchies. The theater owner, watching the profits of the outside concessionaires grow, realized that by selling munchies himself inside his lobby, he could keep all that revenue to himself.

Voilà! The modern theater concession stand was born.

For reasons only a psychologist could explain, patrons are willing to pay incredible mark ups for refreshments and show-related souvenirs, as long as they can buy them in a theater lobby before and after the show and during intermission. It doesn't even matter whether the theater will actually allow them to eat their snacks during a performance, as long as the theater owner is willing to charge them high prices for soft drinks, cocktails, candy, etc. It is not uncommon for concession stands to mark up merchandise two, three, and even four times its cost. (The profits for soft drinks and popcorn are obscene by any standards, except those of the theater owner.)

So why shouldn't you get in on the action?

There are two ways to handle theater concession stands. Under the first way, the theater maintains the concession stand itself. The advantages? The theater controls all concession sales, employs and supervises the staff, and keeps all the profits (or swallows the losses—fat chance) for itself. However, this also places all the responsibility on the shoulders of management,

which is very likely overworked from doing what it is supposed to do, namely, creating and presenting shows in the first place. In addition, management must also deal with staffing the enterprise, keeping careful watch on the money, and maintaining the concessions inventory. This, by itself, is a great deal of work and in many theaters requires the employment of a concessions manager.

Alternatively, it may be desirable to contract with a professional concessions company to maintain your refreshment stand. This relieves the theater of staffing worries, inventory control, and the like. However, it also means much smaller profits. Most profits go to the professionals, with the theater receiving a small cut. It also means the theater will have less control over refreshments.

In the case of small theaters, management may not have a choice. Few professional concessionaires will even want your business unless you can meet a certain minimum level of sales expectations. Therefore, the small theater may have to handle concessions on its own, if it wants those extra dollars.

Theaters also must determine whether to permit patrons to bring munchies into the auditorium during the performance. In motion picture operations, the issue was settled decades ago. Patrons consume their popcorn, candy, drinks, etc., while the show goes on. For decades, few live theaters permitted this. Refreshments had to be eaten or drunk in the lobby. In live theater, this policy makes sense, since the unwrapping of candy and other consumables can be distracting to the actors, while in films it makes no difference. In addition, live theater just seemed too classy for that kind of conduct. However, just as society has relaxed its standards for virtually every kind of behavior in the last decades, live theater is gradually allowing patrons to bring their refreshments into the auditorium. In addition, profits from concessions have become too substantial to let a little thing like the performance get in the way. I mention it, because it's a policy decision each theater must make for itself.

If you decide to engage a professional concessionaire to handle your operations, you must draw up a written agreement to codify your arrangement.

CONCESSIONS AGREEMENT ESSENTIALS

1. *Product identification.* Identify the products the concessionaire is permitted to sell to your patrons, i.e., candy, soft drinks, mixed alcoholic beverages, beer, wine, etc. It is not necessary or desirable to specify brand names, such as Milk Duds or Pepsi, unless you have separate exclusive agreements with those particular manufacturers. It is becoming quite common for large brands to enter into arrangements with theaters, whereby the manufacturer pays big money to have its name associated with the theater or the particular production. In such cases, if the product also lends itself to refreshment sales, the manufacturer expects you or your concessionaire to sell only its product in your lobby. For instance, if Coca-Cola puts up sponsorship dollars for your show, it will expect you to sell Coca-Cola products (not Pepsi) out of your refreshment stand. And, if you are bound by separate sponsorship agreements to sell only a certain brand in your lobby, your concessionaire may want, well, some concessions from you. (Bear in mind, your concessionaire may have its own deal with particular suppliers of refreshment products.) Gets complicated, doesn't it?

   In this regard, therefore, you may wish to restrict the kind of products the concessionaire may sell out of your facilities. For instance, you may wish to prohibit the display and sale of souvenir merchandise from shows not playing at your facility, as well as illegal or immoral items, or products that may be offensive to your patrons.

2. *Exclusive sales.* Concessionaires typically—and quite justifiably—demand the exclusive right to sell refreshments and merchandise in your theater. No professional company will want to compete with another concessionaire for your patrons' business.

3. *Product pricing.* In most instances, leave product pricing up to the concessionaire. There are only two circumstances under which you may reasonably interfere with pricing:

   a. To restrict the maximum price the concessionaire may charge your patrons. Your justification here is a wish not to offend patrons. Even here, however, I would leave the decision making to the professional, whose business it is to know optimal pricing, and who, after all, has its own margins to maintain. A cynic would also point out your patrons are, well, a captive audience, especially since you can forbid them from bringing outside food and beverages into your facilities.

   b. With show-related merchandise you are supplying. Since you know your own costs of manufacturing the products, as well as your own desired profit margins, you may set a minimum price you want the concessionaire to charge. Here, again, though, I would still leave ultimate decision making to the professional. Remember, also, prices may have to be adjusted depending on demand for individual products.

4. *Concession stand locations.* The theater is justified in restricting the locations, size, and number of concession stands that may safely and properly be operated in its facilities. Fire and building codes may play a part in these decisions.

5. *Cloakrooms.* The professional may also demand the license to operate your cloakroom facilities. In such cases, he will split coat check charges with you, according to the percentage formula you negotiate. Tips belong to cloakroom staff and are never split with anyone.

6. *Fees.* Concessionaires do not pay or guarantee set fees to the theater owner. Instead, gross sales are split according to formulas the parties establish in their agreement. Commonly, the parties negotiate different formulas for different products. Soft drinks, alcoholic beverages, candy, and souvenir programs are subject to one formula. Cloakroom fees are governed by a second formula.

   In the case of show related merchandise that the producer of a visiting attraction provides, the concessionaire will keep a percentage of the gross sales, while remitting the balance to the producer. The concessionaire will pay you a percentage of the share he keeps. (See paragraph 7 below for more details.) All splits are based on gross sales less sales tax.

7. *Show-related souvenirs.* If another producer is licensing your space and he desires to sell show-related merchandise, he must do so through your concessionaire in the same manner discussed in paragraph 6 above.

8. *Permits/licenses.* The professional concessionaire is always responsible for obtaining permits and licenses and to comply with all city and state laws, governing the sales of such merchandise. The concessionaire must also report all sales and remit taxes thereon to the appropriate sales tax authorities. Make sure your concessionaire agrees to indemnify and hold you harmless for all of these duties and taxes. The taxes are particularly important, since the fines and penalties for failure to pay can add up very quickly, to substantial amounts. You do not want to inadvertently be held responsible to the taxing authorities for the concessionaire's failure to pay its obligations. If you are, inadvertently, held responsible for the taxes, the indemnity and hold harmless provisions mean the professional must reimburse you for any money you must pay out.

9. *Concession stand employees.* By the same token, make it clear that the concessions staff is employed by the professional and not your company. You do not want to be responsible if the concessionaire fails to pay federal, state, and local employment taxes. Again, require that the concessionaire indemnify and hold you harmless for these costs, if you incur any.

10. *Governmental authorities.* Demand that the concessionaire comply with all the rules and regulations of all governmental authorities having jurisdiction over its operations. This especially includes the proper handling of food under health codes, and the proper storage and use of equipment under fire codes.

11. *Payment schedules.* Commonly, concessionaires settle up payments to you on a once per month basis. In a particularly large operation, like an arena, in which substantial sums of money may be involved, you may demand biweekly or even weekly settlements. In any case, establish the specific periods of time for which sales will be computed, such as from the first day of the month to the last day of the month. Then establish a reasonable date after which the concessionaire must report all sales for the period to you and make its payment. In the past, when much counting was done by hand, the concessionaire might demand as much as twenty days after the close of a month (if the sales period was monthly) to settle up. With computers, tallies can be made even on a daily basis, so giving the concessionaire that much time is ridiculous and merely allows it to

earn interest on money that rightfully belongs to you. I would not give more than fourteen days, and even that is stretching it in the concessionaire's favor. The concessionaire must provide you with a detailed written accounting of sales during the settlement period.

12. *Insurance.* Require that the concessionaire maintain, at its own expense, product and food liability insurance, as well as coverage for public liability and property damage, and workers' compensation. He must name you as co-insured on all policies. The insurance should cover all of your patrons, employees, guests, and licensees. Consult with your own agent to determine the appropriate dollar amounts based on the size of your facilities and expected sales. The concessionaire must furnish you with proof of coverage and premium payment before you allow him to begin business on your premises.

The concessions company must also take full responsibility for any injuries to persons or property arising out of its sales. For instance, the concessionaire sells spoiled food to a patron, who becomes ill. Or the cloakroom staff loses or damages a patron's mink coat. In such event, the patron's attorney will sue both you (as theater owner or producer) and the concessionaire. Again, if you must bear any of these expenses, your contract with the concessions company should call for it to indemnify and hold you harmless for them.

In connection herewith, post visible signs either on or above each concession stand that clearly state: "Concessions are owned and operated by The Botulism Concessions Company, an independent business." It wouldn't hurt to print a similar notice inside your programs either.

13. *Rules and regulations.* The concessionaire must also comply with all of your own rules and regulations for operating within your facilities, whether in effect at the time the contract is signed or which you may later adjust. You also should reserve the right to amend the rules as you, in your sole discretion, will deem desirable and necessary. It should be the concessions company's responsibility to communicate your rules and regulations to its staff, as well as train them in compliance and to take responsibility when they fail to observe them.

14. *Reservation of rights.* Reserve the right to cancel performances or change attractions as you, in your sole discretion, deem desirable and necessary

without being held liable for the concessionaire's real (or imagined) lost sales. Reserve also the right to schedule, reschedule, and designate the times and dates of all performances.

15. *Inspection of books.* You have the right to inspect and audit the concessionaire's books, during normal business hours, to verify the gross receipts, out of which your share is computed.

16. *Employee image.* Make sure the concessionaire employs persons whose image and decorum fit with the image you want to maintain for your theater. Employees should all be of legal age. In addition, employees who handle and sell alcoholic beverages must have attained the minimum age the law requires for such duties. Remember, however, you do not want to exert any control or dominion over the concessions staff such that the law may deem you a co-employer for tax and other purposes. If a member of the concession staff behaves improperly or otherwise requires supervision, the concessionaire should be told and should handle the matter itself. In other words, other than informing the concessionaire, stay out.

17. *License restrictions.* You may wish to restrict the concessionaire's license to only certain events. For instance, you may run main productions eight per-formances per week. But, in your otherwise dark time, you may license your space for special events, such as corporate meetings, or to charitable organizations for fundraisers. Concession sales at these events may not be appropriate or wanted by the groups licensing your space.

18. *Start/End dates.* Specify the term of the license and the starting dates and the date when the concessionaire's rights expire.

19. *Options to renew.* An option to renew (on either side) is a toss up. The concessionaire may want you to include it in your contract, but you may want to keep your own options open when the concessionaire's license expires. You may want to seek bids from other concessionaires. Of course, if the experience has been mutually agreeable, you may want to continue doing business with the same professional.

An option to renew on the same terms may not be desirable, either, since this locks both of you into merely continuing the same relationship. It would be better, if you want to give the professional any kind of option, to state that any renewal "will be on terms to be negotiated." This gives both of you the right to consider conditions existing when you are ready to negotiate any renewals.

Form 6 Concessionaire License

THE PARTIES:

A. _____ ("Theater Company") owns and operates the _____
Theater ("Facility"), which is located at _____ _____.

B. _____ ("Concessionaire"), whose business headquarters are located at
_____, is in the business of supervising and operating concession stands
in facilities similar to those owned by the Theater Company, for the purpose of selling food, beverages, souvenirs, and
similar merchandise to the patrons of such facilities during regular performance times.

Whereas the Theater Company desires to grant, and the Concessionaire desires to obtain, an exclusive license to the
Concessionaire to supervise and operate any and all concession and refreshment centers [and cloakroom facilities] in
and about the facility, upon the following terms and mutual promises and covenants:

1. The Theater hereby grants to the Concessionaire the license to supervise and operate any and all concession and
   refreshment centers/stands [and cloakroom facilities] in and about the Facility. Such license to begin such operations will begin on _____ and terminate on _____, unless the parties will subse-
   quently agree in writing to terminate sooner.

2. During the term hereof, said license to the Concessionaire will be exclusive. The Theater will not grant or permit any
   other persons or entities any rights or licenses to operate any concession stands and/or sell the merchandise listed
   in paragraph 3 below in or about its Facility. In the event the Producer or Presenter of any attraction playing at the
   Facility during the term hereof desires to offer attraction-related merchandise and/or souvenirs to patrons, he will
   do so only through sales conducted by the Concessionaire, upon terms to be agreed upon between the
   Producer/Presenter and the Concessionaire.

3. This license confers upon the Concessionaire the right to sell soft drinks, food, candy, alcoholic beverages, and the
   following merchandise, provided it is related to the attraction playing at the facility: librettos, recordings, wearing
   apparel, souvenir books, posters, sheet music, and any other souvenir type products (hereinafter collectively
   "Merchandise"). The Concessionaire may not offer for sale any souvenir type merchandise for any attraction not
   playing at the facility. The Concessionaire is strictly forbidden at all times to offer, attempt to sell, or sell any illegal,
   immoral, or improper merchandise of any kind whatsoever. The Theater Company reserves the right to approve of
   all products offered for sale by the Concessionaire at its Facility.

4. The Concessionaire will have the sole right to determine the appropriate pricing for each item sold or offered for
   sale under this license.

5. The Theater will permit [has available] _____locations for concession stands/refreshment centers [and cloakroom facilities]. They are located [will be established] at approximately the following places within the Facility:
   _____
   _____.

6. The Concessionaire will be responsible, at its own expense, for obtaining all permits, licenses, and other authoriza-
   tions, which are required by law, from the government bodies having jurisdiction. The Concessionaire will comply
   with all city and other state laws governing the sale and handling of all merchandise (including sanitary and health
   laws governing food and drinks), which it sells from the Facility.

7. In particular, the Concessionaire will collect and remit, and otherwise be responsible, for all sales, employment, or
   other taxes imposed upon its operations by all governmental bodies having jurisdiction hereof. The
   Concessionaire will hold the Theater Company harmless and indemnify it for any losses caused by its failure or
   omission to do so.

8. All revenues earned by the Concessionaire from the sales conducted at the Facility will be divided between the
   Concessionaire and the Theater Company on the following basis:
   _____% of [gross] [net] receipts to the Concessionaire; and _____% of [gross] [net] receipts to the
   Theater Company, for all sales of food, soft drinks, alcoholic beverages, and souvenir books;

_____% of [gross] [net] receipts to the Concessionaire, and _____% of [gross] [net] receipts to the Theater Company, for all other souvenir type merchandise.

[Gross] [Net] receipts will be defined as follows: _____
_____.

On or before the _____ day of each month during the term of this license, the Concessionaire will remit all payments due to the Theater Company for its operations for the month preceding. Each payment will be accompanied by an itemized accounting statement and such other documentation as may be required to support all remittances. Theater Company or his agents will have the right to audit the Concessionaire's books and records, during normal business hours, to verify and compare the computation of sales and all sums due to the Theater Company. In the event such verification determines a shortage of more than _____ dollars ($_____), the Concessionaire will, in addition to immediately remitting the shortage, be responsible for the costs of the Theater Company's audit and inspection.

9. Concessionaire will, at all times, obey all of the rules and regulations that may, from time to time, be established by the Theater Company and will instruct, and be responsible for, its employees to likewise obey all said rules and regulations. Concessionaire and its employees will at all times conduct their business and behavior in an honest manner. Concessionaire will employ only persons of legal age for the activity in which they are engaged and will require all employees to be appropriately attired, as the Theater Company may, from time to time, require. Concessionaire will be solely responsible for its employees and agents and their conduct hereunder, as well as all wages, workman's compensation, employment taxes, and other matters incidental to their employment by the Concessionaire.

10. The kind, type, and scheduling of attractions and performance days and times will be solely in the discretion of the Theater Company. The Concessionaire understands that, from time to time, the facility may be "dark," with no attractions or performances scheduled. The Theater Company, in its discretion, may restrict or limit the times during which the concession stands may be open for business, particularly during the actual performances, and may even prohibit sales during particular performances. The Concessionaire will have no claim or recourse for expenses or lost profits for any such times in which its operations are restricted or canceled.

11. The Concessionaire, at its own expense, will purchase public liability, food liability coverage, and property damage insurance covering all patrons, employees, the public, and any other persons and property in connection with its operations on and about the facility. The Concessionaire will name the Theater Company (and such other persons and entities as the Theater Company designates) as co-insured and will provide the Theater Company with evidence of same. Coverages will be in not less than the following amounts:

Injury or death to one person: $_____

Injury or death to more than one person: $_____

Property Damage (Per occurrence): $_____

Property Damage (Aggregate): $_____

The Concessionaire will also maintain, at its own expense, such workman's compensation as may be necessary and appropriate for its employees, agents, and other parties under its control.

12. The Theater will furnish the Concessionaire with waste removal, reasonable utilities and storage space, all without additional charge.

13. In the event of a claim, suit, or other action against the Concessionaire by any person claiming to be injured as a result of its actions, products sold, or omission to act, the Concessionaire, at its sole expense, will defend such proceedings, including providing defense for the Theater Company, if the Theater Company is named as a defendant in such action, or if such claim is made against the Theater Company. Although the Theater Company agrees to cooperate with the Concessionaire in all such proceedings, the Concessionaire agrees to be solely liable for any judgments, settlements, or other payments to such parties, including their costs and attorney fees and will hold the Theater Company harmless and indemnify it therefore. The Theater Company will, in no event, be responsible for any debts, obligations, judgments, or settlements against the Concessionaire.

14. The Concessionaire agrees to post signs in conspicuous places in and about its concession stands [and cloakrooms], stating that all concession stands [and cloakrooms] are under its sole operation and control.

15. This Agreement will not be construed as creating a joint venture and/or partnership between the parties, and the Theater Company and the Concessionaire hereby expressly disavow any intention or desire to create same.

16. This Agreement may not be modified, amended, or changed, except by a written instrument signed by the parties hereto.

17. This Agreement will be binding on the parties, their heirs, legal representatives, and assigns.

18. Notwithstanding paragraph 17 above, this agreement may not be assigned by either party except with the consent of the other party.

19. In the event of a dispute, breach, or claim hereunder, which the parties cannot settle, either party may submit the matter to binding arbitration in the County of _____, State of _____, which arbitration will be conducted by a member of the American Arbitration Association, under its Commercial Rules. Any court of competent jurisdiction may enforce judgment awarded thereon by the arbitrator. The arbitrator will require the losing party to pay the prevailing party's costs and attorney fees of arbitration.

20. The laws of the State of _____ shall govern this agreement.

21. All notices required hereunder will be mailed by certified mail, return receipt requested, to the parties at the addresses following their names on page one of this Agreement, or at such other address, as either may, in writing, from time to time so notify the other. All notices will be effective on the date of receipt.

In Witness Whereof, the parties have hereunto set their hands and seals.

_____ (Theater Company)

By: _____ (Title)

_____ (Concessionaire)

By: _____ (Title)

chapter **6**   Programs and Souvenir Books

Let's define our terms here. We use *program* to refer to the booklet distributed to each patron as he takes his seat. Ushers often pass out these programs as they take the tickets or they simply put one on each seat before the audience is let into the auditorium. Sometimes these are glossy little magazines or simply the product of somebody's desktop computer. They contain show information and sometimes other editorial material (usually theater related). Some programs contain advertising, others not.

Souvenir books are created for the particular show. They are ordinarily sold—not given away—at the concession stand. For producers, they represent an additional source of revenue. They contain photographs, often in color, of the production and the creative team. They may or may not contain biographical information of the cast. Souvenir books are always glossy, handsome publications; they have to be, when one considers they are fairly expensive. They usually do not contain any editorial material not pertaining to the particular show. They may contain advertising material, though usually this relates to other souvenirs the producer is hawking for the production. The producer pays the concessionaire a percentage of the gross profits from these.

Financial arrangements for programs vary. Many theaters contract out with program suppliers. The publisher may give these to the theater free or at little cost, instead keeping the revenue from any advertising it can sell. Some publishers split advertising revenue with the theater, while others, instead, charge the theater for the programs.

Many theaters, especially smaller ones that the major publishers ignore, choose to publish their own programs. In many cases, they can make an additional profit off the advertising revenue, which they may or may not split with the producer of the particular attraction.

Form 7, which follows, is a simple advertising contract that theaters will find useful if they self-publish their programs.

PROGRAM ADVERTISING ESSENTIALS

1. *Advertising particulars.* Specify the particulars of the advertiser's purchase, including the rate, size, number of insertions, and location. Except for cover advertising, the theater should not guarantee the actual location of the ad.
2. *Camera-ready copy.* Advertisers may provide their own camera-ready copy. For an additional charge, they may require typesetting.
3. *Cost.* Total up the actual cost of the advertisement, which then becomes the value of the contract.
4. *Deadlines.* Establish deadlines for providing copy and/or approving of proofs.
5. *Limited liability.* A theater that publishes its own programs should always limit its liability to advertisers. Printing errors do occur. At the same time the theater may encounter problems that prevent it from publishing a particular issue. In either event, the theater does not want to be saddled with a large claim from an advertiser for lost profits or any other consequences of an error or failure to publish. The theater can offer two choices. The easiest choice is to simply publish a corrected advertisement in a subsequent issue (which the theater should always choose). The second alternative is to refund a percentage of the advertiser's charge, but it may be difficult to apportion the amount of the refund to which the advertiser may be entitled.

6. *Third party claims.* A theater also needs to protect itself against any claims by third parties that the advertiser has misappropriated someone else's copyrighted material, trademark, or service mark. Likewise, the theater does not want to become embroiled in an invasion of privacy or right of publicity case.

7. *Approval of content.* Finally, the theater should reserve the right to reject any advertising material it deems unsuitable for its audience. (Would you advertise condoms to an audience of churchgoers?) And of course you do not want to promote any illegal activities or merchandise.

8. *Cancellations.* Disclose your cancellation policies, to prevent any misunderstandings.

Form 7 Program Advertising

THIS AGREEMENT made this _____ day of _____, by and between _____ ("Theater") and _____ ("Advertiser").

The Theater publishes a program which it distributes free of charge to its patrons at all performances.

The Advertiser herein agrees to purchase advertising space in the aforesaid program upon the following terms and conditions.

1. The Advertiser hereby purchases advertising space, at the following rate, size, location, and number of insertions:
   _____ Full Page _____ Insertions _____ Total price
   _____ ½ Page _____ Insertions _____ Total price
   _____ ¼ Page _____ Insertions _____ Total price
   The Advertiser understands and agrees that the Theater does not guarantee location for any of the above.
   The Theater guarantees location for the following advertisements only:
   _____ Inside Front Cover _____ Insertions _____ Total price
   _____ Inside Back Cover _____ Insertions _____ Total price
   _____ Outside Back Cover _____ Insertions _____ Total price

2. The Advertiser [will] [will not] provide camera-ready copy.
   [The Advertiser requires typesetting, at an additional cost of _____ dollars ($_____).]
   [The Advertiser requires additional specifications, as follows: _____
   _____
   _____
   The cost of the additional specifications is _____.]

3. The total cost to the advertiser is _____ dollars ($_____), payable upon the following schedule:
   _____.

4. The deadlines for providing copy for the advertising for each issue is:
   Issue _____ Deadline _____
   Issue _____ Deadline _____
   Issue _____ Deadline _____
   [If the Advertiser requires typesetting, Theater will provide proofs to the advertiser not later than _____ days before printing. Advertiser will thereupon return same with necessary corrections or approval not later than _____ days before printing. Advertiser may correct only printer's errors; the advertisement itself may not be changed without additional charge. If the Advertiser fails to return corrected proofs or approve of same within the aforesaid time limit, it is conclusively agreed and understood that the Advertiser approves of same.]

5. The Theater's liability in the event of an error in printing, or a failure to print advertisement for any reason, is limited only to [printing a corrected advertisement in a subsequent issue of the program of the Theater's choosing at no charge to the Advertiser] [refund to the Advertiser of not more than _____% of the charge for the particular advertisement in error]. The Theater will not be liable under any circumstances for the Advertiser's incidental or consequential damages, lost profits, expenses, claims by third parties against the Advertiser, or any other costs incurred by the Advertiser as a result of the error.

6. The Theater reserves the right to reject advertising at any time which it deems unsuitable for its publication, defames or libels any person or entity, infringes upon any trademark, copyright, or service mark owned by others, violates the right to publicity or privacy of any person or entity, or promotes or offers for sale any illegal or unlawful substance or thing of any kind or any unlawful or illegal activity.

7. Advertiser represents and warrants that it has the right or license to use any trademarks, copyrights, or service marks owned by others, the likenesses of any persons living or dead, featured in its advertising and, upon request of the Theater, agrees to furnish proof of same. However, regardless of whether the Theater requests proof of Advertiser's

authority, the Advertiser will hold the Theater harmless and indemnify it against any claims, causes of action, judgments, settlements, attorney fees, costs, or any other expenses incurred by the Theater as a result of a breach of this paragraph.

8. The Advertiser may cancel or change any advertisement purchased under this Agreement upon _____ days written notice in advance of the publication of same and will be entitled to a refund for any unused portion of any fees paid, except fees paid for typesetting and other services rendered. The Advertiser may not cancel or change any advertisement once the particular program has [been typeset] [been printed, even if not distributed].

9. The laws of the State of _____ will govern this Agreement.

10. All notices required hereunder will be sent to the parties at the addresses following their signatures below.

In Witness Whereof, the parties have hereunto set their hands and seals this day and date.

_____ (Theater)

By: _____ (Title)

Address: _____

_____

_____ (Advertiser)

By: _____ (Title)

Address: _____

_____

part 2 **Literary Talent**

chapter **7** Simple Production License

Regional and small theaters frequently desire to present a production of an unpublished play in a simplified arrangement with the author. Often, the play has already received its world premiere elsewhere; thus the theater is contemplating the second, third, or even fourth production. (This has happened to me with several of my plays.) Or perhaps the company is unwilling or unable to offer the playwright the level of production that would call for a more complete agreement. Both the producer and the playwright need a simple license agreement.

Form 8, which follows, is tailor made for such circumstances, regardless of whether the theater company is professional or amateur. Most of its clauses are boilerplate and should not be negotiated. Negotiable terms are "fill in the blank" clauses.

THE SIMPLE LICENSE

Under a simple license, the theater is merely acquiring a one time, limited right to present the play at a date certain, upon easily negotiated royalties. The level of production is not such that the theater would be entitled to ask for or receive any ancillary or subsidiary rights in the play. (See chapter 9, "Option to Present Play.")

SIMPLE LICENSE ESSENTIALS

1. *Producer representations.* At the outset, during the initial negotiations, the theater must make certain warranties to its contemplated level of production, seating capacity, professional or amateur status, and contemplated ticket prices. In determining the terms for and granting the license, the author will rely upon these representations.

2. *Grant of rights.* The author, in turn, grants the license to the theater for the production as desired.

3. *Royalty formulas.* Form 8 provides for royalties according to several possible formulas:

   a. If a limited ascertainable number of performances are contemplated, royalties may be a flat sum per performance. This is particularly common in amateur, community, or school productions.

   i. For instance, a community theater may intend to present the play for eight performances at a fee of $60 for the first performance and $50 for each succeeding performance. Royalties are easily determined: $60 plus (seven times $50) is $410.

   b. Another formula that is *de rigeur* in professional productions calls for guaranteed royalties plus a percentage of weekly box office sales from all sources.

   i. For instance, the theater contemplates producing my play *Sex Marks the Spot* for eight performances in a facility that seats five hundred. The producer will price tickets at $10. Thus, the producer's total box office take at capacity ($5,000 per performance) times eight performances is $40,000. The producer expects to sell out 90 percent of his tickets. Now 90 percent of $40,000 is $36,000. We negotiate a royalty rate of 10 percent of the gross box office sales. Thus my guaranteed royalty is $3,600 (10 percent of $36,000). The producer pays me this figure.

   ii. If, however, he sells out the full eight performances, the production grosses $40,000. My total royalties of 10 percent will be $4,000. Since he has already paid me $3,600, he owes me $400. If the production fails to sell out even 90 percent, i.e., fails to earn back the advance royalties, that is the producer's loss. Guaranteed royalties are always nonrefundable.

c. All guaranteed and flat fee royalties should be paid at least ten days before the first public performance (preview or otherwise). It is usual for an author to ask the producer to pay the guaranteed royalties by the first day of rehearsal.

d. The author is always entitled to an appropriate accounting of the box office receipts.

4. *Script changes.* Theaters are never permitted to alter the author's script without her permission. The Dramatists Guild is very firm about this. So am I.

5. *Author's rights.* If the author does accept suggestions or changes to her manuscript, she owns them absolutely, regardless of who contributed them.

After the Lynn Thompson *Rent* case, I believe theaters have a duty to protect authors from ownership claims by personnel who are under the theater's control and supervision. Therefore, as a playwright, I would never give up paragraph six of Form 8, even if it meant losing a production. Absolute and total ownership of my copyrights is more valuable to me than any single production.

6. *Archival recordings.* Many small theaters want to record their productions "for the archives." Absent the author's express consent, this is a violation of copyright. (For further information, see chapter 15.)

Form 8 Simple Production License

THIS AGREEMENT, made this _____ day of _____, 20_____, ("Effective Date"), by and between _____ ("Theater") and _____ ("Author"):

1. (A) The Author is the creator of the copyrighted Play entitled _____ ("Play"), which Theater desires to present as part of its _____ season. Upon the following mutual terms, covenants, and considerations, the Author hereby grants the Theater this license to present the Play.

   (B) The Theater represents and warrants that it is organized and operated as a _____ Theater, as that term is generally understood in the industry. Its actors and directors _____ [are] [are not] paid for their services in connection with the Theater's production. [Theater does not operate under a contract with Actors' Equity Association.] [Theater operates under the Actors' Equity Association contract known as _____.] The Theater further understands that the terms of this agreement and the Author's grant of a production license are based upon said representation.

2. Theater will present the Play commencing on or about _____ for [a run of _____ consecutive performances through _____.] [an open end run of _____ evening and _____ matinee performances, per week.] All performances will take place at the Theater's primary facility located at or about

   _____.

3. [Flat fee royalties: Theater will pay to the Author nonrefundable royalties of _____ dollars ($_____), for {*each performance*} {the full run consisting of _____ performances}. Said royalties will be due and payable no later than _____ days before the first public performance, regardless of whether same is labeled as a preview. Royalties will be due for all public performances, regardless of whether admission is charged.] [*Alternate*]

3. [Guaranteed royalties plus a percentage: Theater will pay to the Author nonrefundable advance guaranteed royalties of _____ dollars ($_____), which will be due and payable upon the signing of this agreement. In addition, Theater will pay to the Author the sum of _____ % of gross weekly ticket sales (as further defined) for all performances after first deducting all guaranteed royalties heretofore paid. Gross ticket sales will be defined as to the total of all weekly ticket sales, from all sources whatsoever. Royalties will be paid weekly and will be due on the Wednesday following the week in which they are earned. Royalties will be due and payable for all attendees at all public performances, regardless of whether admission is charged to the attendee. In the event the Theater elects not to charge admission for any attendee or performance, royalties will be computed as follows: Theater will count attendance at the free performance and pay royalties as if the attendees had all purchased their tickets at the highest ticket price for that type of performance—matinee, evening, Saturday, etc. Theater will accompany each royalty payment with a detailed box office statement, certified by the treasurer and the producer attesting to the accuracy of ticket sales and attendance so reported. The Author or [his] [her] representative may further inspect the books of the Theater during normal business hours to verify the accuracy of all royalty payments and box office statements. Notwithstanding the foregoing, no admissions will be charged for attendance by the bona fide press and no royalties will be payable thereon.

4. Theater will not make any changes, alterations, and/or omissions to the Play, from the Author's manuscript, without the Author's written consent. The Theater will take reasonable steps to advise its artistic personnel of its obligation in this respect.

5. Any changes, alterations, suggestions, or additions to the Play, to which the Author consents, will become the Author's sole property, regardless of who contributed such changes or suggestions. Author may, at [his] [her] sole discretion, incorporate same, or any portion of same, into [his] [her] copyright, as well as into future productions and/or publication of the Play without owing compensation to anyone. Theater will take reasonable steps to advise its artistic personnel of its obligation in this respect.

6. (A) Theater agrees to hold Author harmless for any material copyrighted and/or owned by others used in its production of the Play and to obtain permission for and pay any fees as may be necessary for same. Theater will indemnify and hold Author harmless from any liability occasioned by Theater's failure to secure said permissions.

(B) Author hereby represents and warrants that [he] [she] is the sole creator of the Play; that no part of it, to [his] [her] knowledge, infringes upon or violates the rights of other persons or entities; or infringes upon or violates the rights or privacy or publicity of any other persons or entities; that there are no claims or liens against the Play that would prevent Theater's production thereof; and that [he] [she] has the full right and authority to enter into this license. Author further agrees to indemnify and hold Theater harmless for any breaches of this paragraph.

7. Theater may photocopy Author's manuscript, at its own expense, for distribution to its artistic and production personnel, solely in connection with this run of the Play. Theater may make only as many copies of the manuscript as are necessary for its production. No copies of the manuscript may be distributed, sold, or given away to the general public or persons not directly connected with Theater's production, without the Author's express written consent.

8. This license is on a nonexclusive basis.

9. (A) The Author will receive prominent billing credits in all programs, advertising, and publicity within the Theater's control in a type size not less than _____ % of the title substantially as follows:

   " _____

   A play by _____ "

   (B) Upon notice by the Author of an error in [his] [her] billing credit, the Theater will promptly rectify said error.

10. The Author reserves all rights not expressly granted to the Theater by this agreement. This Agreement does not, expressly or by implication, grant to the Theater any implied or ancillary rights, subsidiary or merchandising rights. Theater is acquiring merely a simple license to present the Play or the number of performances and during the time period stated in paragraph 2 above.

11. Except as specified in paragraph 12 below, Theater will not, for any reason, make, cause, or allow any recording of the Play, or excerpt thereof, by audio, videotape, or other means, by itself, its personnel, or any other individual or organization without the Author's express written consent. In all its programs and by announcement prior to each performance, Theater will notify its patrons that all recordings, by audio, videotape, or other means, are expressly forbidden. Recordings "for the archives" are specifically prohibited, regardless of the means by which they are made.

12. Notwithstanding paragraph 11 above, the Theater may authorize an excerpt from the Play, not to exceed 300 (three hundred) seconds, to be recorded/filmed by a commercial or public radio or television station, for the sole purpose of publicizing the production of the Play, provided, however, the Theater will receive no compensation, or profit, directly or indirectly, for authorizing any such radio or television presentations. Any such excerpt may not include material that may require the permission of persons other than the Author.

13. Author may attend all performances without cost and will be entitled to _____ additional complementary tickets for each performance during the run. Author may, in addition, attend all rehearsals of the Play.

14. In the event the Theater desires the Author to attend rehearsals and/or performances of the Play, or to otherwise appear in its community for publicity or other purposes, the Theater will compensate the Author for the expenses of reasonable travel and accommodations, in the amount of _____, which will be payable no later than fourteen days prior to the desired appearance date(s).

15. Theater will provide Author with a minimum of _____ copies of all promotional/publicity material, including press releases, flyers, posters, and programs; _____ sets of production photographs; _____ copies of all newspaper and magazine articles regarding its production; and _____ copies of all review not later than _____ days after the final performance.

16. This document constitutes the entire agreement between the Theater and the Author and may not be modified, except by an instrument in writing, signed by both parties. All disputes will be resolved through arbitration to be held in _____ County, State of _____, by a professional arbitrator, in accordance with the Commercial Rules of the American Arbitration Association. The arbitrator shall require the losing party to pay the reasonable costs and attorney fees of the prevailing party. Any court of competent jurisdiction may enter judgment upon the arbitrator's award.

17. Notices and correspondence hereunder will be sent to the parties at the following addresses:

    Author: _____

    Theater: _____

IN WITNESS WHEREOF, each of the parties has signed this contract as of its Effective Date herein above stated.

_____ (Author)

_____ (Date of signing)

_____ (Theater)

By:
_____ (Authorized officer)

_____ (Date of signing)

chapter 8 Commissions

Producers and theater companies frequently commission playwrights to create brand new works especially for them. This arrangement gives the producer a great deal more input into shaping a project than presenting an already written piece. The playwright follows certain, often very specific, guidelines, thereby writing a play that is suitable to the commissioning party's needs and desires.

Commissions often come about due to one or more reasons:

1. The producer has a specific idea or theme he wishes to develop into a play.
2. Money is available for that purpose. For instance, the producer's nonprofit company has gotten a government or foundation grant to create the new work.
3. The producer wants to work with a particular playwright. Perhaps the playwright is a major or an emerging name, and the producer is eager to present her newest work.
4. The producer has acquired underlying rights to a novel, short story, or screenplay that he now wants to adapt for the stage.
5. The producer wants the prestige and status of presenting a wholly new work.
6. A theater company's mission is to foster and develop new plays and playwrights.

Whatever the reasons for the commission, the producer and the playwright are entering into a complex business and legal arrangement, which must be as carefully structured as the play itself.

TWO AGREEMENTS

When entering into a commission arrangement, both the playwright and her producer must negotiate two separate, yet interdependent contracts:

1. The Commission Agreement
2. The Production Agreement (also known as the Option Agreement)

Although it is possible to combine the two into a single agreement, this is not a desirable procedure. The purpose of each contract is different. In order to maintain clarity and the most efficient documentation of the understanding between the parties, two separate instruments are best.

However, it is desirable and highly recommended that the playwright and producer negotiate both contracts at the same time. While it is possible to negotiate and fulfill the commission agreement first, while leaving the production option for later, I discourage this practice. By negotiating both arrangements at the outset, the parties know exactly the terms and course their association will take. Leaving the production option open to negotiation until after the play has been written and accepted invites uncertainty, misunderstandings, and, possibly, a collapse of the relationship. (What if, for instance, after the play is finished and accepted, the parties cannot agree on the terms of the production itself?)

Some commission agreements attempt to obviate this problem by providing that the parties will negotiate "in good faith" the terms of the production contract when the producer exercises his option to present the play. I have trouble with "good faith." While it is admittedly a term bandied about quite commonly in the law, it is difficult to define and sometimes requires a court to decide whether a party has acted "in good faith." I believe that, if there is any way to avoid the issue (by negotiating all the terms of the arrangement up front, for instance), why not do so and get it over with?

A second argument for negotiating both contracts at the same time is pragmatic. It gives both parties a chance to see how well they can navigate difficult issues together, before one party invests money and the other devotes time and talent into developing the material. After all, if you can't find common ground here, how will you be able to work together during the production process?

Bottom line: negotiate both contracts at the beginning. Then, in the commission agreement, incorporate your production option by reference and attachment thereto.

The production agreement (Option) should be based on the appropriate models I have provided in Forms 10 and 11, below.

COMMISSION ESSENTIALS

1. *Commission fee.* The commission fee is payment for the writing itself. It is not an advance against the author's royalties, which themselves are set forth in the option agreement. The author earns her fees by actually writing the script, regardless of whether it is accepted or produced by the theater company. (She earns her royalties as any other author would: as payment for allowing each performance of the play.) As such, these fees are also nonrefundable. Thus the producer bears the risk the work may not be suitable or satisfactory to his needs.

2. *Research/Travel fees.* Many plays require a great deal of research. Research itself often involves expenses. For instance, if the show is based on a famous court case, the playwright will have to purchase a transcript of the trial, a cost that can run into hundreds, sometimes even thousands of dollars. In addition, the playwright may have to travel to the locations where the story is set, interview real life participants in the drama, or otherwise incur necessary expenses in the creation of the work. The commissioning producer must bear these expenses. The parties negotiate either reimbursement of the expenses or jack up the fee appropriately.

3. *Deadlines.* The playwright must estimate how much time she will need to research and write the first draft, based on the work to be done, research involved, her own work habits, and her professional and personal responsibilities. The producer must calculate when he would like to present the script, based on his own schedule, needs, commitments, and any strings attached to the grant money. Keeping all these factors in mind, the par-

ties must negotiate a deadline for the writer to turn in her first draft.

Once the playwright delivers her first draft, the producer must commit to a time when he will review the material and request changes. The parties should consider the time needed to arrange an actors' reading of the draft. Anywhere from sixty to ninety days is standard for this review period. The producer should never keep the writer in limbo unnecessarily.

Once the producer gives the playwright his notes for revision, the playwright will need additional time to prepare her second draft. Again, this is an individual matter, depending on the extent of the revisions needed, and the playwright's work habits.

At the end of this time, the playwright turns in her second draft.

4. *Number of drafts.* Everyone agrees the producer is always entitled to at least two drafts of the project. But is he entitled to more than two drafts?

Some producers want and expect more than two drafts. I believe a producer should request more than two drafts only if he is willing to pay the writer additional fees. Some producers are indecisive, unable to make up their minds, constantly expecting rewrites. I believe that if the producer has enough confidence in the writer to commission her in the first place, then she should be able to create a playable script in two drafts. By the second draft, moreover, the producer knows whether he has something he wants to present. Besides, in the normal production process, most scripts undergo rewrites anyway. Therefore, two drafts should be the limit!

After the second draft, the producer must decide either to present the play (at which point the terms of the production option govern), or to pass on the project.

5. *Copyright.* Copyright always belongs to the playwright. Some producers argue that, because the original idea was theirs, they deserve, at least, a piece of the copyright. No way! The playwright is the sole author and therefore entitled to ownership of the copyright.

6. *Playwright's independent contractor status.* Traditionally and legally, the playwright has always been viewed as an independent contractor, not as an employee of the producer. (That is fundamental to the author's claim of ownership of the copyright. Under a work-for-hire, or employer-employee arrangement, the

employer owns the copyright. In Hollywood, the writer is an employee of the producer who commissions her to write the screenplay. Therefore the producer owns the copyright. Such is not the case in the theater.) The commission does not change this arrangement.

An independent contractor works on her own schedule. She is not controlled by or supervised by the person who pays her. (Input into the script by the producer does not constitute control or supervision.) Usually she works out of her own facilities and not on the producer's premises, using her own equipment. She is responsible for her own taxes. If she is injured while working on the script, she bears the responsibility. The producer is not liable.

Although it is not commonly a part of commission agreements, because of the playwright's traditional role as an independent contractor, I would specify this arrangement anyway. We live in a litigious society.

7. *Commission formulas.* The parties negotiate the amount of the commission fee, which depends upon the amount of money available; the reputation of the playwright; the level of production; the travel and other expenses involved; and similar factors. There are two formulas commonly used for payment of the commission fees:
    a. The first calls for paying the author as follows:
        i. One-half of the fee when the parties sign the commission agreement.
        ii. The remaining half when the author delivers the first draft.
    b. The second payment schedule is as follows:
        i. One-half of the fee when both parties sign the commission agreement.
        ii. One-quarter of the fee when she delivers her first draft.
        iii. The remaining quarter of the fee when she delivers he second draft.
    c. Under the second schedule, two additional scenarios come into play:
        i. If the first draft is satisfactory to the producer, he will immediately pay the author the additional half of the fee.
        ii. However, if the producer requests rewrites, he is not obligated to pay the final quarter of the fee until the author delivers her second draft.

From the author's point of view, the first schedule allows her to receive full payment by the time she delivers her first draft. (She is still committed to delivering a second draft.) The second schedule allows the producer to hedge his bets. He does not have to make the last payment until and unless the author gives him a second draft. If, for any reason, he abandons the project before she delivers her final draft, he does not have to pay the final installment. In other words, the first schedule may be more favorable to the playwright, while the second is more protective of the producer's money.

8. *Abandonment.* A producer may abandon the project when he believes it is not working out. Commonly, this occurs because the playwright's drafts are not what the producer hoped for. Or he has lost interest in the project. His needs may have changed. If the commissioning producer is a theater company, a change in artistic directors, or artistic direction, may cause the company to abandon a project.

When a producer abandons a project, the rights to the material belong to the playwright. Whether she receives her final payment of the commission fee depends on the payment schedule selected, as discussed above, as well as the point at which the producer calls it quits. She may freely take the project elsewhere. The producer relinquishes his rights to the work.

9. *Producer exercises his option.* When the producer pays the author the final balance of her commission fees, he is free to choose to produce the play. If he does so, then, if the parties have already negotiated a production agreement, it takes effect, and they proceed as they normally would under any production circumstances. If the parties have only agreed "in good faith" to negotiate the production contract, now is the time to do so.

10. *Underlying Rights.* As we will discuss in chapter 12, "Underlying Rights," after the producer purchases the right to adapt an existing work from another field, he commissions the writer.

As part of the Commission Agreement, the producer will transfer over to the playwright his rights to the underlying work, so that the playwright may create the adaptation. These rights inure to the playwright, even once the producer's run of the show closes.

If the producer abandons the play prior to presenting it, the playwright retains ownership of both her script and the underlying rights. However, the producer may reasonably request reimbursement of any money he has paid for the underlying rights from the playwright once she finds a new producer. (Her new producer will likely pay for these rights anyway.)

11. *Producer's rights.* Under the commission agreement, the commissioning producer acquires the right to present the world premiere of the work.

Note that the world premiere right is exclusive to the commissioning producer. The playwright cannot give any other producer the world premiere of the play, unless, of course, the commissioning producer abandons it. The world premiere run lasts for as long as the production agreement does, whether it is for a limited or an open run. Once the world premiere production by the commissioning producer has closed, the playwright is free to offer her script to other producers. The commissioning producer no longer has exclusivity, with one exception. He may require exclusivity in a limited geographic area (usually within a two hundred mile radius of his facility) for a second production within a limited time period.

However, I urge playwrights to resist the "exclusivity" part of this arrangement. While it is acceptable to give the commissioning producer the right to present the play again for a second (and even a third production) during a limited time period, this right should not be exclusive to the community. And the right should *never* be "world" or "United States" exclusive in perpetuity. The commissioning producer gets exclusive rights only to the *world premiere*, not to the play forever. And the parties should negotiate separate production licenses (and royalties) for any subsequent productions by the commissioning producer.

12. *Subsidiary rights.* Some producers believe that merely because they have commissioned a piece, they are also entitled to participate in a share of the subsidiary rights income. This is as wrong as seeking a share of the copyright. A commission by itself does not entitle the producer to any part of the author's subsidiary rights. A producer *earns* participation in the subsidiary rights only by the terms of the production agreement, by presenting the play at a certain level of production, and for the requisite number of performances. (See chapter 9.)

13. *Artistic control.* Since the author is creating a piece specifically to meet the needs of the commissioning producer, she must expect notes and requests for rewrites. But this can become a tricky situation. Just as in the case of an already written script accepted by a producer, the author maintains absolute artistic control over her work in a commission. She does not have to change one word. The problem arises: What happens if she refuses to go along with her commissioning producer's requests? There is the very real danger she may blow the commission. The producer may decide to abandon the project and send her packing.

It's a tough situation. The only guideline I can give is this: stay as close as you can to the producer's desires as you work on the script. Consult often along the way and try to reach accommodation where there are artistic differences. One other point: The commission agreement must specify that all ideas, notes, suggestions, and the like coming from the producer and his staff, which the writer incorporates into the material, belong to the writer, whether or not the commissioning producer actually presents the show.

Form 9 Commission Agreement

THIS AGREEMENT dated this _____ day of _____, 20_____, by and between _____ ("Producer") and _____ [*and* _____]
(the "Playwright") [(collectively the "Playwright")].

1. (A) The Producer hereby engages the Playwright to create an original stage play, presently entitled _____ (the "Play").

   (B) In consideration of the mutual covenants and agreements set forth herein, the Playwright hereby grants to the Producer the right to purchase an exclusive option to present the Play on the live stage, in a world premiere engagement [upon the terms and conditions the Parties agree to negotiate in good faith upon the acceptance of the completed work for production by the Producer] [upon the terms and conditions contained in the Production Agreement attached hereto and incorporated herein]. Provided the Producer is not otherwise in default in his obligations under this Agreement and will have made all payments as set forth herein, said exclusive right will continue during the First Draft and Second Draft review periods, as set forth in paragraphs 4(A), (B), (C); and 5(A) and (B) below.

2. The parties understand and agree that the present title of _____ is for identification purposes only. Said title may be changed by mutual consent of the parties at a subsequent time. In the event the parties cannot agree upon a final title for the Play, the author's decision will be final.

3. [Said Play will consist of a minimum of _____ typewritten pages.] The Play will be:

   (A) Based on an original idea of the _____ [Producer] [Playwright].

   (B) Based on an underlying _____ [novel, short story, screenplay, etc.], written by _____; the copyright to which is owned by _____; and the rights to adapt same for the live stage are owned by _____.

4. (A) On or before _____, the Playwright will deliver to the Producer a first draft of the script. After said delivery the Producer will have the right to read the script for a period of _____ days (the "First Draft review"). During the period permitted for said first review, the Producer may, at [his] [her] option and sole expense, arrange as many table and/or staged readings of the script as [he] [she] deems necessary, utilizing such actors and directors as [he] [she] may deem desirable. Playwright will have the right of approval of actors and the director. Playwright will at all times be permitted to attend same. Admission will not be charged and the readings will not be open, advertised, or publicized to the general public. Only persons directly connected with the theater company and/or such industry professionals as the Producer and Playwright may invite will be permitted to attend. Within the said first review period, the Producer must advise the Playwright in writing that:

   (i) The first draft, in its present form, is suitable and acceptable for [his] [her] needs and expectations; and the Producer now wishes to present the Play on the live stage, under the terms and conditions of the option referred to paragraph 1(B) above.

   Or

   (ii) The Producer desires revisions or modifications in the script to be prepared by the Playwright in a second draft. The Producer will give the Playwright detailed notes and guidance as to [his] [her] requirements for same. Upon said notice, the Playwright will have an additional period of _____ days thereafter, in which to write the second draft and deliver same to the Producer. Upon delivery of the second draft, the Producer will have _____ days thereafter (the "Second Draft review"). During said Second Draft review period, the Producer will have the right in [his] [her] sole discretion and expense, to arrange table and/or staged readings of the second draft, on the same terms as paragraph 4(A) above.

5. On or before the expiration of the Producer's Second Draft review period, he will notify the Playwright in writing as follows:

   (A) [He] [She] intends to present the Play on the live stage, under the terms and conditions of an option he wishes to purchase from the Playwright;

   Or

(B) The Producer elects not to produce the Play. If the Producer fails to give timely notice under paragraph 5(A) above of [his] [her] intentions to produce the Play, said failure will be the same as an election not to produce the Play. In either event, the Producer will have no further rights or interest in the Play. The Playwright will have no further obligations hereunder to the Producer. The Play will become the sole property of the Playwright, free and clear of any claims or encumbrances by the Producer. The Playwright may then offer it to other, even competing producers and/or publishers without restriction or limitation. Upon said election or failure to give timely notice, as aforesaid, all sums unpaid hereunder will immediately become due and owing. The Producer will pay said sums to the Playwright immediately. It is expressly understood and agreed that said election and termination of the Producer's rights will not relieve or excuse him from his obligation to pay all sums required hereunder.

6. In full consideration of the covenants herein, the Producer will pay to the Playwright the sum of _____ dollars ($_____) (the "Commission Fee"), according to the following payment schedule:

_____

_____

_____

[*Alternate #1*]
[(A) Not less than _____ dollars ($_____) upon the date wherein the parties have first entered into this Agreement; and
(B) The balance of _____ dollars ($_____) when the Playwright delivers the first draft of the Play.]
[*Alternate #2*]
[(A) Upon the execution of this agreement, not less than _____ dollars ($_____); and
(B) Upon delivery of the Playwright's first draft, not less than _____ dollars ($_____) of the total sum; and
(C) Upon the first to occur of the acceptance by the Producer of the Playwright's first draft; or the delivery of the second draft by the Playwright, not less than the remaining _____ dollars ($_____) of the total amount.]

7. The sums as set forth in paragraph 6 above are intended as payment for work performed by the Playwright in creating the script. They are not intended as, nor should they be construed, as advances against the royalties or option payments as set forth in any option or production agreements contemporaneously or subsequently negotiated and entered into by the parties. Therefore, they are not recoupable against advances, royalties, or other payments due under said option or production agreement. All sums paid hereunder are considered earned by the Playwright when [he] [she] creates the Play and are therefore nonrefundable. In the event the Producer deems the Play unsuitable or unacceptable to his needs and expectations, the Producer will have no recourse against the Playwright for sums paid, except to abandon the project. Said abandonment, however, will not relieve him from his obligations to complete all payments due hereunder, as per paragraph 5(B) above.

8. In the event the Producer shall fail to timely make all payments and reimbursements required hereunder, all of its rights and interest in the Play will immediately and automatically terminate, without further notice or action by the Playwright.

9. [This Commission Agreement will entitle the Producer to the exclusive right to present the Play on a one-time basis only. In the event the Producer will desire to present subsequent productions of the Play, he must negotiate additional options and/or production agreements with the Playwright at such subsequent times. Said options and/or agreements will be on a nonexclusive basis, unless otherwise agreed to at that time by the parties. Playwright will have no obligation by reason of this Commission to negotiate and/or authorize subsequent productions of the Play.]
[*Alternate*]

9. [This Commission Agreement will entitle the Producer to the exclusive right to present the Play in its world premiere on a one-time basis only. However, upon twelve months notice, the Producer may exercise the right to present _____ additional productions, on a nonexclusive basis, for a period of _____ years, from the date of execution of this agreement. For each additional production, the parties agree in good faith to negotiate terms and conditions of a production agreement.]

10. (A) Copyright to the Play will belong solely to the Playwright, and the Producer will not, by virtue of this agreement, be entitled to or claim any interest or right therein. This Agreement does not create, bestow, or otherwise give the Producer any claim right, or interest in any subsidiary rights to the Play, all of which are strictly reserved by the Playwright.
(B) All other rights not specifically and expressly granted herein to the Producer are reserved by the Playwright.

11. The Producer acknowledges, first, that the Playwright is the exclusive author of the Play. Second, in the normal course of this agreement and any subsequent production he or any of his employees or persons under his control, may offer suggestions, ideas, dialogue, and other material, which the author at [his] [her] sole discretion may incorporate into the script for use in the contemplated production, subsequent productions (whether or not produced by the Producer), and in publication of the script. All such material that the Playwright chooses to retain in the script will become the exclusive property of the Playwright to use as [he] [she] sees fit. In such event, the Producer, his employees and persons under his control, will have no rights or claims thereto. The Producer will notify, in writing (and provide a copy thereof to the Playwright), all of its employees and others within his control of the author's rights and the Producer's obligations under this paragraph. Further the Producer will not, privately or publicly, or permit other persons under his control, represent that anyone other than the Playwright created or wrote any part of, or the whole, of the Play. The Producer will indemnify and hold the Playwright harmless against any claims, encumbrances, judgments, costs, or attorney fees incurred in violation of this paragraph.

12. Although the Producer may offer guidance, suggestions, and requests for changes, additions, deletions, or modifications to any part of, or all of, the Play, the Playwright will not be obligated to make or incorporate such alterations. No such changes, additions, deletions, or modifications may be made without the consent of the Playwright. In the event the Playwright refuses to make any requested changes, the Producer may deem the material unacceptable and refuse to exercise his right to option the Play.

13. Provided that the Producer has made all of his payments hereunder and provided that the Producer is not otherwise in default hereunder, the Playwright will use [his] [her] best efforts (but will not guarantee) to secure billing credit for the Producer in all subsequent productions and publications of the Play. The Producer's billing credit will appear in substantially the following form:
"Originally Produced by _____"

14. The Playwright represents and warrants that [he] [she] is the sole owner and creator of the Play. Except as noted below, all material, characters, incidents, dialogue, and stage directions are wholly original with [him] [her] and do not violate or infringe upon the copyrighted work of others and/or infringe upon, or violate, the rights of privacy or publicity of any persons, and except as noted in (D) below, does not depict any real life person:
(A) _____ The Play contains or is based on certain material in the public domain.
(B) _____ The Play contains or is based upon certain material created by others for which the author is not required to obtain permission.
(C) _____ The Play contains or is based upon certain material created or owned by others for which the Playwright [Producer] has obtained permission, a copy of which is attached hereto as evidence thereof.
(D) _____ The Play depicts real life persons and contains incidents and information occurring to them, for which the Playwright has obtained permission, a copy of which is attached hereto as evidence thereof.
The Playwright further represents and warrants that [he] [she] has the full right and authority to grant the rights herein conveyed to the Producer.

15. The laws of the State of _____ will govern this agreement.

16. All notices required hereunder will be addressed to the parties at the addresses printed below their names, until other notice of change of address is given in writing, and will be by certified mail, return receipt requested. Notices so given will be effective on the date of receipt thereof.

17. This document contains the entire Agreement between the parties. No changes, modifications, or alterations thereof will be effective unless contained in a writing signed by both parties.

18. This Agreement, and all written modifications, alterations, supplements, and amendments hereto contained in writing signed by the parties, will be binding on the parties, their executors, administrators, personal representatives, successors, and assigns.

19. Notwithstanding anything contained in the foregoing paragraph, it is agreed and understood that neither party may assign this Agreement without the written consent of the other party hereto, except that the Producer may assign this Agreement to a Joint Venture and/or Limited Partnership, of which he will continue to be a party, which will produce the Play. In addition hereto, the Playwright may assign this Agreement by will, trust, or other testamentary instrument, for the purposes of estate planning.

20. In the event of a claim or dispute between the parties, which cannot be settled by the parties themselves, either party may submit this dispute to arbitration in _____ County, in the State of _____ in accordance with the Commercial Arbitration Rules of the American Arbitration Association and conducted by a member thereof. Judgment upon the award so rendered by the arbitrator may be entered by any court of competent jurisdiction. The arbitrator will require the party losing such dispute to pay the reasonable costs and attorney fees of the prevailing party.

21. Nothing contained herein is intended or should be construed as creating an employer-employee and/or work-for-hire relationship between the parties. At all times during the term of this agreement, the Playwright will be an independent contractor, over whom the Producer will not exercise any supervision or control. The parties expressly stipulate and agree that the Producer's payment of any fees hereunder, writing guidelines, or requests for changes and modifications in the Play will not constitute such supervision or control as to create an employer-employee or work-for-hire relationship.

22. As of the execution of this agreement, the Producer owns or holds the option on the live stage rights to adapt the underlying work _____, written by _____, copyrighted by _____, into the Play, which is the subject of this Agreement. Contemporaneous with the execution hereof, the Producer will assign all said options and/or rights to the Playwright to be [his] [her] sole property, now and forever, regardless of whether the Producer will ultimately choose to produce the subject Play. A copy of said assignment will be attached hereto.

In Witness Whereof, the parties have this date affixed their hands and seals hereto.

_____ (Playwright)

_____ (Address)

_____

_____ [(Producer)] [(Theater Company)]

By: _____ (Title)

_____ (Address)

_____

chapter 9 Options to Present a Major Production

When a producer discovers an original play he wishes to present as a world premiere, it is incumbent upon him to tie up the exclusive rights to the script before his competitor does. To do this, the producer ordinarily purchases an *option* from the author.

OPTION VS. SIMPLE LICENSE

An option differs from a simple license in several ways. A producer usually *options* a work when he intends to present its world premiere in a *major* production. A producer *licenses* a script when his is one of many productions of the show, or he cannot mount the play at a level such that he would be entitled to the greater rights producers ordinarily acquire in the typical option.

A summer stock theater will likely license a play, even if it is the world premiere. A regional theater will option a play for a main stage production, while it may license the play for a studio presentation. A storefront theater may attempt to option a play, but in such case, the author should not grant exclusivity and should never give it a piece of her subsidiary rights. (See below.) The storefront simply cannot give the author the level of production that entitles it to subsidiary rights.

A simple license is a very straightforward arrangement to present a script for (ordinarily) a limited time period in a single, modest production. Heavily weighted in the playwright's favor, the license, in exchange for flat or guaranteed royalties or a percentage of the gross ticket sales merely gives the producer the right to present the play and nothing more. Once the particular presentation is over, the producer's rights in the piece terminate. It is ordinarily a nonexclusive right versus the exclusivity of the option. The playwright reserves the right to license her piece for any number of other productions running concurrently.

For more information about simple licenses, see chapter 7.

A producer options a play when he does not want anyone else presenting it anywhere else in the geographic territories and during the time period specified in the option. In other words, the producer wants exclusivity to the work until after his production has completed its run.

OPTION FEES

Options are not free. (Some producers try to wangle free options from writers, especially from newcomers. I would advise any playwright who is offered this kind of arrangement to run for the hills and take her script with her.) The producer must pay for an option. In addition, each time the author extends the option—that is, each time the author gives the producer additional time to present the show—the producer must pay the author more money. Each option payment (including the first) is treated as an advance against royalties. The producer pays the author X number of dollars. Later, when the production starts earning money, the producer first deducts these advance payments against any subsequent royalties due to the playwright.

The initial option fee is due when the parties sign the contract. Additional options for extensions are due when the producer requests—and the author grants—the extension.

The size of the option fee varies according to the level of production, the length of time the producer wants for the option, and the size of the theater. In general, the parties should estimate what the author's royalties for one week might be at the contemplated ticket prices, if the play sells 75 to 85 percent of capacity. This figure should be the minimum option fees. (Notice I said "minimum.")

The reason for the payment is simple: The producer is asking the author to take her play off the market during the time period granted in the option. The author deserves to be compensated, since this means she must forego any other opportunities that might come up for production during this time period. When a producer takes a license, he does not ask the playwright to take the script off the market. Under a mere license, the author may pursue as many productions as she desires concurrently.

Since the author is granting the producer something of value—taking her script out of the market—option fees are nonrefundable. If, for any reason, the producer does not go ahead and actually present the show, the author retains the option fees as her sole property. This is her payment for keeping the script out of the market. (I know one playwright who has yet to see a production, yet makes a very good living off option fees.)

TIME PERIOD

The time period specified in the option is the time the producer wants in order to mount his production. This period is negotiable. Playwrights do not want to take their scripts out of the marketplace for too long, especially because the producer may not be able to actually get the show up and running. (Under an option the producer only promises to *try* to present the show. He does not guarantee production.) This time period can be relatively short—six months or less for a regional production. Or it can extend for years. A Broadway or off Broadway producer would not be unreasonable if he asked for two years from the date of signing the option agreement to first rehearsal.

The time period is often in increments. For instance, a producer may acquire a first option for a period of six months. The original option may give him the right to purchase a second extension for an additional six months. He may even acquire a third extension for still another six months. Each time he requests an extension he must, as noted above, pay additional sums to the author in consideration of the additional time he is seeking. But purchasing option time in increments gives the producer a way to hedge his bets. Instead of committing himself to one large lump sum payment up front for, say, eighteen months, he purchases three shorter option periods of six months each for smaller sums. If, at the end of each six months period, he chooses to move ahead, he can do so by paying a fee for another six months. If, at any time, he chooses to quit, he has not expended too much money.

An option gives the producer a chance to "test the waters" without making a substantial up-front commitment—which usually comes out of the producer's own pocket and he cannot get back if he can't mount the production. Most often, a producer options a play for the period of time he thinks he will need to raise funds to actually produce the script. During the first six months, he can gauge investor interest. If interest is there, he can purchase a second and even a third six-month time period to complete the financing. If there is a lack of interest, he can drop the project at only minimal cost. Likewise, the producer may want time to interest a major star or director in the project.

Producers frequently ask for automatic extensions in the original option agreement. This is not unusual. It assures the producer that, if he wants the additional time, he can have it—as long as he pays the author the agreed upon extension fees.

REVERSION OF RIGHTS

If a producer cannot present the show at the level of production promised in the option agreement during the option period (and any extensions), his rights terminate when the option time period runs out. At that point, all rights granted by the author in the option revert back to her. The producer has no further claim or interest in the play. The author is free to offer her script to another producer.

Remember I noted that a producer takes an option when he hopes to mount a major production. Any old production won't do, even if it is a world premiere. (A community theater may present the world premiere of a play, but that is not a major production, as that term applies to options.)

Here's why the level of production is so important. Unlike a mere license, which gives the producer only minimal rights, an option is a complex arrangement, under which the producer may, if his production meets certain standards, acquire an interest in the subsidiary rights to the script.

"CHAMPAGNE" MONEY

One of the most important factors attracting investors and producers to new plays is the opportunity to participate in its attendant subsidiary rights.

A play earns money in a number of ways. First and foremost, its initial production, if it runs long enough at sufficient capacity, throws off profits over and above its costs to present and run. I call these profits "eating money." But the real money—the "champagne" profits—comes out of the producer/investors share of the show's subsidiary rights.

A successful play can earn champagne profits for decades, after its initial run. Even though *Oklahoma!* is sixty years old, it still generates substantial income each year from dinner theater, school and community productions, major professional revivals, touring companies, and sales of the cast albums. The same can be said of *The Odd Couple, Bye Bye Birdie, Arsenic and Old Lace, Dial M for Murder, Fiddler on the Roof,* and hundreds and hundreds of other shows.

How?

Each play has ancillary rights, which can provide very substantial profits during the life of its copyright. Each time your local high school or community theater presents a copyrighted show it must pay royalties to the copyright owners. The same is true of your favorite dinner theater and anyone else who produces it. These are a fraction of the subsidiary rights to a show.

Actually, subsidiary rights encompass just about any use you can make of a show. Besides the aforementioned stock and amateur rights, there are revivals, touring companies, foreign productions, motion picture adaptations, television adaptations, television series, publication of the script and the music and lyrics, original cast albums, videocassettes, DVDs, concert versions, radio productions, First Class Productions, Second Class Productions, readings . . . stop me, I'm running out of breath! (But not out of types of subsidiary rights.) Earnings from these rights run into the millions and millions—heck, even tens of millions—of dollars. With all this potential money involved, you can imagine the number of fingers that want into the pie.

Of course, the author benefits, but so does the original producer. And so do the original investors.

In fact, investors love to participate in subsidiary rights. If the investors have already gotten back their investments out of the original run, these are the champagne profits. But even if a show loses money in its original production, sometimes, it can make back enough income out of the subsidiary rights, such as a movie sale, to cushion any losses and maybe even show a profit. (There are lots of shows that lost money during their run on Broadway, yet made it all back, and then some, out of subsidiary rights.) So subsidiary rights act as a hedge to help minimize losses.

As part of the option agreement, therefore, the producer will insist upon participating in any of the net income earned from the sale of subsidiary rights. In an ordinary license, the producer will not expect, nor be entitled to, an interest in the subsidiary rights.

Bear in mind, however, a producer and his investors do not automatically participate in the subsidiary rights. They must earn their share. And there are three conditions they must meet:

1. The production must be—as I have emphasized—a MAJOR one.
2. The producer must keep the show running for a minimum number of performances.
3. The producer must not otherwise be in default under the contract.

Let's examine these conditions more closely.

OPTION ESSENTIALS

1. *Level of production.* A production is a major production—for purposes of subsidiary rights participation by the producer/theater company and investors—only when it contributes substantial value to the play. Usually this means it attracts a lot of attention. A Broadway or off Broadway production contributes substantial value because both of these levels of production are attention-getters. They are the gateways to the world. They lead to foreign productions, movie sales, and substantial interest in the aftermarket of regional, stock, and amateur productions. Presentation on the main stage at a large regional theater of national note may also add substantial value to the script. Often a well-received regional theater production may attract a commercial production on or off Broadway.

   And I realize one could argue that a community theater adds value to the play, since it gives the author a chance to test out the work before an audience. But this is not the kind of "substantive" value that entitles it to subsidiary rights participation.

2. *Length of production.* A producer must earn his participation in the subsidiary rights by keeping the show running for a minimal number of public performances. "One performance and we close" does not cut it. The minimal number of performances is a negotiable item. Commonly, on Broadway, it is at least twenty-one paid public performances. There must be an official opening. And you don't count previews. The reason? The play must *run* in order to add value to the script. A quick closing does not help anyone, least of all the playwright. In negotiating the minimum number of performances, incidentally, keep in mind that the fewer the performances, the smaller the producer's participation will—and should—be. In

short, both the level and the run of the production are the two tests the producer must meet to earn participation in the author's subsidiary rights. And both of these terms should be clearly and specifically laid out in the option agreement.

Although Forms 10 and 11, which follow, provide for subsidiary rights participation, I leave the level of production and the minimum number of performances open to negotiation between the parties, based on the foregoing factors as they may apply to any particular situation.

3. *Producer default.* If the producer defaults in his obligations under the contract, he forfeits any interest in the subsidiary rights. The most common producer default: failure to pay the author her royalties.

4. *Percentages.* This is the trickiest area to navigate because there is a wide divergence of opinion as to what constitutes a fair percentage of the author's subsidiary rights that a theater may claim. It follows that the percentage formula varies, according to the viewpoint one holds. There are, however, some specific industry guidelines, as follows:

a. Amateur, community, and small professional theater level: zero participation.

b. Regional Main stage: ranges from 1 percent all the way up to 5 percent.

Some regionals attempt to recover at least some of their royalty payments to the author by asking for the equivalent percentage back of the subsidiary rights. So, for example, if the regional pays the author 7 percent of the box office take during the run, it asks for 7 percent of her subsidiary rights income. This occurs most often when the regional pays the author more than the standard royalty. Personally I believe this is reprehensible. Period. I advise playwrights to resist. The regional pays the author royalties based on the box office because, just as with every work not in the public domain, it must pay a license fee for the right to present the script. That it agrees to pay royalties higher than normal should not, by itself, entitle the regional to a higher piece of the author's subsidiary rights.

Problems arise when two theaters coproduce a show. Or when first one regional mounts the production and then a second regional produces it—all before it moves to a commercial transfer. All of the theaters (as well as the commercial producer) will want a share of the author's income. But there is only so much of the pie to go around. In such cases, the author must count her percentage give-aways carefully, or else she may find herself giving away a lot more than she should.

All percentages are based on the author's "net" income from the subsidiary rights. That is, first the author deducts her agent's commissions off her gross income before she begins splitting up the pie with the commercial producer and the other subsidiary rights participants.

5. *Subsidiary rights window.* Except as noted below, the time period during which the original producer or theater company may participate in the subsidiary rights is strictly limited, both by industry practice and, when the playwright is a member of the Dramatists Guild, by the terms of the Guild contracts. The reason for limiting the theater's window is simple and rooted in common sense. The value of any particular production diminishes with time. Remember that the theater justifies its participation in subsidiary rights by the value its production added to the script. However, as time passes, that original production fades into little more than newspaper clippings. The "heat" the production generates cools down. As time goes on, it becomes less likely the original production helped the author dispose of the subsidiary rights.

Here's a simple example: Suppose the New Lincoln Theater produces the world premiere of Charles Grippo's play *A Wife's Tale* on February 1, 2005. That production attracts so much attention that Samuel French purchases the stock and amateur licensing rights on March 1, 2005. Obviously, the New Lincoln's production added such value that the sale to Samuel French can be attributed to it.

But, suppose the New Lincoln Theater presents *A Wife's Tale* on February 1, 2005, but no one acquires the stock and amateur licensing rights until March 1, 2015—ten years later. Chances are, no one will even remember the New Lincoln production. So how could it result in the rights sale? The key is this: You must be able to link up the original production with the disposition of the subsidiary rights (or the acquisition by a commercial producer). As time goes on, the play may receive several productions at several different theaters before the commercial producer takes it on or before there is any interest in the subsidiary rights.

Which production, therefore, resulted in the rights deal? To obviate this problem, the industry has come up with standard formulas. I am deliberately omitting the Broadway formula, as codified in the Dramatist Guild Approved Production

Contracts for Plays and Musicals. The formula is so complex—varying according to the different categories of subsidiary rights—that it would require an entire chapter by itself. The other categories are as follows:

LEVEL OF PRODUCTION	SUBSIDIARY RIGHTS WINDOW
Regional	Five years
Off Broadway	Ten years

The time period starts to run on the day after the last performance. It applies to the date when the author enters into the contract of sale of the rights, not when she actually starts to earn income.

Here's an example: The New Lincoln Theater's main stage production of *A Wife's Tale* closes on February 1, 2005. Under its contract with playwright Grippo, it participates in the sale of subsidiary rights for five years, beginning on the date after the last performance—that is, February 2, 2005. On February 1, 2010, Grippo contracts with Samuel French for the sale of the stock and amateur licensing rights. Since Grippo sold the rights within the five years period, New Lincoln owns a piece of my income from the sale, even though I won't even receive my first royalty check until, let's say, October 1, 2010—more than five months after the sale.

On the other hand, if I sell the rights to Samuel French on February 3, 2010, New Lincoln's five years have expired. It is no longer entitled to any of my Samuel French income.

6. *Kinds of subsidiary rights.* Under "Champagne Money" above, I listed a portion of the kinds of subsidiary rights attached to every play. However, it is important to specify in the option agreement exactly which subsidiary rights the author will share with the producer.

7. *Geographic territories.* Broadway and off Broadway producers generally share in the author's subsidiary rights income from productions throughout the world. However, regional theaters—even major ones—commonly share only in the author's subsidiary rights income earned from productions in the United States and Canada. Some regionals also try to weasel their way into subsidiary rights income earned from productions in Britain, Australia, and New Zealand. But I advise authors and agents that this demand is over-

reaching. Regional theaters never share in the sale of motion picture or television rights. These are considered worldwide rights. Commercial producers participate in this income in perpetuity. This was the exception to the limiting of rights I noted above.

8. *Copyright.* Copyright always belongs to the author. Period.

9. *Billing.* All producers want billing credit for producing the world premiere (and sometimes the second production). Producers consider this a perk to which they believe themselves entitled. It is often more than mere ego, especially for nonprofits. Billing credits on subsequent productions and publications of a particular play look awfully good on grant applications. The problem is, authors are not in a position to guarantee billing in subsequent productions and publications. In all such arrangements they are dealing with third parties who were not involved in the original option. Producers and theater companies need to recognize these limitations on the author. The most any playwright can do is to use her best efforts to obtain billing credits in future productions and publications.

10. *Grant of rights.* A producer will naturally seek the broadest grant of rights he can get, while the author should try to narrow those rights as much as possible. It is always wisest for both parties to be realistic and up-front with each other. A producer may really, sincerely, want to present the play on Broadway—and of course Broadway is every playwright's goal. But does the producer have a realistic shot at delivering? Can he raise the funds? Can he attract Broadway level actors and directors to the piece?

The parties should aim first for what they can realistically achieve. Start with the level that is possible. If success comes, it is possible to structure the option agreement in such a way that the parties can move the show up, level by level, until it reaches their shared highest goals. In such an event, the parties should negotiate each contract at the appropriate time, rather than creating a one-size-fits-all arrangement. This is because each different level demands different kinds of terms, including whether and how much the producer will participate in the subsidiary rights. In giving the producer options to move the play up, the author should demand that the producer:

a. Specify the level of each production

b. Accept a small window of opportunity in which to exercise the option, so as not to tie up the author's script longer than necessary

c. Expect a smaller participation in the subsidiary rights (or perhaps none) at the lowest levels; with participation widening only as the level of production moves up

d. Pay the author for each option at a rate commensurate with the level of production

11. *Author warranties*. The author must warrant that:

a. She is the sole creator of the work.

b. It does not infringe upon the copyrighted works of others.

c. It does not violate anyone's rights of publicity or privacy.

She agrees to hold the producer harmless and indemnify him for any breaches of these clauses.

12. *Cast and director approval*. An author has the absolute right to approve of the cast and the director.

13. *Script approval*. No changes, modifications, additions or deletions may be made to the script without the author's sole approval. This means by anyone—especially directors.

14. *Rehearsals, casting, and production meetings*. The playwright must have the absolute right to attend all rehearsals, casting sessions, and production meetings. In connection therewith, the producer must, obviously, give her reasonable notice in advance of the time and place when they are to occur. Common sense must prevail here. While I require producers to give reasonable advance notice, the means of notice cannot, as a practical matter, always be by certified mail, return receipt requested. A telephone or face-to-face notice is sufficient here, since many meetings are scheduled on the fly, especially in the crush of production.

For instance, after a preview performance, the producer and director may decide they need to hold a production meeting in the middle of the night. It would suffice for the producer to simply say, "Charles, we're meeting at 2:00 A.M. in Gower's room to discuss the second act." And I have heard too many horror stories of ego-mad directors barring authors from attending the rehearsals of their own plays. This is absolutely inexcusable behavior, and I don't care if the director has three Tonys to his credit and the playwright is a rank unknown. Nobody—absolutely nobody—should keep the playwright out.

(I digress, but this story is so good I have to share it. David Merrick once attempted to bar Jule Styne from a rehearsal of a show for which Styne had composed the score. Now Styne was no dummy and not about to let Merrick push him around. Knowing that the producer had not yet signed his composer's contract, Styne told him: "If you keep me out of my own rehearsal, I'm leaving the show and taking my music with me." Since the press opening was only two nights away, this would have left Merrick presenting a musical without any music. Of course, Merrick caved and never tried that trick again with another writer.)

So I make the playwright's attendance at rehearsals and productions meetings a matter of contractual right.

15. *Changes belong to author*. Any changes, bits of business, or other ideas that the author does choose to incorporate into her script belong to her, as her sole property. See also chapters 7 and 8.

16. *Assignment*. A playwright-producer relationship is like a marriage. Presumably both parties share the same vision and goals for the work. It is a personal relationship. A producer should not be permitted to assign his rights under the option to anyone, except to a limited partnership or joint venture of which he remains a partner. If a playwright permits a producer to assigns his rights to someone not of the playwright's choosing, the new producer may not view the work in the same way the playwright does—Uh-uh. No way.

17. *Royalties*. I've saved the best for last. Royalties may either be a flat fee, a percentage of the gross weekly box office, or a combination. The gross weekly box office includes all income the show earns from all sources—not just the physical box office, but also group sales, ticket brokers, Ticketmaster, etc. The royalty percentages depend upon industry practice for the particular level of production.

OPTIONS TO PRESENT A MAJOR PRODUCTION

Form 10 Option to Produce Play (Nonmusical)

THIS AGREEMENT, dated this _____ day of _____, 20_____, by and between
_____ ("Producer") and _____
("Playwright"), wherein the Producer desires to present on the live speaking stage the world premiere production
("Production") of the play, created by the Playwright, presently entitled _____ ("Play").

Now, in consideration of the mutual covenants, considerations, and promises contained herein, the parties hereby
agree as follows:

1. The Playwright hereby grants the Producer the sole and exclusive right to present on the live speaking stage the
   world premiere production of the Play during the times, at the level(s) of production, and in the geographic territories, as stated herein. During the term of this agreement and as long as the Producer will retain any rights or options
   to present the Play on the live speaking stage and provided that the Producer will not otherwise be in default or
   breach hereof, the Playwright will not grant, license, or permit any other person or entity to present or perform the
   Play in any other medium (excluding motion pictures) within the geographic territories stated herein. Nothing contained herein, however, will prevent the Playwright, during the term hereof, from entering into any licenses, grants, or
   other agreements to permit the Production of the Play by other persons on the live speaking stage, so long as such
   Productions do not occur during the period in which the Producer retains the right to present the Play.

2. Nothing contained herein will prevent the Playwright from entering into the sale of the motion picture rights to the
   Play, provided, however, that said motion picture version of the Play is not released, distributed, or otherwise made
   available for viewing by the general public during the time herein [and subject to the consent of the Producer, as
   described in paragraph _____ herein.]

3. Copyright, and any extensions thereof, to the Play and all elements contained therein will belong solely to the
   Playwright. The Playwright will control the disposition of all rights and uses thereto, except as otherwise provided
   hereunder. All rights not expressly granted to the Producer herein are reserved by the Playwright. All ideas, suggestions, modifications, bits of business, dialogue, and any other material contributed by the Producer or any other
   Party under his control will belong to the Playwright as [his] [her] sole property, free and clear of any claim, interest,
   or lien thereon. Producer will be under an affirmative duty to communicate and notify all persons under his control
   of the Playwright's rights in this respect.

4. (A) Except as otherwise provided herein, in all programs, advertising, houseboards, flyers, signs, and other promotional material under the control of the Producer, the Playwright will be entitled to billing credit as author of the
   Play, substantially as follows:
   "_____

   A play by _____"
   (B) Playwright's name will appear in a typeface and style that is at least 75% of the size of the title of the Play, or the
   size and prominence of the star, whichever is larger. No other names or credits may appear before or be given
   greater prominence than the Playwright's name, except those of a major star or a director of prominence.
   (C) The Playwright's name may be omitted from billing only in the following case: in teaser, small, or ABC ads in
   which only the title of the Play, the name of the theater, and the name of a star of prominence appear. In no event
   may the Playwright's name be omitted from any materials in which the Producer's name appears.
   (D) In all advertising, publicity, and promotional materials (including marquee signs) the Producer's name may
   appear before the Playwright's only in his capacity as a presenter of the Play—for example:
   "_____ [Producer]

   Presents
   "_____

   A play by _____"
   (E) In the event of an error occurring in the Playwright's billing, the Producer, upon receipt of written notification by
   the Playwright thereof, will promptly rectify such error.

(F) This being the world premiere production of the Play, the Producer desires billing credit in all programs, flyers, advertising, and promotional materials on all future productions, including motion picture, video, and broadcast television adaptations, and billing credit on all publications of the Play. Said credit will appear substantially as follows: "Originally presented on the _____ stage by _____" [Producer]

The Producer recognizes, however, that said credits will not always necessarily be a matter under the Playwright's control and authority, but may instead be under the control and authority of third persons or entities not a party to this Agreement. Playwright agrees, however, to use [his] [her] best efforts to secure same for the Producer.

5. The Playwright hereby represents and warrants that [he] [she] is the sole creator of the Play; that all characters, dialogue, plot, incidents, and other elements contained therein are original with [him] [her], except for those elements which are in the public domain; that [except as noted below] the Play has not been copied in whole or in part from any other copyrighted work; that the Play does not infringe upon or violate any other person or entity's right of publicity, trademarks, or rights of privacy.

[The Play is based in whole, or in part, upon the copyrighted work entitled _____, by _____, ownership of which is presently held by _____.

The Playwright has obtained full rights and permissions to use elements from _____, or to base the present Play upon elements and materials contained therein. A copy of said rights and permissions is attached hereto and made a part hereof.]

The Playwright further represents and warrants that there are no claims, liens, or other encumbrances upon the Play or any part hereof. The Playwright has not previously granted, assigned, encumbered, or otherwise disposed of any of the rights or interest in the Play that [he] [she] is herein granting the Producer. That there are no claims, liens, grants, dispositions, or exploitations of the Play, or any interest therein, which would in any way diminish, encumber, or invalidate any of the rights, or the exploitation thereof, herein granted to the Producer.

The Playwright has the sole authority and right to enter into this Agreement and to grant the rights conveyed hereby.

The Playwright will hold the Producer harmless and indemnify [him] [her] from any breach or violation of this paragraph of this Agreement, including costs, attorney fees, judgments, recoveries, and/or settlements (with the Playwright's consent) which the Producer may incur.

6. The Producer hereby represents and warrants that [he] [she] has the capability and the authority to present the Play in the territories and at the level of Production stated herein. However, by this Agreement, the Producer is taking a mere option to present the Play upon the terms herein stated. Nothing contained herein is intended or will be construed as a guarantee by the Producer that [he] [she] will in fact present the Play in the territories and at the level of production herein stated during the term herein.

7. The Producer's production being the world premiere of the Play, the Playwright will provide services to the Producer as follows:

(A) Deliver a completed draft of the Play within _____ days of the execution of the Agreement in generally accepted industry manuscript form;

(B) Rewrite and revise the Play as many times and as much as may be reasonably appropriate and necessary;

(C) Assist with the selection of the director, cast, and designers;

(D) Assist and advise the Producer, Director, and all members of the Production staff with any matters, problems, or issues for which it may be appropriate or necessary to consult with the Playwright;

(E) Attend rehearsals of the Play, as well as any preview performances, for the purpose of resolving any problems that may become apparent during same.

8. (A) The Producer will pay the Playwright an advance of _____ dollars ($_____), upon the execution of this Agreement.

(B) In consideration of the payment made in (A) above, the Producer will have the option to present the Play as a professional production on the live speaking stage on or before _____ (the "First Option Period") in the geographic location of _____, at the _____ level of production.

(C) At any time prior to expiration of the first option period, the Producer may purchase a "Second Option Period" by paying to the Playwright the sum of _____ dollars ($_____). Said Second Option Period will begin _____ [the day after the First Option Period expires] and terminate on _____.

(D) At any time prior to the expiration of the Second Option Period, the Producer may purchase a Third Option Period by paying to the Playwright the sum of _____ dollars ($_____).

The Third Option Period will begin on the _____ [day after the Second Option Period expires] and will terminate on _____.

(E) If, by the expiration of all the option periods purchased by the Producer hereunder, the Producer has not presented the Play as aforesaid in section (B) above, all of his rights hereunder will terminate and revert back to the Playwright.

(F) All advances paid hereunder as described in sections (A) through (D) above will be consideration for the Playwright granting the exclusive options for the times as stated herein. Said advances will be nonrefundable, if the Producer fails to present the Play.

(G) If the Producer presents the Play, then all advances paid hereunder will be recoupable against royalties due and owing to the author as described in paragraph 9 below.

(H) Notwithstanding the foregoing or any other terms of this agreement, the Producer does not guarantee production of the Play during the term of the option or any extensions thereof.

(I) Failure to pay advances to the Playwright when due and owing will be a material breach of this Agreement.

9. (A) In consideration of all the rights herein granted by the Playwright and for the Playwright's services in connection with the Producer's Production, as described in paragraph 7 above, the Producer will pay to the author royalties, on a weekly basis, as follows:

Prior to recoupment: _____% of the gross weekly box office receipts

After recoupment: _____% of the gross weekly box office receipts

Recoupment will mean the date when the Play has earned back all of its costs to produce, regardless of whether the Producer has distributed all or any part of the Play's capitalization back to its investors.

(B) Royalties to the Playwright will be due and payable on the Wednesday of the week succeeding the week during which the royalties are earned. Failure to pay royalties in full when due and owing will be a material breach of this agreement.

(C) Gross weekly box office receipts will be defined as all earnings from the play from all sources of ticket sales, including, but not limited to, box office, telephone, mail order, groups, theater parties, ticket brokers, Telecharge, Ticketmaster, discount ticket outlets, and any and all sources of ticket sales, less any taxes and sales commissions due thereon.

(D) Prior to the payment of royalties, Producer will first deduct all advances paid under paragraphs 8(A) through (D).

(E) Royalties will be due and payable, based on the full box office price, even on complementary tickets given away by the Producer, whether as gifts or as part of group or subscription sales promotions. Notwithstanding the foregoing, no royalties will be paid on the following complementary tickets:

(i) Tickets given to bona fide members of the press;

(ii) Tickets given away for the official opening of the Play for the purpose of "padding" the house;

(iii) Tickets given to the Playwright for [his] [her] personal viewing of the performance.

(F) Each weekly payment of royalties will be accompanied by a detailed box office statement, for each performance during the subject week, accounting for the disposition of all tickets available for said performance, signed by the treasurer or business manager of the theater in which the Play is being presented and countersigned by the Producer. If the Playwright is a member of the Dramatists Guild, a duplicate copy of each statement will be forwarded to the Guild.

(G) Playwright or [his] [her] designated representative may inspect the Producer's records, during normal business hours, for the purpose of verifying the accuracy of all royalty payments and box office statements.

10. In the event the Playwright must travel to a rehearsal or production location more than _____ miles from [his] [her] place of residence, the Producer agrees to pay for the Playwright's reasonable costs of travel, including economy airfare, and the Playwright's accommodations while at the said rehearsal and/or production locations. Accommodations provided the Playwright, at the Producer's expense, will be at least equivalent in value and living conditions and standards as the Producer's own accommodations. Accommodations will include the cost of hotel/motel rooms, meals, local calls, and transportation to and from the rehearsal/production location from the Playwright's hotel/motel.

11. Playwright will be entitled to attend all performances free of charge. In addition thereto, the Playwright will be entitled to _____ pairs of adjoining house seats for each performance, located as follows _____. Said house seats will be held until _____ prior to each evening performance and until _____ prior to each matinee performance.

   After such time, if the Playwright fails to use them, they will be released for sale to the general public. All house seats will be purchased at the regularly established box office price. Playwright agrees not to resell such tickets at a premium or otherwise; to maintain accurate records therefore; and to comply with all state and/or local laws applicable to the use thereof.

12. The Producer reserves the right to assign his rights under this Agreement to a general partnership, joint venture, limited partnership, or other entity owned or controlled by the Producer, as long as the Producer remains an active principal therein. Any other assignment will require the consent of the Playwright in writing.

13. The Playwright hereby grants the Producer the right to present an excerpt or excerpts from the Producer's Production of the Play in a radio or television broadcast, whether live, taped, or on motion picture film, for the purpose of promoting and publicizing the Production. Each presentation may not exceed a total of _____ [minutes] [seconds]. The Producer may not receive any direct or indirect compensation or profits therefrom, other than reimbursement for expenses incurred in preparing and presenting the broadcast excerpt, including any payments to the cast required by the appropriate unions or otherwise by contract. In all such presentations, the Producer will use his best efforts to assure appropriate billing credit for the Playwright.

14. Except as provided in paragraph 13 above, no part of the Play may be recorded, by audio, video, motion picture film, or any other means, whether now known or hereinafter invented, for "archival" purposes, "for the archives," or any other purpose, without the Playwright's additional written consent. Any such unauthorized recording will be, prima facie, a willful violation of the Playwright's copyright.

15. Notwithstanding anything to the contrary contained herein, Playwright will have the absolute right (but not the obligation) to attend all rehearsals, auditions, and casting sessions, and production meetings, and the Producer will provide the Playwright with reasonable advance notice thereof. For purposes of notice herein, telephone or face-to-face in person notice will suffice. Any attempt to prevent or otherwise deprive the Playwright of [his] [her] rights herein will be, prima facie, a material breach of this agreement.

   [Paragraph 16 Alternative #1 in which Producer obtains share of subsidiary rights]

16. [Except for the production license herein granted to the Producer, the Playwright owns and controls all of the rights, uses, and interests in the Play and may dispose of same at {his} {her} sole discretion. However, the parties recognize that Producer's successful production of the Play contributes to the value of its uses and rights in other media. By reason thereby, the Playwright recognizes therefore that the Producer will be entitled to certain percentages of the net receipts paid to the Playwright in any or all of the following uses: worldwide motion picture rights; net receipts paid to the Playwright within the continental United States and Canada from any or all of the following: touring, Broadway performances, and off Broadway performances (except those presented by the Producer pursuant to paragraph _____ herein); stock, amateur, foreign language productions; concert tours or productions; condensed tabloid productions; commercial and merchandising uses; audio, video, or other visual or sound recordings, whether by means now known or hereinafter invented; radio or television broadcasts (collectively the "subsidiary rights").

   The parties, recognize, however, that the Producer will only be entitled to share in the afore described net receipts under the following conditions:

   (A) The Producer's production must run for at least the following consecutive paid performances in order to entitle the Producer to the following percentages of the aforesaid rights:

   _____ performances: _____%
   _____ performances: _____%
   _____ performances: _____%
   _____ performances: _____%

   In computing the number of performances, only _____ paid previews may be counted in the computation.

(B) The Playwright must enter into the contract for the disposition of the aforesaid rights prior to the expiration of _____ years beginning on the date of the last performance of the Producer's production. Producer will be entitled to the aforesaid share of the Playwright's net receipts whenever thereafter same are earned or received.

(C) Playwright will remit the Producer's share of the net receipts within thirty days after receipt by the Playwright, accompanied by a copy of the statements received by the Playwright for same.

(D) Producer or his representative may, during normal business hours, inspect the Playwright's records to verify the correctness of all payments and accompanying statements.

(E) In the event the Producer fails to make any payments owed to the Playwright under any of the terms of this Agreement when due and payable, the same will be a material breach hereunder. Upon receipt of written notice by the Playwright of said failure, the Producer will have thirty days thereafter to rectify the situation. In the event the Producer fails to rectify the situation within said thirty days, all of his rights, interest, and claims to any of the aforesaid net receipts under this paragraph 16 will terminate, and he will have no further claim or right hereunder.

(F) Playwright's net receipts will be defined as Playwright's gross receipts less agent's commission.

(G) Nothing contained herein will obligate the Playwright to dispose of any of the aforesaid subsidiary rights at any time.]

[*Paragraph 16 Alternative #2. Playwright does not give Producer any share of subsidiary rights.*]

16. [The Producer will not be entitled to any share of the Playwright's subsidiary rights.]

17. No changes, additions, deletions, or modifications of any kind may be made to the text of the Play without the Playwright's consent.

18. The Playwright or [his] [her] designee has the right to approve the choice of director, cast, permanent replacements, and designers, which approval will not be withheld unreasonably. In cases in which the Playwright is physically unavailable to give aforesaid approval or not reachable by telephone, the Producer will send the Playwright a telegram requesting approval of any of the aforesaid matters. If, after forty-eight hours have expired, the Playwright fails to respond, approval will be deemed to have been given.

19. This Agreement will be governed and interpreted by the law of the State of _____.

20. Except as otherwise provided herein, all notices required hereunder will be given to the parties at their respective addresses following their signatures below, by certified mail, return receipt requested. Notice will be effective as of the date of receipt.

21. In the event of a dispute or disagreement arising under this Agreement, the parties agree to submit this matter to binding arbitration before a member of the American Arbitration Association. The Arbitrator will have the right to award attorney fees and costs to the prevailing party thereunder. Any court of competent jurisdiction may enter judgment thereon.

IN WITNESS WHEREOF, the parties have hereunto set their hands and seals this day and date.

_____   _____
Producer   Address

_____   _____
Playwright   Address

Form 11 Option to Produce Play (Musical)

THIS AGREEMENT, dated this _____ day of _____, 20_____, by and between _____
("Producer") and _____ ("Book writer"), and _____
("Composer") and _____ ("Lyricist") (hereinafter collectively the "Authors") wherein the
Producer desires to present on the live speaking stage the world premiere production ("Production") of the Musical,
created by the Authors, presently entitled _____ ("Musical").

Now, in consideration of the mutual covenants, considerations, and promises contained herein, the parties hereby
agree as follows:

1. (A) The Authors hereby grant to the Producer the sole and exclusive right to present on the live speaking stage the
   world premiere production of the Musical during the times, at the level(s) of production, and in the geographic territories, as stated herein. During the term of this agreement and as long as the Producer will retain any rights or
   options to present the Musical on the live speaking stage and provided that the Producer will not otherwise be in
   default or breach hereof, the Authors will not grant, license, or permit any other person or entity to present or perform the Musical in any other medium (excluding motion pictures) within the geographic territories stated herein.
   Nothing contained herein, however, will prevent the Authors, during the term hereof, from entering into any
   licenses, grants, or other agreements to permit the Production of the Musical by other persons on the live speaking
   stage, so long as such Productions do not occur during the period in which the Producer retains the right to present
   the Musical.
   (B) Nothing contained in paragraph 1(A) above shall interfere with or in any way restrict the Composer and Lyricist
   from licensing, using, or otherwise granting the so-called small performing rights to any or all of the music and lyrics
   contained within the Musical concurrent with the Producer's presentation of the Musical. Small performing rights
   will be defined as the recording, publishing, synchronization, and use of the music and/or lyrics in any way, other
   than a dramatic performance.
2. Nothing contained herein will prevent the Authors from entering into the sale of the motion picture rights to the
   Musical, provided that said motion picture version of the Musical is not released, distributed, or otherwise made
   available for viewing by the general public during the time herein [and subject to the consent of the Producer, as
   described in paragraph _____ herein.]
3. Copyright, and any extensions thereof, to the Musical and all elements contained therein will belong solely to the
   Authors. The Authors will control the disposition of all rights and uses thereto, except as otherwise provided hereunder. All rights not expressly granted to the Producer herein are reserved by the Authors. All ideas, suggestions,
   modifications, bits of business, dialogue, and any other material contributed by the Producer or any other Party
   under his control will belong to the Authors as their sole property, free and clear of any claim, interest, or lien
   thereon. Producer will be under an affirmative duty to communicate and notify all persons under his control of the
   Authors' rights in this respect.
4. (A) Except as otherwise provided herein, in all programs, advertising, houseboards, flyers, signs, and other promotional material under the control of the Producer, the Authors will be entitled to billing credit as author of the
   Musical, substantially as follows:

   "Book by _____"
   "Music by _____"
   "Lyrics by _____"
   ["Based on _____ by _____"]

   (B) Authors names will appear in a typeface and style that is at least 75% of the size of the title of the Musical, or the
   size and prominence of the star, whichever is larger. No other names or credits may appear before or be given
   greater prominence than the Authors' name, except those of a major star or a director of prominence.

(C) The Authors' names may be omitted from billing only in the following case: in teaser, small, or ABC ads in which only the title of the Musical, the name of the theater, and the name of a star of prominence appear. In no event may the Authors' names be omitted from any materials in which the Producer's name appears.

(D) In all advertising, publicity, and promotional materials (including marquee signs) the Producer's name may appear before the Authors only in his capacity as a presenter of the Musical, for example:

"_____ (Producer)

Presents

_____" (Title of Musical)

(E) In the event of an error occurring in the Authors' billing, the Producer, upon receipt of written notification by the Authors thereof, will promptly rectify such error.

(F) This being the world premiere production of the Musical, the Producer desires billing credit in all programs, flyers, advertising, and promotional materials on all future productions, including motion pictures, video, and broadcast television adaptations, and billing credit on all publications of the Musical. Said credit will appear substantially as follows:

"Originally presented on the _____ stage by _____" (Producer)

The Producer recognizes, however, that said credits will not always necessarily be a matter under the Authors' control and authority, but may instead be under the control and authority of third persons or entities not a party to this Agreement. The Authors agree, however, to use their best efforts to secure same for the Producer.

(G) Whenever one of the Authors receives billing credit, the other Authors shall likewise receive the same billing credit.

5. [Each of the Authors, for himself and not the others, represents and warrants that _____ {he} {she} is the sole creator of each element contributed by _____ {him} {her} to the Musical; that each element contributed by _____ {him} {her} respectively is original with _____ {him} {her}, except for those elements which are in the public domain; that [except as noted below] none of the respective elements of the Musical have been copied in whole or in part from any other copyrighted work; that the Musical does not infringe upon or violate any other person or entity's right of publicity, trademarks, or rights of privacy.]

[*Alternate*]

5. [The Musical is based in whole, or in part, upon the copyrighted work entitled _____, by _____, ownership of which is presently held by _____. The Authors have obtained full rights and permissions to use elements from _____, or to base the present Musical upon elements and materials contained therein. A copy of said rights and permissions is attached hereto and made a part hereof.]

The Authors further represent and warrant that there are no claims, liens, or other encumbrances upon the Musical or any part hereof. The Authors have not previously granted, assigned, encumbered, or otherwise disposed of any of the rights or interest in the Musical that they are herein granting to the Producer. That there are no claims, liens, grants, dispositions, or exploitations of the Musical, or any interest therein, which would in any way diminish, encumber, or invalidate any of the rights, or the exploitation thereof, herein granted to the Producer.

The Authors have the sole authority and right to enter into this Agreement and to grant the rights conveyed hereby.

The Authors will hold the Producer harmless and indemnify him from any breach or violation of this paragraph of this Agreement, including costs, attorney fees, judgments, recoveries, and/or settlements (with the Authors' consent) which the Producer may incur.

6. The Producer hereby represents and warrants that he has the capability and the authority to present the Musical in the territories and at the level of Production stated herein. However, by this Agreement, the Producer is taking a mere option to present the Musical upon the terms herein stated. Nothing contained herein is intended or will be construed as a guarantee by the Producer that he will in fact present the Musical in the territories and at the level of production herein stated during the term herein.

7. The Producer's production being the world premiere of the Musical, the Authors will provide services to the Producer as follows:

(A) Deliver a completed draft of the Musical within _____ days after the execution of the Agreement in generally accepted industry manuscript form;

(B) Rewrite and revise the Musical as many times and as much as may be reasonably appropriate and necessary;

(C) Assist with the selection of the director, choreographer, cast, and designers. The composer will have the sole right to select the musical director, conductor, arrangers, orchestra members, and rehearsal pianist.

(D) Assist and advise the producer, director, and all members of the production staff with any matters, problems, or issues for which it may be appropriate or necessary to consult with the Authors;

(E) Attend rehearsals of the Musical, as well as any preview performances, for the purpose of resolving any problems that may become apparent during same.

8. (A) The Producer will pay the Authors collectively an advance of _____ dollars ($_____), upon the execution of this Agreement.

(B) In consideration of the payment made in (A) above, the Producer will have the option to present the Musical as a professional production on the live speaking stage on or before _____ (the "First Option Period") in the geographic location of _____, at the _____ level of production.

(C) At any time prior to expiration of the First Option Period, the Producer may purchase a "Second Option Period" by paying to the Authors collectively the sum of _____. Said Second Option Period will begin _____ [the day after the First Option Period expires] and terminate on _____.

(D) At any time prior to the expiration of the Second Option Period, the Producer may purchase a Third Option Period by paying to the Authors collectively the sum of _____ dollars ($_____). The Third Option Period will begin on the _____ [day after the Second Option Period expires] and will terminate on _____.

(E) If, by the expiration of all the option periods purchased by the Producer hereunder, the Producer has not presented the Musical as aforesaid in section (B) above, all of his rights hereunder will terminate and revert back to the Authors.

(F) All advances paid hereunder as described in paragraphs (A) through (D) above will be consideration for the Authors granting the exclusive options for the times as stated herein. Said advances will be nonrefundable, if the Producer fails to present the Musical.

(G) If the Producer presents the Musical, then all advances paid hereunder will be recoupable against royalties due and owing to the authors as described in paragraph 9 below.

(H) Notwithstanding the foregoing or any other terms of this agreement, the Producer does not guarantee production of the Musical during the term of the option or any extensions thereof.

(I) Failure to pay advances to the Authors when due and owing will be a material breach of this Agreement.

9. (A) In consideration of all the rights herein granted by the Authors and for the Authors' services in connection with the Producer's Production, as described in paragraph 7 above, the Producer will pay to the author royalties, on a weekly basis, as follows:

Prior to recoupment:

_____% of the gross weekly box office receipts to the Book writer

_____% of the gross weekly box office receipts to the Composer

_____% of the gross weekly box office receipts to the Lyricist

After recoupment:

_____% of the gross weekly box office receipts to the Book writer

_____% of the gross weekly box office receipts to the Composer

_____% of the gross weekly box office receipts to the Lyricist

Recoupment will mean the date when the Musical has earned back all of its costs to produce, regardless of whether the Producer has distributed all or any part of the Musical's capitalization back to its investors.

(B) Royalties to the Authors will be due and payable on the Wednesday of the week succeeding the week during which the royalties are earned. Failure to pay royalties in full when due and owing will be a material breach of this agreement.

(C) Gross weekly box office receipts will be defined as all earnings from the Musical from all sources of ticket sales, including, but not limited to, box office, telephone, mail order, groups, theater parties, ticket brokers, Telecharge, Ticketmaster, discount ticket outlets, and any and all sources of ticket sales, less any taxes and sales commissions due thereon.

(D) Prior to the payment of royalties, Producer will first deduct all advances paid under paragraphs 8 (A) through (D).

(E) Royalties will be due and payable, based on the full box office price, even on complementary tickets given away by the Producer, whether as gifts or as part of group or subscription sales promotions. Notwithstanding the foregoing, no royalties will be paid on the following complementary tickets:

(i)   Tickets given to bona fide members of the press;

(ii) Tickets given away for the official opening of the Musical for the purpose of "padding" the house;

(iii) Tickets given to the Authors for their personal viewing of the performance.

(F) Each weekly payment of royalties will be accompanied by a detailed box office statement, for each performance during the subject week, accounting for the disposition of all tickets available for said performance, signed by the treasurer or business manager of the theater in which the Musical is being presented and countersigned by the Producer. If any one of the Authors is a member of the Dramatists Guild, a duplicate copy of each statement will be forwarded to the Guild.

(G) Authors or their designated representatives may inspect the Producer's records, during normal business hours, for the purpose of verifying the accuracy of all royalty payments and box office statements.

10. In the event any one of the Authors must travel to a rehearsal or production location more than _____ miles from [his] [her] respective place of residence, the Producer agrees to pay for the Author's reasonable costs of travel, including economy airfare, and the Author's accommodations while at the said rehearsal and/or production locations. Accommodations provided to the Author, at the Producer's expense, will be at least equivalent in value and living conditions and standards to the Producer's own accommodations. Accommodations will include the cost of hotel/motel rooms, meals, local calls, and transportation to and from the rehearsal/production location from the Author's hotel/motel.

11. Authors will be entitled to attend all performances free of charge. In addition thereto, each of the Authors will be entitled to _____ pairs of adjoining house seats for each performance. Said house seats will be held until _____ prior to each evening performance and until _____ prior to each matinee performance. After such time, if the particular Author fails to use them, they will be released for sale to the general public. All house seats will be purchased at the regularly established box office price. Authors agree not to resell such tickets at a premium or otherwise; to maintain accurate records therefore; and to comply with all state and/or local laws applicable to the use thereof.

12. The Producer reserves the right to assign his rights under this Agreement to a general partnership, joint venture, limited partnership, or other entity owned or controlled by the Producer, as long as the Producer remains an active principal therein. Any other assignment will require the consent of the Authors in writing.

13. The Authors hereby grant to the Producer the right to present an excerpt or excerpts from the Producer's Production of the Musical in a radio or television broadcast, whether live, taped, or on motion picture film, for the purpose of promoting and publicizing the Production. Each presentation may not exceed a total of _____ [minutes] [seconds]. The Producer may not receive any direct or indirect compensation or profits therefrom, other than reimbursement for expenses incurred in preparing and presenting the broadcast excerpt, including any payments to the cast required by the appropriate unions or otherwise by contract. In all such presentations, the Producer will use his best efforts to assure appropriate billing credit for the Authors.

14. Except as provided in paragraph 13 above, no part of the Musical may be recorded, by audio, video, motion picture film, or any other means, whether now known or hereinafter invented, for "archival" purposes, "for the archives," or any other purpose, without the authors additional written consent. Any such unauthorized recording will be, prima facie, a willful violation of the Authors individual and respective copyrights.

15. Notwithstanding anything to the contrary contained herein, Authors individually and collectively will have the absolute right (but not the obligation) to attend all rehearsals, auditions and casting sessions, and production meetings, and the Producer will provide the Authors with reasonable advance notice thereof. For purposes of notice herein, telephone or face-to-face in person notice will suffice. Any attempt to prevent or otherwise deprive the any Author of these rights herein by the Producer or any persons under his control or in his employment will be, prima facie, a material breach of this agreement for which monetary damages shall not be a sufficient remedy. In addition to, or in lieu of monetary damages, the Authors, individually or collectively, may seek injunctive relief.

[Paragraph 16 Alternate #1, in which Authors give Producer share of subsidiary rights.]

16. [Except for the production license herein granted to the Producer, the Authors own and control all of the rights, uses, and interests in the Musical and may dispose of same at their sole discretion. However, the parties recognize that Producer's successful production of the Musical contributes to the value of its uses and rights in other media. By reason thereby, the Authors recognize therefore that the Producer will be entitled to certain percentages of the net receipts paid to the Authors in any or all of the following uses: worldwide motion picture rights; net receipts paid to the Authors within the Continental United States and Canada from any or all of the following: touring, Broadway performances, and off Broadway performances; stock, amateur, foreign language productions; concert tours or productions; condensed tabloid productions; commercial and merchandising uses; audio, video, or other visual or sound recordings, whether by means now known or hereinafter invented; radio or television broadcasts (collectively the "subsidiary rights").

The parties, recognize, however, that the Producer will only be entitled to share in the afore described net receipts under the following conditions:

(A) The Producer's production must run for at least the following consecutive paid performances in order to entitle the Producer to the following percentages of the aforesaid rights:

_____ performances: _____%

_____ performances: _____%

_____ performances: _____%

_____ performances: _____%

In computing the number of performances, only _____ paid previews may be counted in the computation.

(B) The Authors must enter into the contract for the disposition of the aforesaid rights prior to the expiration of _____ years beginning on the date of the last performance of the Producer's production. Producer will be entitled to the aforesaid share of the Authors' net receipts whenever thereafter same are earned or received.

(C) Authors will remit the Producer's share of the net receipts within thirty days after receipt by the Authors, accompanied by a copy of the statements received by the Authors for same.

(D) Producer or his representative may, during normal business hours, inspect the Authors' records to verify the correctness of all payments and accompanying statements.

(E) In the event the Producer fails to make any payments owed to the Authors, individually or collectively, under any of the terms of this Agreement when due and payable, the same will be a material breach hereunder. Upon receipt of written notice by the Authors, individually or collectively, of said failure, the Producer will have thirty days thereafter to rectify the situation. In the event the Producer fails to rectify the situation within said thirty days, all of his rights, interest, and claims to any of the aforesaid net receipts under this paragraph 16 will terminate, and he will have no further claim or right hereunder.

(F) Authors' net receipts will be defined as Authors' gross receipts less agent's commission.

(G) Nothing contained herein will obligate the Authors to dispose of any of the aforesaid subsidiary rights at any time.]

[Paragraph 16 Alternative #2 in which the Authors do not share subsidiary rights with Producer.]

16. [The Producer will not be entitled to any share of the Authors subsidiary rights.]

17. No changes, additions, deletions, or modifications of any kind may be made to any element of the Musical without the consent of the author of that individual element.

18. The Authors or their designee have the right to approve the choice of director, cast, permanent replacements, and designers, which approval will not be withheld unreasonably. In cases in which any one of the Authors is physically unavailable to give aforesaid approval or not reachable by telephone, the Producer will send to that Author a telegram requesting approval of any of the aforesaid matters. If, after forty-eight hours have expired, the Author has failed to respond, approval will be deemed to have been given.

19. This Agreement will be governed and interpreted by the law of the State of _____.

20. Except as otherwise provided herein, all notices required hereunder will be given to the parties at their respective addresses following their signatures below, by certified mail, return receipt requested. Notice will be effective as of the date of receipt.

21. In the event of a dispute or disagreement arising under this Agreement, the parties agree to submit this matter to binding arbitration before a member of the American Arbitration Association. The Arbitrator will have the right to award attorney fees and court costs to the prevailing party thereunder. Any court of competent jurisdiction may enter judgment thereon.

IN WITNESS WHEREOF, the parties have hereunto set their hands and seals this day and date.

_____   _____

Producer   Address

_____   _____

Book writer   Address

_____   _____

Composer   Address

_____   _____

Lyricist   Address

chapter 10 Collaborations

When two or more persons join together to create a work of art, they are entering into a *collaboration*. In the theater, two or more writers may author a play together, e.g., George S. Kaufman and Moss Hart in such works as *The Man Who Came to Dinner* and *You Can't Take It With You*. More frequently, a book writer, composer, and lyricist will create a musical together. In fact, the vast majority of musicals have been written by two or more people, with each person responsible for separate elements of book, music, and lyrics.

However, increasingly, a third model is being added into the mix. A theater company, composed of actors, decides to create a piece, to which all of the members contribute material.

This is the company-created play. This, too, is a collaboration. Because of the larger number of authors involved, it is on a much grander scale than the traditional models.

In all of these cases, the authors must negotiate a separate written collaboration agreement among themselves. They are advised to do so well before they actually begin work. If they delay until the project is underway or is even finished, they may find they are unable to agree on such business terms as the division of royalties or the marketing of the work. If they cannot reach accommodation on such matters, all of their work may be for naught. A promising project may bog down for years in legal controversies.

These are the primary issues the parties must address.

COLLABORATION ESSENTIALS

1. *Copyright.* In the case of a straight play all the authors share equal ownership of the copyright, which is taken out in all their names. In a musical the book writer owns the book while the composer and lyricist (or their music publisher) hold the copyright on the musical numbers.

2. *Voting mechanism.* The parties must agree upon a mechanism by which they will decide artistic and business matters. Commonly, each author is entitled to one vote. In the case of a musical, voting usually is apportioned according to the respective elements—that is, the book writer, composer, and lyricist each have one vote.

   Musicals, however, are not always necessarily so straightforward. Sometimes, two people create a single element: for instance, two persons may author the book. (The book of the musical *Chicago* was authored by Bob Fosse and Fred Ebb.) In that case, each person can still have one vote. Or each element has one vote; even though there are two book writers, they share one vote. This can become tricky. What if the two authors of the one element don't agree?

   And what if one person wears more than one hat? For instance, Alan Jay Lerner wrote both the book and the lyrics to such musicals as *My Fair Lady* and *Camelot*, while Frederick Lowe wrote only the music. In such event, Lerner would have two votes to Lowe's one; Lowe would always be outvoted. That isn't fair, is it?

   In the case of company-created works, the parties may (but are not required to) leave business decisions up to the producer or business manager, reserving artistic decisions for themselves. And is voting to be by majority rule? Or by a quorum? If the quorum is the preferred method, then what constitutes a quorum? I can't give you an easy answer. Each team of collaborators must thrash out these issues for themselves and agree upon a satisfactory solution.

3. *Deadlocks.* It is also wise to establish a means for settling deadlocks. A neutral third party should be appointed, whom all the collaborators can respect.

In artistic matters, a playwright or director of note may be chosen. In business matters, a theatrical lawyer, agent, or accountant may be the way to go. First ask your third party if he wishes to participate, before appointing him in your agreement.

4. *Merger.* Merger is the concept by which all of the creative contributions to a work finally come together to form a unified whole. Until merger occurs, each collaborator is free to remove his material from the piece. Once merger occurs, the work is frozen and no party may remove his contribution.

Merger does not occur automatically. Merger occurs when the parties say it does, on the merger date. This may be the first press preview, the last technical rehearsal, or the traditional opening on Broadway. (Today, most Broadway collaborations specify the merger date as the first press preview, because the traditional opening on Broadway isn't really the press opening anymore.) The choice of date is up to the parties. There is no right or wrong answer. However, the date must be selected in the collaboration agreement, since, as you will see, many other terms of the agreement depend on it.

5. *Representatives.* The parties should decide upon the appropriate representatives for the piece—agent, attorney, and accountant. Usually, only one attorney and one accountant will be selected. However, when each collaborator has his or her own agent, all of the agents may wind up marketing the piece on a nonexclusive basis. Agents are accustomed to working together in such instances and producers are likewise accustomed to dealing with multiple agents for a single work.

6. *Removal of a collaborator.* The trickiest clauses of a collaboration agreement relate to the removal or addition of a collaborator prior to the merger date. (After the merger date, since the work is now completed, you don't remove or add collaborators.) A collaborator may voluntarily—or be requested to voluntarily—leave a project at some time prior to merger. But what happens to the material she has created up to that point? May she take it with her to another project? May she create another work in competition with her former collaborators? Must she leave the material in the work? Do the other collaborators want the material? Can the parties even ascertain specifically her contributions up to the time of her departure?

If the show is a musical and the departing collaborator is the composer, obviously it is an easy task to determine what element she has contributed. Or is it? Suppose she thought of an idea that, while not a piece of music, in fact relates to the show as a whole? For example, when Rodgers and Hammerstein were transforming the Molnar play *Liliom* into *Carousel,* Rodgers suggested changing the locale of the piece to Maine from Budapest. Not a musical idea, certainly, yet important to the finished work. If it is a straight play, it becomes almost impossible to ascertain each person's specific contributions. Yet you must answer the above issues.

Moreover, a collaborator may leave a piece for any number of reasons, besides a voluntary departure. She may die. She may become disabled such that she can no longer participate in the show. In either case, does she retain any rights to the show? Certainly, if the collaborators wish to keep any of her contributions, she should retain some interest in the play. But by what formula? How do you quantify a creative work? By the amount of time she has thus far put into the project? By the amount of work? But what if she has contributed a single idea that defines the show? Or at least substantially helps it—like changing the setting from Budapest to Maine?

Ooh! These are vein-busting issues, aren't they? And ya better figures 'em out at the outset, folks! Or else you're gonna have real trouble in River City.

7. *Addition of a collaborator.* If a collaborator dies or becomes disabled before the work is finished, the remaining authors may choose to bring in another writer to finish her work. The parties must create a formula to modify the deceased/disabled collaborator's interest in the show, so they may fairly compensate her replacement. They will not change her billing credits, but they will have to make room for the new writer. The remaining collaborators should not have to seek the consent of the legal representative of the deceased/disabled collaborator to replace her, since that may be difficult to obtain.

8. *Division of royalties.* The collaborators must decide on a formula for dividing up the net income the work will (hopefully) generate. Net income is the total of all income earned by the work, from all sources, less agent's commissions, the expenses incurred in marketing the work, the producer's share of the subsidiary rights, and royalties due to the owner of the underlying rights. (See "Underlying Rights," chapter 12.) The most common formula is an equal division. However, a

different formula may be desirable. For instance, one of the collaborators may be more famous than the others and therefore may demand a greater share of the income.

9. *Small/Grand rights.* The *small rights* are to the rights to record and perform the songs outside of the show. For instance, Barbra Streisand wants to record your show's ballad, "Love Up Your Nose." Or Tony Bennett wants to use it as part of his act. The small performing rights are always controlled by the composer and lyricist, or their publisher. The *grand rights* are the rights to perform the songs as part of a dramatic presentation of the show—with action, incident, characters, and plot. They are controlled by all of the authors. Your col-laboration agreement must distinguish between the two and account for the money earned from these separate sources.

10. *Sale/Assignment of interest.* At some point during the life of the copyright, one of the collaborators may want to sell out her interest in the show. Maybe she needs immediate cash for medical bills, to send her children to college, or any number of reasons. However, the other collaborators may not want a stranger stepping into her voting shoes. Or they may want to own the show themselves. The parties must create a mechanism, so that, if a col-laborator wants to sell her interest, the other authors have the first chance to buy her out. The price should be whatever a third party would pay.

Form 12 Collaboration Agreement (Nonmusical)

THIS AGREEMENT is made and entered into this _____ day of _____, 20_____ ("Effective Date") by and between _____, (all collectively hereinafter "Authors"); all of whom desire to collaborate with each other to create a play presently entitled _____ (the "Work").

Therefore, in consideration of the mutual covenants, promises, and agreements contained herein, the parties agree as follows:

1. Each party will write and create the Work and join with the others to complete the said Work.
2. Copyright in the play will be taken out and owned as follows _____.
3. After deductions for agents' commissions (as defined below), the producer's share of subsidiary rights, and any other percentages of the gross revenues which the parties must share with others, then all of the net revenues, money, and income from the commercial exploitation of the Work, its adaptations, derivations, translations, and use in any media or format, whether now in existence, or hereinafter developed, will be divided among the parties as follows:
   _____%
   _____%
   _____%
   "Agent's commissions" will refer to the agent for the Work as a whole and not to the respective agents for the individual parties, each of whom will be responsible for his own agent's commissions.
4. All contracts dealing with the Work will require that, whenever authorship credit is given to one author, all of the collaborators must also be duly credited and provided in the same size and style of type as the others. Authorship credit will appear in the following order:
   _____
   _____
   _____
5. Merger of the respective contributions of the parties hereto will, for all purposes, occur on the happening of the following:

   _____
   The Merger Date

   Upon the happening of the Merger Date, all of the material that the parties have agreed will constitute the Work will thereupon be incorporated into and become an essential part of the Work forever. After the Merger Date, the merged material may not be removed, or otherwise used in any manner outside of the Work.
   Any material created for or considered for the Work, but not actually a part of the Work on the Merger Date, will not be merged into the Work and will remain the individual property of its creator/collaborator, whose control over it will be absolute. All rights to the same are reserved by its creator/collaborator. None of the other collaborators will have any rights, claims, entitlement or interest thereon.
6. All of the parties must agree upon and execute any contracts for all productions, presentations, publications of the Work, and for the sale or license of any rights therein. Except with the consent of the other parties, no party may sell, license, or otherwise dispose of any of the rights to the Work or authorize or grant the rights to produce or present the Work in any manner whatsoever.
7. Whenever the consent of the author is required or desired, the parties intend and agree that voting rights on matters will be apportioned as follows:
   Each collaborator will have one vote and there will be as many votes as there are collaborators. All decisions will be by [majority] [unanimous] vote.
   In the event the parties cannot agree upon a decision, the collaborators hereby appoint the following persons to break deadlocks:

Artistic Decisions: _____

Business Decisions: _____

8. In the event that merger has not occurred and one party dies or becomes disabled such that he cannot effectively collaborate, the remaining parties may continue the Work. They will have unbridled discretion to modify or change any or all parts of the Work, including any material contributed by the deceased or disabled party. If the remaining parties determine that additional material or contributions are needed for the element which the deceased or disabled party had heretofore been creating, they may bring in another person to finish the element, including changing or deleting any material heretofore created by the deceased or disabled party, or otherwise to contribute to the Work.

   In the event the surviving parties bring in a third person collaborator, they may compensate the new collaborator by changing [decreasing] the deceased or disabled party's compensation according to the following formula: _____. They will not be required to obtain the consent of the disabled party or his representative or of the representative of a deceased party. However, they may not change or reduce any billing credits for the deceased or disabled party. Otherwise, all other compensation due to the deceased or disabled party will be duly paid, as heretofore agreed upon. In addition, copies of all contracts or other agreements affecting the Work will be furnished promptly to the disabled party or [his] [her] representative, or to the legal representative of the deceased.

9. At any time prior to merger, any of the parties may be removed by [majority] [unanimous] vote of the other parties. [For this purpose, and this purpose only, the parties will not vote by unit. Instead each party will have one vote.] The removed party will be entitled to due written notice. All rights to any of the material created or contributed by the removed party will revert immediately to [him] [her], to use and exploit as [he] [she] will see fit, and the remaining parties will have no claim, interest, or entitlement to the use of the same, whether in this Work or in any other. The removed party will have no claim, interest, or entitlement to the Work, or any revenues earned by it.

10. If, pursuant to any of the provisions of paragraph 8 or 9 above, the parties agree to add or replace a collaborator, the new collaborator will be required to sign this agreement and to be bound hereto. However, such new, additional, or replacement collaborator will not be entitled to any revenues or other receipts earned by the Work, including advances even for uncompleted work, prior to the date of his signing of this agreement.

11. The parties hereby appoint _____ as [exclusive] [nonexclusive] agent for the Work. The parties hereby appoint _____ as attorney for the Work.

12. The parties hereby warrant and represent that all material each has or will contribute to the Work is and will be original with each party (except for public domain sources) and has not been adapted or derived from any other copyrighted and/or trademarked material owned by a third person or entity not a party to this Agreement. Furthermore, to the best of knowledge of the contributing party, his material does not infringe upon or violate the rights of others, including any rights of publicity or privacy belonging to any third persons or entities.

13. Any collaborator hereunder may sell, pledge, lease, assign, encumber, or otherwise dispose of his interest of net receipts to a third party, provided, however, he first gives written notice of his intention, including the terms and conditions of said sale or encumbrance, to the other collaborators. Said notice must be by certified mail, return receipt requested, and will be effective only upon receipt by the other collaborators. The other collaborators will have _____ days after receipt, as a first option, to purchase the Selling Collaborator's interest, on either an individual or joint basis, upon the terms and conditions so stated in the notice. If, during the said time period, the Purchasing Collaborators either fail to exercise said option, or complete the purchase, the Selling Collaborator may offer and transfer his rights to a third party upon the same terms and conditions as contained in the notice to the other Collaborators, provided; however, he transfers only his right to receive the net revenues. Upon receipt of a copy of the sales contract to a third party, the remaining collaborators must honor the Third Party Purchaser's interest in the net receipts. The Selling Collaborator may not transfer voting or other rights to the Third Party. Upon transfer of his interest in the net receipts, the Selling Collaborator's voting rights, in all matters, business and artistic, will cease (but not his rights to billing credit).

14. The parties expressly deny any intention or agreement to form a partnership or joint venture between them, and this agreement will not be construed as creating same.

15. This agreement may not be assigned or transferred (except an interest in the net receipts as provided in paragraph 14 above), without the express written consent of the other parties. Nothing contained herein, however, will prevent a party from transferring or assigning his rights by will, trust, or other testamentary instrument to any person(s) and/or entities, for estate planning purposes.

16. This agreement will bind the parties hereto, their executors, administrators, personal representatives, successors, and assigns.

17. In the event of the death or disability of a collaborator, after merger has occurred, the following provisions will prevail:

    (A) All artistic decisions, for which the Authors' decision may be required, requested, or permitted, will be made by the surviving collaborators, according to the voting formula herein described in paragraph 7 above. If a collaborator is disabled but still competent to make artistic decisions, his voting rights will not change, and he will be entitled to vote as if disability had not occurred.

    (B) The legal representative of the deceased or the disabled collaborator will not be permitted to vote on artistic matters.

    (C) All business decisions, which the Authors may be required, requested, or permitted to make, will be made by the surviving collaborators and the legal representative of a disabled collaborator who is not competent to make such decisions and the legal representative of a deceased collaborator.

18. This constitutes the entire agreement of the party. No modification, or amendment hereto, will be effective except by the written consent of the parties.

19. The parties agree and understand that the creation and/or marketing of the Work may entail expenses. The parties must agree in advance upon any expenses incurred and they agree to share such expenses, pro rata. In the event any party advances expenses, to which all of the parties have mutually agreed, he will be entitled to reimbursement from any monies earned by the Work before such revenues are divided up among the parties. In the event it becomes apparent, within a reasonable time, that the Work may not earn revenues sufficient to repay him, the other parties agree to reimburse the advancing party, in full, pro rata according to their shares in the Work.

20. The laws of the State of _____ will govern this agreement.

21. In the event a dispute or disagreement arises out of this Work, or in the event of a breach hereof, and it becomes apparent the parties cannot settle the same among themselves, then any party may require the other parties to submit to arbitration in _____ County, State of _____, in accordance with the Commercial Arbitration Rules of the American Arbitration Association. All such arbitration will be binding upon the parties. Any court of competent jurisdiction may enter judgment upon the award rendered by the arbitrator. In all such arbitrations, the losing party agrees to pay the costs of arbitration, as well as the prevailing party's reasonable costs and attorney fees.

22. All notices required hereunder will be in writing and will be given by personal delivery or certified or registered mail (return receipt requested). Said notices will be effective upon the receipt thereof. All notices will be addressed to the parties at the addresses following their signatures below or to such other addresses as any party may specifically, in writing, direct.

IN WITNESS WHEREOF, the parties have hereunto affixed their hands, seals, and signatures below.

Name: _____ Address: _____

Name: _____ Address: _____

Name: _____ Address: _____

Form 13 Collaboration Agreement (Musical)

THIS AGREEMENT is made and entered into this _____ day of _____, 20_____ ("Effective Date") by and between _____, ("Book writer"), _____ ("Composer"), and _____ ("Lyricist") (all collectively hereinafter "Authors"); all of whom desire to collaborate with each other to create a musical play presently entitled _____ (the "Musical").

Therefore, in consideration of the mutual covenants, promises, and agreements contained herein, the parties agree as follows:

1. Each party shall write and create his respective element of the Musical and join with the others to complete the said Musical.

2. (A) Copyright in the respective elements of the play shall be taken out and owned as follows:
   Book: _____
   Music: _____
   Lyrics: _____
   (B) Nothing contained herein—including those provisions relating to merger below—shall be construed or intended as creating a "joint work," as that term is used under the United States Copyright Act of ____, and any amendments, modifications, or supplements thereof. The parties expressly agree and understand the book, music, and lyrics of the play shall each be deemed a separate work for copyright and other purposes. The copyright to each such element shall belong solely to its respective creator as set forth in section (A) above.

3. (A) After deductions for agent's commissions (as defined below), producer's share of subsidiary rights, and any other percentages of the gross revenues which the parties must share with others, then, except as provided in (B) below, all of the net revenues, monies, and income from the commercial exploitation of the Musical, its adaptations, derivations, translations, and use in any media or format, whether now in existence, or hereinafter developed, shall be divided among the parties as follows:
   Book writer: _____%
   Composer: _____%
   Lyricist: _____%
   "Agent's commissions" shall refer to the agent for the Work as a whole and not to the respective agents for the individual book writer, composer, and lyricist, each of whom shall be responsible for his own agent's commissions.
   (B) The parties understand and agree that the music and lyrics may be used separate and apart from the play and said separate uses will earn revenues thereon. Such uses may include but not be limited to the separate publication, mechanical reproduction, synchronization, small performing rights, motion picture, television, radio, video, cast albums, recordings of any kind, all of which may occur and be presented in any format of sound reproduction and/or publication, whether now known or hereinafter developed. Except as provided in (C) below, the composer and/or lyricist, as the case may be (or an entity owned or licensed by each of them respectively), shall have sole control, authority, and direction over such uses, and the book writer shall have no control, authority, or direction thereon. All revenues earned from such uses shall (except as provided in (C) below) inure to and belong to the composer and lyricist respectively and the book writer shall not be entitled to any of said revenues (except as provided in (C) below). All such revenues shall be divided according to the following formula:
   (i)   If both music and lyrics are used, then _____% to the Composer and _____% to the Lyricist;
   (ii) If only the lyrics are used, then _____% to the Lyricist and _____% to the Composer;
   (iii) If only the music is used, then _____% to the Composer and _____% to the Lyricist.
   (C) In the event _____% of the book is used in any presentation of the separate music and/or lyrics, as stated above in section (B), then the book writer shall be entitled to _____% of the net receipts. The book writer shall further be entitled to _____% of the direction and authority over the use of the book, in connection therein.
   (D) In any publication of the book, net receipts therefrom shall be divided as follows:

(i) If only the book is used, then 100% of the net receipts shall inure to the book writer. Only the book writer shall have direction and authority over the use of the book in such publication.

(ii) If only lyrics are included in the publication of the book, then net receipts shall be divided as follows: _____% to the Book writer and _____% to the Lyricist [and _____% to the Composer]. The book writer shall have _____%, the Lyricist shall have _____%, [and the composer shall have _____%] of the direction and authority over such use of the book and lyrics respectively.

(iii) If the music and lyrics are included in the publication of the book, then net receipts shall be divided according to the formula, as stated in section (A) above. The book writer shall have _____%, the Lyricist shall have _____%, and the composer shall have _____%, of the direction and authority over such use of the book, lyrics, and music respectively.

4. All contracts dealing with the Musical Play, or any of the elements contained therein, shall require that, whenever authorship credit is given to one author, all of the collaborators must also be duly credited and provided for in the same size and style of type as the others. Authorship credit shall appear in the following manner:

Book by _____

Music by _____

Lyrics by _____

5. Merger of the respective elements of book, music, and lyrics, shall, for all purposes, occur on the happening of the following:

_____

The Merger Date

Upon the happening of the Merger Date, all of the material—whether elements of the book, music, or lyrics—that the parties have agreed will constitute the Work, will thereupon be incorporated into and become an essential part of the Work forever. Said merged material may not be removed, or otherwise used in any manner outside of the Work (except as noted in paragraph 3 (B) above).

Any material created for or considered for the Work, but not actually a part of the Work on the merger date, shall not be merged into the Work and shall remain the individual property of its creator/collaborator, whose control over it shall be absolute. All rights to same are reserved by its creator/collaborator. None of the other collaborators shall have any rights, claims, entitlement, or interest thereon.

6. The book writer shall have sole rights of approval to the book element, including any additions, and/or deletions thereto. The composer shall have sole rights of approval to the musical elements, including any additions, and/or deletions therefrom, as well as to the choices of orchestra members, rehearsal pianist, musical orchestrations, and arrangements. The lyricist shall have sole rights of approval to the lyric elements, including any additions, and/or deletions thereto.

7. All of the parties must agree upon and execute any contracts for all productions, presentations, publications of the Work, and for the sale or license or any rights therein (except as otherwise provided in paragraph 3 (B) herein). Except with the consent of the other parties (and as otherwise provided in paragraph 3 (B) herein), no party may sell, license, or otherwise dispose of any of the rights to the Work or authorize or grant the rights to produce or present the Work in any manner whatsoever.

8. Whenever the consent of the author is required or desired, the parties intend and agree that voting rights on matters shall be apportioned as follows:

[Each collaborator shall have one vote and there shall be as many votes as there are collaborators. All decisions shall be by {majority} {unanimous} vote.]

[Except as provided herein in paragraph 10 below, the respective elements of the Work—Book, Music, and Lyrics—shall be divided into 3 separate units. (It shall be irrelevant the number of persons actually making up a particular unit.) Each unit shall be entitled to one vote. All decisions shall be by {majority}{unanimous} vote.

(A) In the event two or more persons constituting a unit cannot agree upon a voting decision, then the vote of that unit shall be the will of the majority.

(B) In the event there is a tie vote within a unit, containing an equal number of persons, the parties within the unit appoint _____ to determine the result of the vote.]

In the event the parties cannot agree upon a decision, the collaborators hereby appoint the following persons to break deadlocks: Artistic Decisions: _____ Business Decisions: _____]

9. In the event that merger has not occurred and one party dies or becomes disabled such that he cannot effectively collaborate, the remaining parties may continue the Work. They shall have unbridled discretion to modify or change any or all parts of the Work, including any material contributed by the deceased or disabled party. If the remaining parties determine that additional material or contributions are needed for the element which the deceased or disabled party had heretofore been creating, they may bring in another person to finish the element, including changing or deleting any material heretofore created by the deceased or disabled party, or otherwise to contribute to the Work.

   In the event the surviving parties bring in a third person collaborator, they may compensate the new collaborator by changing [decreasing] the deceased or disabled party's compensation according to the following formula: _____.

   They shall not be required to obtain the consent of the disabled party or his representative or the representative of a deceased party. However, they may not change or reduce any billing credits for the deceased or disabled party. Otherwise, all other compensation due to the deceased or disabled party shall be duly paid, as heretofore agreed upon. In addition, copies of all contracts or other agreements affecting the Work shall be furnished promptly to the disabled party or his representative, or to the legal representative of the deceased.

10. At any time prior to merger, any of the parties may be removed by [majority] [unanimous] vote of the other parties. [For this purpose, and this purpose only, the parties shall not vote by unit. Instead each party shall have one vote.] The removed party shall be entitled to due written notice. All rights to any of the material created or contributed by the removed party shall revert immediately to him, to use and exploit as he shall see fit, and the remaining parties shall have no claim, interest, or entitlement to the use of same, whether in this Work or in any other. The removed party shall have no claim, interest, or entitlement to the Work, or any revenues earned by it.

11. If, pursuant to any of the provisions of paragraph 9 or 10 above, the parties agree to add or replace a collaborator, the new collaborator shall be required to sign this agreement and to be bound hereto. However, such new, additional, or replacement collaborator shall not be entitled to any revenues or other receipts earned by the Work, including advances even for uncompleted work, prior to the date of his signing of this agreement.

12. The parties hereby appoint _____ as [exclusive] [nonexclusive] agent for the Work. The parties hereby appoint _____ as attorney for the Work.

13. The parties hereby warrant and represent that all material each has or will contribute to the Work is and will be original with each party (except for public domain sources) and has not been adapted or derived from any other copyrighted and/or trademarked material owned by a third person or entity not a party to this Agreement. Furthermore, to the best of knowledge of the contributing party, his material does not infringe upon or violate the rights of others, including any rights of publicity or privacy belonging to any third persons or entities.

14. Any collaborator hereunder may sell, pledge, lease, assign, encumber, or otherwise dispose of his interest of net receipts to a third party, provided, however, he first gives written notice of his intention, including the terms and conditions of said sale or encumbrance, to the other collaborators. Said notice must be by certified mail, return receipt requested, and shall be effective only upon receipt by the other collaborators. The other collaborators shall have _____ days after receipt, as a first option, to purchase the Selling Collaborator's interest, on either an individual or joint basis, upon the terms and conditions so stated in the notice. If, during the said time period, the Purchasing Collaborators either fail to exercise said option, or complete the purchase, the Selling Collaborator may offer and transfer his rights to a third party upon the same terms and conditions as contained in the notice to the other Collaborators, provided, however, he transfers only his right to receive the net revenues. Upon receipt of a copy of the sales contract to such third party, the remaining collaborators must honor the Third Party Purchaser's interest in the net receipts. The Selling Collaborator may not transfer voting or other rights to the Third Party. Upon transfer of his interest in the net receipts, the Selling Collaborator's voting rights, in all matters, business and artistic, shall cease (but not his rights to billing credit).

15. The parties expressly deny any intention or agreement to form a partnership or joint venture between them, and this agreement shall not be construed as creating same.

16. This agreement may not be assigned or transferred (except an interest in the net receipts as provided in paragraph 14 above), without the express written consent of the other parties. Nothing contained herein, however, shall prevent a party from transferring or assigning his rights by will, trust, or other testamentary instrument to any person(s) and/or entities, for estate planning purposes.

17. This agreement shall bind the parties hereto, their executors, administrators, personal representatives, successors, and assigns.

18. In the event of the death or disability of a collaborator, after merger has occurred, the following provisions shall prevail:

    (A) All artistic decisions for which the Authors' decision may be required, requested, or permitted shall be made by the surviving collaborators, according to the voting formula herein described in paragraph 8 above. If a collaborator is disabled but still competent to make artistic decisions, his voting rights shall not change, and he shall be entitled to vote as if disability had not occurred.

    (B) The legal representative of a deceased or a disabled collaborator shall not be permitted to vote on artistic matters.

    (C) All business decisions, which the Authors may be required, requested, or permitted to make, shall be made by the surviving collaborators and the legal representative of a disabled collaborator who is not competent to make such decisions and the legal representative of a deceased collaborator.

19. This constitutes the entire agreement of the party. No modification, or amendment hereto, shall be effective except by the written consent of the parties.

20. The parties agree and understand that the creation and/or marketing of the Work may entail expenses. The parties must agree in advance upon any expenses incurred and they agree to share such expenses, pro rata. In the event any party advances expenses, to which all of the parties have mutually agreed, he shall be entitled to reimbursement from any monies earned by the Work before such revenues are divided up among the parties. In the event it becomes apparent, within a reasonable time, that the Work may not earn revenues sufficient to repay him, the other parties agree to reimburse the advancing party, in full, pro rata according to their shares in the Work.

21. The laws of the State of _____ shall govern this agreement.

22. In the event a dispute or disagreement arises out of this Work, or in the event of a breach hereof, and it becomes apparent the parties cannot settle same among themselves, then any party may require the other parties to submit to arbitration in _____ County, State of _____, in accordance with the Commercial Arbitration Rules of the American Arbitration Association. All such arbitration shall be binding upon the parties. Any court of competent jurisdiction may enter judgment upon the award rendered by the arbitrator. In all such arbitrations, the losing party agrees to pay the costs of arbitration, as well as the prevailing party's reasonable costs and attorney fees.

23. All notices required hereunder shall be in writing and shall be given by personal delivery or certified or registered mail (return receipt requested). Said notices shall be effective upon the receipt thereof. All notices shall be addressed to the parties at the addresses following their signatures below or to such other addresses as any party may specifically, in writing, direct.

IN WITNESS WHEREOF, the parties have hereunto affixed their hands, seals, and signatures below.

Name: _____   Name: _____

Address: _____   Address: _____

_____   _____

Name: _____   Name: _____

Address: _____   Address: _____

_____   _____

chapter 11   Agreement Canceling Collaboration

In the event the collaborators do part ways, it is wise to cancel the arrangement in a writing signed by all of the parties.

Collaborations usually dissolve before the parties have exploited the particular work. Once the work receives any level of production or publication—that is, it is actually exploited—the collaboration is frozen and not dissolvable, even if the joint authors can't stand being in the same room with each other.

Therefore, the need for a written cancellation agreement will most likely occur, at any time before the work is exploited.

It is, of course, easiest to break up as collaborators before the work has taken any substantial shape. However, if the parties have invested considerable time and talent in a project that is very nearly completed, or at least nearing the point where it may be ready to showcase to prospective producers or publishers, the parties may want to rethink whether dissolving the collaboration at this point is even desirable. Is it worth losing all that time and effort when success may be near? Are the differences such that they cannot be compromised or even set aside long enough to finish the project? Obviously, there is no set answer, just as there is no set reason why any given team of authors may choose to go their separate ways.

If the work has not been exploited, merger should not as yet have occurred, and therefore the piece has not become a unified whole. The parties therefore are free to take their respective contributions and do with them as they wish. This may mean finding new collaborators to work on the particular project; simply taking their material on to other projects; or discarding their work into the circular file altogether. It is the individual's choice.

Actually, it is not unusual for two or more writers to begin work on a particular project, but then, when they find that either the project or the collaboration is not working as they had hoped, decide to part company. After the death of Oscar Hammerstein, for instance, Richard Rodgers and Alan Jay Lerner (who had dissolved his collaboration with Frederick Lowe) joined forces to create a musical called *I Picked A Daisy*. Unfortunately, after beginning work together, Rodgers decided he had picked a lemon in Lerner and called it quits. (Lerner subsequently went on to develop the same project with composer Burton Lane. Retitled *On A Clear Day You Can See Forever*, it enjoyed a modest, if unspectacular, Broadway run and later became a movie with Barbra Streisand.)

Why is it necessary to draw up a separate cancellation agreement? A separate agreement releases each party from any obligations created by the original collaboration arrangement. In addition, it sets forth each party's rights to the unexploited material. It is written proof of the parties' intentions.

There are two other approaches one might take to canceling the collaboration agreement, neither of which is desirable nor appropriately protective. I call them the "lazy man's" approach to the law—sort of like not brushing your teeth after every meal and hoping nothing goes wrong. The first of these approaches involves merely tearing up the written collaboration agreement and calling it terminated. The second approach involves writing the word "Canceled" across the face of the collaboration agreement, under which each party signs her name or ascribes her initials. This does only a patchwork job.

CANCELLATION ESSENTIALS

1. *Project description*. Describe the project by the title used in the original collaboration agreement. If you have subsequently changed the title, include the later title(s) also. For instance: "*Man in the Moon*, formerly known as *The Green Cheese Guy*."

2. *Identification.* Name the collaborators.

3. *Reference.* Refer to the original collaboration agreement. State that by mutual agreement, the parties are canceling the original contract. It is not necessary or desirable to state the reasons the collaboration is breaking up.

4. *Contributions.* Describe as specifically as possible the contributions of the respective authors. In a musical, this is easy: the composer, the music; the lyricist, the lyrics; and the book writer, the book. (Granted, there may be some overlap: for instance, the book may contain a line of dialogue, which, the lyricist appropriates, with the book writer's consent, to turn into a song.) Since merger has not yet occurred, these materials belong to their respective creators. It is this material the parties are taking away with them. You list each collaborator's contribution in an attachment to the Cancellation Agreement called Exhibit *A.* This document becomes part of your Cancellation Agreement.

5. *Costs.* If the parties have incurred any substantial costs in developing the work to this point, state how these costs are to be apportioned and made up. Costs usually occur in preparing the individual elements, and so it may simply be desirable for the creator of that particular element to swallow the costs for it. Since the parties have not yet begun to exploit the work, no marketing or other costs attributable to the work as a whole have yet been incurred. Therefore, there are no costs of this kind to be divided up.

6. *Termination.* Once the collaboration terminates, none of the parties may exploit material belonging to another collaborator.

7. *Underlying rights.* If the project is based on an underlying work, such as a novel or a play, the question arises: which of the collaborators retains the rights to the underlying work? Obviously, the collaborator who still desires to proceed with the project, albeit with other parties. If all of the collaborators pitched in toward the purchase or option of the underlying rights, then the collaborator wishing to retain the rights should, at the minimum, reimburse the others for their share of the moneys expended.

Form 14 Agreement Canceling Collaboration

THIS AGREEMENT dated this _____ day of _____, 20____, concerns the unexploited work (the "Work"), known as _____, and previously the subject of a certain collaboration agreement dated _____, by and between the following parties [as joint authors:

_____

_____

_____]

[*Alternate*]

[_____ (Composer of the music: "Composer")

_____ (Author of the lyrics: "Lyricist")

_____ (Author of the book: "Book writer")]

All of whom are of legal age and sound mind, as of this date, time, and place.

1. In consideration of the mutual covenants herein subscribed, it is hereby mutually agreed and understood by and between the above joint authors, on behalf of themselves, their heirs, assigns, trustees, and/or executors, that the aforesaid collaboration agreement is hereby canceled and terminated, as of this date, time, and place.

[*Alternative paragraph 2 for a musical collaboration*]

2. [The parties specifically agree that merger of their respective contributions of music, book, and lyrics has not taken place. Title to the respective elements will vest and hereinafter by owned solely by the following:

Music _____

Lyrics _____

Book _____]

[*Alternative paragraph 2 for a nonmusical collaboration*]

2. [The parties specifically agree that merger of any of the creative elements contributed by each of them respectively has not taken place. These contributions are described more particularly in Exhibit A, which is attached hereto and made a part hereof.]

3. Each owner of the respective elements is hereby free to use, exploit, publish, record, or produce said element in any way he sees fit, now and forever, in any medium, whether now known or hereinafter discovered. Each owner may enter into an agreement of collaboration with another person(s), not a party to the original collaboration agreement, to use all or any part of his respective element in another work. None of the owners will be liable to the others for any such use, and none of the owners will claim or have a right to claim any rights, title, interest, earnings, or other benefits in elements belonging to another owner.

4. To date, the parties have incurred certain costs in conjunction with the aforesaid collaboration agreement. Said costs are, approximately, as follows: _____

[Music _____

Lyrics _____

Book _____]

[The owner of each said element will be solely responsible for the costs of her element only.] None of the parties will be responsible as to the costs of elements not created by [him] [her].

5. None of the parties will have the right—or give the appearance of having any right—to market, publish, exploit or otherwise deal with elements not owned by [him] [her].

6. The Work is based, in whole or in part, upon an underlying _____ (novel, screenplay, etc.), entitled _____, the copyright to which is owned by _____. Prior to beginning the creation of the Work, a license to adapt said underlying _____ was entered into by separate agreement with the copyright holder, by the undersigned _____. Fees totaling _____ dollars ($_____) were paid to the copyright holder by _____. The undersigned _____ wishes to pursue adaptation of the underlying _____ with other persons, whose identities may not be known at this time.

(A) All of the joint authors hereby consent, now and forever, to the undersigned _____'s continued use of the underlying _____.

(B) The joint authors hereby assign and transfer to the undersigned _____ any and all rights to said underlying _____, which they may have acquired by the aforesaid written license with the copyright holder of the underlying _____ and/or by reason of partial or full performance under the collaboration agreement.

7. This agreement will be governed by the laws of the State of _____.

IN WITNESS WHEREOF, the parties hereby affix their signatures hereto.

_____

_____

_____

12 Underlying Rights

Many stage productions have been adapted from other works. Think of *Auntie Mame*, *The Woman in Black*, *Bang the Drum Slowly*, and *The Grapes of Wrath*—all stage plays coming from novels.

Even more so, musicals tend to be based on other works. Just look at this list:

MUSICAL	UNDERLYING WORK
Hello, Dolly!	*The Matchmaker* (Play)
Thoroughly Modern Millie	*Thoroughly Modern Millie* (Screenplay)
South Pacific	*Tales of the South Pacific* (Short stories)
My Fair Lady	*Pygmalion* (Play)
Phantom of the Opera	*Phantom of the Opera* (Novel)
Oliver!	*Oliver Twist* (Novel)
The Producers	*The Producers* (Screenplay)

In fact, original musical successes are rare—*Urinetown* and *They're Playing Our Song* notwithstanding. The reason: It is so hard to create a successful musical that it helps to base the show on already proven material.

In all of these cases, the writers of the musical took material created by someone else—a novel, screenplay, or play—and transformed it into a new form, a new work. Unless the author of the adaptation is also the creator of the original story, the adaptor is using material owned by another person or entity (such as a Hollywood film studio). In all such cases, the adapting writer or her producer must first obtain the rights to make such an adaptation from the owner of the original material. These are called the *underlying rights*—so named because the original novel, play, etc., underlies the new adaptation.

In most cases, this is not a simple process. In fact, it is fraught with legal peril.

THAT CRUCIAL FIRST STEP

I caution writers and producers to acquire the underlying rights FIRST before they commit a word to paper or compose the first song. I cannot emphasize this point too strongly—but I will anyway.

Purchase the underlying rights first!

You are a fool if you don't.

Too many writers commit months, even years, of hard work, writing an adaptation of a favorite work for the stage, only to learn too late that the rights to the underlying work are not available to them and never will be. It is a heartbreaking pill to swallow. In such a case, there is nothing the writer can do, except to junk her work. It is absolutely ridiculous, when life is so short and productions are tough enough to come by, to throw away all of that time on a hopeless project. With a little effort at the beginning, one can ascertain the availability or unavailability of the rights.

And make no mistake about it. If you can't get the rights to the underlying material, even if your adaptation is the best show since *My Fair Lady*, you will not get produced—by anyone, unless you can find a bigger fool than you are. Producers—and their lawyers—always want concrete written proof that you own the underlying rights. Hollywood studios will slam the door in your face if you cannot provide this proof. And remember our preliminary contract discussions about our old friends, Mr. Hold Harmless and Ms.

Indemnity Clause. Oh, and don't forget that you (as author) must warrant that your work does not infringe on the rights of others.

So get the damn rights first.

Okay?

PUBLIC DOMAIN

Anyone seeking to adapt another work should first ascertain if the rights have fallen into the public domain. In such a case, the material is freely available to all. You don't have to pay royalties on it either. The works of Shakespeare, Dickens, Poe, and the like are all public domain. That's why no one needed permission to create *Pickwick* (*The Pickwick Papers* by Dickens), *West Side Story* (*Romeo and Juliet* by Shakespeare) or *Phantom of the Opera* (*Phantom of the Opera* by Gaston Leroux).

Whether a work has fallen into the public domain is not a simple question. In general, any work published or registered with the Copyright Office before 1923 is public domain. Any work published or registered between 1923 and 1963 may or may not still be subject to copyright, depending on whether a renewal registration was filed when the initial term of copyright (twenty-eight years at that time) expired.

Two advantages emerge from using public domain material:

1. You do not need anyone's permission to use it.
2. You do not need to pay royalties (or even give billing credit) to the original author or her estate.

However, public domain material is fair game for everyone. Thus, if you choose to adapt, let's say, a Shakespeare play into a musical, chances are someone else has also had the same idea. Therefore, there may be several musicals based on the same work competing with yours for productions and audiences. I know of at least six different versions of the *Phantom of the Opera* circulating, besides the Andrew Lloyd Webber show. And we won't even try to count all of the adaptations of *A Christmas Carol* that pop up every year.

COPYRIGHTED UNDERLYING WORKS

The advantage of basing your show on copyrighted material is that you will be acquiring the exclusive rights. Therefore, there will be no other shows competing with yours.

The disadvantages? You must pay both up-front fees and royalties for the rights. And you must give due billing credit to the author.

It is first crucial to ascertain the exact owner of the work. If the author is still alive, chances are he still owns the rights. However, the author may have transferred some or all of his rights—such as to a film studio or another playwright who has beaten you to the project.

Start by looking at the copyright page of a recent edition of the book or play you are considering. (If you are interested in adapting a movie, the film's producer ordinarily owns the copyright, but may/may not own the stage rights. I told you this wasn't going to be easy. For further information on film copyrights, see below.)

Call the publisher's business affairs or rights department. It can tell you who currently owns the rights to the material. The publisher itself may be authorized to negotiate with you. Or it will direct you to the author or his agent or attorney.

(In the case of a play, either the licensing agent or the Dramatists Guild can put you on the right track.)

If the author is deceased, you may have more difficult negotiations. His copyright will have passed by law or by testamentary instrument (such as a will or a trust) to his heirs. These may include his spouse, children, grandchildren, siblings, parents, close friends, or even a favorite charity. (Composer Frederick Lowe, a bachelor, left his interests in shows like *My Fair Lady*, *Camelot*, and *Brigadoon* to several charities.) There may be many persons and/or entities that share interests in the copyright. There may be executors or trustees who administer the estate on behalf of its beneficiaries. You will have to negotiate with all of them (and their attorneys). The parties may be scattered all over the globe and hard to find, let alone reach. Many of them may be unfamiliar with underlying rights negotiations and the theater, which will make your job even harder. Worse still, many of them will have spouses who will want to get their two cents into the matter.

True story #1: I once negotiated an underlying rights agreement with the three sons of a deceased author. The sons were in total agreement on terms. But then the wife of one of the sons—who had absolutely no knowledge or understanding of copyrights and who in fact admitted to me that she had never even seen a live stage show—insisted upon artistic approval of the adaptation. Her husband lived under her control and therefore refused to give his assent without this arrangement. My clients—the would-be book writer and composer/lyricist—who had previously written several successful, published musicals justifiably balked. Nevertheless, this point held up negotiations for months. I mention this, to prepare you for what you may encounter.

True story #2: On behalf of a playwright client, I worked with the agent of an award-winning children's book author to acquire rights so my client could develop the book into a stage musical. However, the rights were the subject of a probate court battle between the author's widow and his mistress—who lived in France! Both women claimed ownership of the rights. In addition, two of Hollywood's top film producers jointly owned the film rights to the book. It just goes to show you how complicated these matters can be.

Your work will be somewhat easier if the heirs have appointed an agent or attorney to represent the copyright. Actually, in the case of a deceased author, this can only help you. Agents carry on these negotiations every day. Although they still must obtain consent from the heirs, they can act as buffers for you.

In any event, be prepared for time-consuming negotiations.

If the author is still alive and mentally competent to handle his affairs, you will negotiate directly with him or his representative.

However, just because the author is still alive, you still do not have a guarantee of success. The author may already have given an option on the rights to another playwright. Or he may intend to adapt the material himself. He may be holding out for a better offer. Or he may simply not want to authorize an adaptation—period.

Once you have ascertained with whom to deal, prepare a short proposal, setting forth your interest in adapting the work; the kind of adaptation you intend (dramatic play or musical); the level of production you are aiming for; and a brief discussion of your artistic vision for the new piece. Attach a current resume, reviews of prior works, and letters of recommendation from artistic directors or literary managers. Do not discuss or offer financial terms in your initial proposal. All you want to do at this point is ascertain whether the copyright holder is interested.

Don't feel intimidated or automatically assume rejection simply because you are not Andrew Lloyd Webber, and can't offer an immediate Broadway production or gobs of money. In particular, if the work you have chosen is obscure or there is little interest being shown in it by anyone else, you may have a good chance.

Then be prepared to wait—possibly for a long time.

If the copyright holder is interested, he may request further details of your artistic intentions. He may even call you personally. At some point, the discussions will turn from art to business.

And that's when the fun begins.

THE OPTION

Obtaining the underlying rights to a work requires two separate agreements: the initial option and a subsequent production agreement. Although these can be combined into a single agreement, I recommend keeping them separate. There are sound reasons for different agreements.

The purpose of the option is to give the adaptor a limited time period in which to write at least one draft of the adaptation and arrange one staged reading. The purpose of the reading, of course, is to determine exactly what shape the project is in. After the reading, you (and the copyright holder) decide whether to go forward with revised drafts and eventually go to a staged production. Subsequently, you hope to interest producers or a theater company in actually presenting a fully realized show.

At the outset, when you obtain the option, there are so many variables to consider that preparing a full production agreement may only bog down negotiations. Until you know what you have (after the staged production), you can't really gauge the level of production that you can realistically hope to achieve—unless, of course, you are Andrew Lloyd Webber.

So stick with the basics first.

HOLLYWOOD

There is a trend right now of adapting Hollywood screenplays into live stage productions: *The Producers, Thoroughly Modern Millie, Hairspray,* etc. In the past, such films as *Meet Me in St. Louis* and *Singing In the Rain* have been transplanted to the stage.

Then there are projects that have a long history with both. *Auntie Mame* started life as a novel by Patrick Dennis. Next it became a stage play by Lawrence and Lee. Warner Brothers turned the stage play into a movie. Then Lawrence and Lee, with Jerry Herman, turned *Auntie Mame* into the musical *Mame*—which Warner Brothers again made into a movie, starring Lucille Ball. Now there is talk of a television adaptation of the musical.

Whew!

When a would-be adaptor seeks to turn a screenplay into a stage play, he must deal with Hollywood—land of palm trees, big bosomed starlets, agents, and bureaucratic film companies that own the copyrights on their screenplays.

The adaptor must ascertain the owner of the stage rights to the particular screenplay he wishes to option. Although the studios own the copyrights, in many cases the screenwriter owns the stage rights—especially on older material and in the rare case that the screenwriter actually had some clout (like Paddy Chayevsky). Thus, the adaptor may have to deal with both the studio and the screenwriter (or his estate).

Trust me. This is a jungle that would have even Tarzan reaching for the Maalox. You absolutely need the services of an entertainment attorney. It is so complex it deserves a book of its own, so this is all you're getting from me here. I mention it only for those of you who want to adapt a favorite movie, like *Psycho*, into a musical.

PRODUCERS AS UNDERLYING RIGHTS PURCHASERS

Thus far, I have discussed the playwright/adaptor as the purchaser of the underlying rights. Often, particularly on Broadway, the producer may acquire the underlying rights to a particular property. Then the producer engages a playwright to turn the project into a dramatic (or musical) adaptation.

A prime example was the late David Merrick, who acquired the underlying rights to *The Matchmaker* and engaged Herman and Stewart to turn it into a musical. Merrick did the same for many of his other shows.

In such a case, the playwright creates the adaptation and the producer then decides if and when it is ready for production. At that point, the producer assigns the underlying rights to the adaptor.

Form 15 and Form 16 provide alternate clauses for the case in which the producer is acquiring the underlying rights. Thus they work for either playwrights or producers, as the case may be.

UNDERLYING RIGHTS ESSENTIALS

1. *Exclusive rights.* The owner of the underlying rights should grant you the exclusive right to adapt her material into your proposed project. I rank exclusivity as the single most important point (yes, even above money) you want. Think about it: The owner grants you nonexclusive rights to the work. This means he in turn can also give dozens of other writers the same rights you have. There can be dozens of adaptations competing with yours. It's the public domain problem, except you are paying for it!

2. *Scope of rights.* Closely related to "exclusive rights" is the scope of the rights the owner is granting. These rights may be limited or very broad and anything in between. For instance, if the adaptor merely wants to do a one-shot piece for a specific theater company in a specific geographic area, she will be seeking a very limited grant of rights. Once her particular production has closed, her rights revert to the owner. She can no longer present her adaptation and cannot market it to anyone else. Few adaptors should think so narrowly. No one can predict the ultimate market for a work. I know of one team of authors who decided, as a lark, to create a musical based on a most absurd premise. They intended only to enter it in a fringe theater festival. The show became the hit of the festival, attracted commercial interest, and, as I write this, it is a sell-out hit on Broadway. Strange things can happen.

An adaptor should try to nail down rights for just such an eventuality. It's not likely to happen (unless he is Andrew Lloyd Webber), but if lightning does strike, he must be prepared to catch it. If his wildest dreams become reality and he has failed to obtain the appropriate rights, he could find the underlying rights holder has him over a barrel. Or, seeing the success of the piece, decides not to deal with him and gives the rights to someone else. Yes, that can happen too. The underlying rights owner may properly retain many rights for herself. In addition, there may be overlapping rights. For instance, a movie company may want to buy the rights to the original underlying work. Yet the adaptation may also attract Hollywood's interest. The parties must take all of these possible rights into account.

3. *Limited time.* The owner will ordinarily give you a limited window to write your script and arrange for a staged reading. You know how fast you write and whether you have other commitments—personal or professional—that may interfere. In addition, you must allow time to round up actors and directors for a staged reading. If you hope to facilitate the reading through a theater company, you must work around their schedule. In short, make sure you negotiate ample time for yourself. Keep in mind the owner will not want to take her work off the market too long, thereby possibly foregoing other opportunities. You must negotiate between yourselves the time period she will accept versus the time period you need.

4. *Manuscript pages.* It is a good idea in your contract to specify the minimum number of pages you must complete before going to the staged reading. If you are writing a musical, estimate the minimum number of songs you must complete. Of course, the length of your script and the number of songs you actually include in the show will change as the project evolves. However, specifying minimums gives both you and the copyright holder some fair measure of how to gauge progress during the option period.

5. *Billing.* The author of the original material is always entitled to billing wherever and whenever the name of the adaptor appears. The size of the type is negotiable and much depends upon her reputation. It should be a minimum of 50 percent of the size of the adaptor's name. If the stage rights are granted by a particular representative of the author, he may demand billing also. Thus:

"Based on the book *The Surprise Autopsy*
By Edgar Allan Poe, Jr.
By arrangement with EAP Enterprises."

The adaptor is responsible for securing the proper billing credit in all contracts for productions of the work.

6. *Right to collaborate.* Even though at the outset you may contemplate authoring the adaptation yourself, you should reserve the right to bring in collaborators if at a later time you choose to do so. This may be tricky. Ostensibly the owner has chosen you to adapt her work, since you have impressed her either with your approach, artistic vision, credentials, or something intangible, like chemistry. In any event, she has confidence in you. Now, if you want to bring in a collaborator, she may want to reserve the right to approve your new partner. Like artistic approvals, this is a difficult question. You may have to grant it.

7. *Right of reversion.* Reversion means to return or to go back. When all is said and done, at some point, your option may terminate. The owner's rights revert to her. Any of the following events may trigger reversion:

a. The required dates for a staged reading have come and gone without the reading occurring.

b. You have failed to perform your obligations under the contract—that is, most likely, you have failed to make the required option payments on time.

c. The required dates for obtaining a third party producer and/or director have come and gone without either occurring.

d. The owner does not approve of the final work.

In such event, there is little you can do, except to attempt to negotiate an extension with the owner. She does not have to give you what you want, however.

8. *Artistic approvals.* Trust me. The question of artistic approvals is the toughest issue you will negotiate— even more so than money. The owner of the underlying rights may demand artistic approvals, since she will want to protect her "baby." The degree of approval she may seek may range from reviewing your adaptation *before* she will even grant the option, to equal say in the standard playwright's approvals of director, cast, etc. Here's the difficulty: If the owner demands approval of your completed adaptation before she will even grant you an option, you risk investing all the time and talent it takes to write the piece with no assurance you will ever even get the rights. If, for whatever reason, the owner disapproves of your adaptation, all of your work has gone for naught. You can't even hope to ever get it produced.

Similarly, if the owner demands equal say in the normal playwright approvals, this may substantially hamper the production process and may discourage producers from taking on the show. This is because now both the owner and the playwright/adaptor have to jointly make decisions that are usually made by the playwright alone. While the playwright may be present during casting, rehearsals, etc., the owner may not make herself so readily or easily available. She may be separated geographically from the location of the production. Worst of all, she may disagree with the playwright on many issues, such as the casting of the lead role, for instance. If there is such disagreement and yet both parties have equal rights of approval, how are conflicts resolved? And can they be resolved so they do not bog down the production process?

And here's another problem: If the owner/author of the underlying rights is still alive, she may have a different vision of the adaptation than the playwright. For instance, in the case of a novel adapted to the stage, often characters and incidents must be compressed, altered, or even dropped, for dramatic and staging purposes. The owner may be possessive of the material. She may want every single scene, character, and incident depicted on the stage, which may make the play unwieldy.

But what if the author is deceased and many heirs now share the copyright? Getting artistic approval may open a hornet's nest of problems. It is difficult enough for two people to agree on any-thing. Can you imagine the problems if you have to get a dozen or more people to agree? What if they are scattered geographically? It could take weeks to obtain a simple decision. Chances are, they are not creative people. Or, worse, some may think they are creative people. And remember my own example of the daughter-in-law of the deceased author who wanted her own artistic approvals. I recommend breaking down artistic approvals into two distinct categories:

a. The first category consists of the author's right to approve the adaptation itself before the adaptor begins marketing the work to third par-ties. The adaptor and author consult during its creation up to and right after the staged reading. At that point, the work should be in enough shape that the underlying rights owner can then either give it her blessings, require additional changes, or simply disapprove entirely. Her approval rights stop at this point.

b. The second category concerns the work once it enters the marketplace. At this point, the work belongs to the adaptor. All artistic decisions belong to the adaptor, just as with an original play. The underlying rights owner does not share in these approvals. However, the owner may legitimately point out that, while she approved of the adaptation as it existed at this point, all works undergo revision—sometimes radically—during the production process. Therefore she should have the right to approve of the final script. But this brings the adaptor back to square one: that now the owner wants to share in the playwright's approval rights during the production process, which then becomes a producer's nightmare, which then—well, do you see what I mean?

Tough, isn't it? Whether you must grant addi-tional approvals depends upon the bargaining power of the parties, the desirability of the project, and the like.

9. *Option payments*. By granting an exclusive right to adapt her work, the owner is taking the material off the market for the term of the option. She will want money for granting this right. The amount of the option payment may range from a few hun-dred dollars into the thousands. Again, the figure depends upon—well, what do you think? The bar-gaining power of the parties, the demand for the underlying work, the length of the option period, the rights being granted, and the level of produc-tion contemplated. Remember also that option payments are nonrefundable. You are paying the underlying rights owner for taking the property off the market. Whether your adaptation goes on to worldwide fame and fortune, or dies at the first staged reading, the owner is entitled to keep the option money. That is a risk the adaptor takes.

Sometimes, an adaptor on a budget may nego-tiate an arrangement, whereby the owner will receive less up-front option money in exchange for a higher percentage of the ultimate royalties from the adaptation. Option payments are advances against subsequent royalties earned. Therefore, as royalties come in, they are recoupable. Option pay-ments usually occur in several stages:

a. A token payment initially when the parties sign the option agreement and the owner grants the license to the adaptor.

b. A more substantial payment, after the staged reading, when the adaptor seeks to extend the option period to allow him to obtain a staged production.

c. A second substantial payment, after the staged production, when the adaptor seeks to extend the option, because a producer, director, and/or a theater company has committed to a full pro-duction agreement for the show.

Structuring option payments to occur in this manner protects the adaptor. He does not have to lay out a substantial amount of money up-front. Instead, he pays money out only if and as the project progresses. If it fails to move past any par-ticular point, he does not have to spend any more money. The project dies at that point.

10. *Royalties*. Once the project begins to earn money for the adaptor, the underlying rights holder is entitled to share in the royalties. The manner in which the owner earns royalties depends on the level of production. For Broadway and off Broadway productions, commonly the owner of the underlying rights receives a small percentage of the gross weekly box office receipts—defined as all the moneys earned from ticket sales from all sources, less taxes and sales commissions. The standard industry range is as follows:

Pre-recoupment	¼ percent to 1 percent
Post-recoupment	¾ percent to 2 percent

These royalties are paid by the producer as part of the writer's share of the gross. Ordinarily, the total writer's share of a production is 5 percent. Some producers, however, in addition, will agree to pay the underlying rights owner's royalties. Therefore the adaptor keeps the entire 5 percent to himself. The total writer's share is 5 percent, plus the underlying rights owner's share. However, other producers insist the adaptor and the owner share the 5 percent, according to whatever arrangements they have made between them. In addition, the underlying rights owner receives a percentage of the adaptor's royalties from all sources such as stock and amateur licensing. These deals range from 5 percent to as much as 25 percent of the adaptor's net earnings. (*Net earnings* means the adaptor's income, after deduction of agent's commissions and the producer's share of the subsidiary rights.)

11. *Copyright.* The adaptation is a new work. Copyright should belong to the adaptor alone. However, be aware that the underlying rights owner may demand part of the copyright. Whether you must grant it again depends upon all of the factors we have previously discussed such as the desirability of the project, etc.

12. *Financial approvals.* This issue is as sensitive as artistic approvals. Although the owner of the underlying work is affected by any business arrangements the adaptor makes for the new work, the adaptor should not share approval over financial matters with her. Sharing financial approvals raises the same problems as sharing artistic approvals.

13. *Merger.* Merger, as an underlying rights matter, works much the same as merger in collaborations (as we have previously discussed). In the case of a work (play or musical) based on another property, it is the point at which the underlying elements become so intrinsically linked to the new piece that the underlying rights owner cannot remove her material. The adaptation now exists as a separate work.

Let's take *Hello, Dolly!* as an example. This Jerry Herman–Michael Stewart show was based on *The Matchmaker* by Thornton Wilder. (*The Matchmaker,* in turn, was based on an earlier Wilder play, which in turn was based on other material, but that is not germane to our discussion.) From *The Matchmaker,* Herman and Stewart took the basic story line, certain characters (like Dolly Levi and Horace Vandergelder) and incidents, and created

their musical. Once merger occurred, those elements from Wilder's play became so much a part of the show Wilder could not take them back without emasculating *Hello, Dolly!* (Imagine, for instance, if Wilder—and now his estate—could remove the Dolly character from the musical. It would become *Hello, Who?*) Merger assures those elements utilized out of the underlying work will remain with the show forever.

Keep in mind, however, that merger does not mean the original work ceases to exist. Far from it. Both shows continue to live independently. Both *The Matchmaker* and *Hello, Dolly!* still coexist very well together in the theater repertoire. So do all of the adaptations and underlying works I mentioned at the beginning of this chapter. And just as in the case of collaborations, merger occurs only when the parties decide that it does. It never occurs on its own. The parties must pick the date when merger will occur.

FORM 15 AND FORM 16

These forms represent mere options only. As I indicated earlier, it is ordinarily unwise to combine the option agreement with the production agreement at the outset.

Form 15 deals with underlying rights for a *dramatic* adaptation. (I define dramatic very broadly to include serious plays, comedies, farces, etc.—anything but a musical.) Form 16 deals with musical adaptations.

Musicals require special treatment because their songs can be performed outside of the show—recordings, cabarets, elevator muzak, etc. These are the small performance rights. Songs are also published separately from the book.

While the underlying rights owner participates in the grand rights—the rights to perform the entire show as a dramatic production—she does not receive any income from the small performing rights of the music and lyrics. These belong to the composer and lyricist.

For instance, suppose you acquire the underlying rights to Edgar Allan Poe Jr.'s, novel *I Was Food for the Maggots.* You turn it into the musical comedy, *The Singing Corpse.* Poe Jr. is entitled to share in the royalties from all productions of your show—that is, the grand rights. However, if Barbra Streisand records your big love ballad, "Bury Me Alive," Poe Jr. does not share in the royalties from the record sales. Those belong to your composer and lyricist (and their publisher).

Form 15 Option for Underlying Rights (Dramatic Play)

This Agreement entered into this _____ day of _____, 20____, by and between _____ [adaptor] [producer] and _____ (owner) for the adaptation of the owner's copyrighted _____ [Novel] [Play] [Screenplay] [Short story], entitled _____ ("Underlying Work") which the _____ [adaptor] [producer] intends to develop into a dramatic play ("Play") for the live stage.

For the mutual covenants and considerations contained herein, the parties agree as follows:

1. (A) The owner hereby grants to the [adaptor] [producer] the right to adapt the Underlying Work into the Play. This right is exclusive during the term of this agreement (and any production agreements resulting herefrom). The owner will not grant this right to any other persons or entities. All other rights not expressly granted herein are reserved by the owner.

   (B) The scope of rights the owner hereby grants will consist of _____ _____.

   (C) The materials contained in the Underlying Work will merge with the Play upon the happening of _____ and will thereafter remain with the Play forever. After merger occurs as aforesaid, the owner will not be entitled to remove any of the materials contained in the Underlying Work that merged with the Play. This in no way restricts the owner's right to exploit or otherwise use his Underlying Work in any way he sees fit, and same will continue to exist as a separate work.

2. [The adaptor may adapt the Underlying Work alone or may bring in other collaborators {without further approval by the owner} {subject to the approval of the owner, which approval will not be unreasonably withheld}.]

   [*Alternate*]

2. [The producer may engage one or more playwrights (adaptor) to adapt the Underlying Work into a script suitable for the live stage. {The choice of playwright will be in the producer's sole discretion.} {The choice of playwright will be subject to the approval of the owner, which approval will not be unreasonably withheld.}]

3. The adaptor will have until _____ to complete the Play, which will consist of a minimum of _____ manuscript pages. The adaptor [producer] will further have until _____ to arrange a staged reading of the Play. In consideration thereof, the adaptor [producer] will pay to the owner the sum of _____ dollars ($_____), due and payable at the time of the signing of this agreement. This sum will be nonrefundable. However, it will be recoupable against any royalties due to the owner (as described in paragraph 12 below).

4. The adaptor [producer] will notify the owner of the date, time, and place of the staged reading and will invite the owner thereto.

5. The owner will have _____ days after the staged reading to signify approval of the Play. If the owner fails to approve of the Play or to give timely notice of approval, all of the adaptor's [producer's] rights will terminate and revert back to the owner. The owner will then be free to negotiate with and grant the same or different rights to third parties without liability or payment to the adaptor [producer]. The adaptor [producer] will not use any material created from the Underlying Work in any other play, screenplay, novel, or other project whatsoever.

6. If the owner approves of the Play following the staged reading, as aforesaid, the adaptor will have the right (but not the obligation) to extend the option period until _____ months after the owner approves of the Play, for the purpose of presenting a staged production. In such event, the adaptor will pay to the owner the additional, nonrefundable sum of _____ dollars ($_____), which is recoupable from any royalties due the owner under paragraph 12 herein. This will be known as the Second Option Period.

7. The adaptor [producer] will have the right (but not the obligation) to further extend the term of this agreement for a Third Option Period, provided the following conditions are met prior to expiration of the Second Option Period:

   (A) The adaptor pays to the owner the nonrefundable sum of _____ dollars ($_____), which will be recoupable against royalties due the owner under paragraph 12; and at least ____ of the following conditions are met:

   (i) A director of stature agrees to direct the Play;

   (ii) A star of stature agrees to perform in the Play;

(iii) A theater company agrees in writing to present the Play;

(iv) [A financially responsible third party agrees in writing to produce the Play.]

[*Alternate*]

(iv) [The producer commits to produce the Play by entering into a production agreement with the owner.]

This Third Option Period shall commence immediately upon expiration of the Second Option Period and shall be for a period of _____ months.

8. The owner will not have the right to approve of the cast, director, designers, or any other personnel necessary to present a staged reading or full production of the Play. Said rights of approval will belong solely to the adaptor.

9. The owner represents and warrants that [he] [she] is the legal owner to the Work, has the full and complete power and authority to convey the rights herein granted; that [he] [she] has not hitherto conveyed, licensed, or otherwise transferred these rights to any other person or entity; that there are no claims or liens against the title to the Work that would interfere with, restrict, or otherwise limit the use and enjoyment of the [adaptor's] [producer's] rights hereto.

10. [In the event the adaptor fails to present a staged reading, or a staged production, within the respective time limits aforesaid, his rights hereunder will terminate, without notice, and revert to the owner.]

[*Alternative*]

10. [In the event the producer fails to present a staged reading or a staged production, or, fails to enter into a production agreement with the owner within the time aforesaid, his rights hereunder will terminate, without notice, and revert to the owner.]

11. The author of the Underlying Work will receive billing credit in all places and at all times in which the adaptor receives credit and will appear in substantially the following form:

"Based on _____ by _____"

Said billing will appear immediately following the name of the adaptor and will be in type size no less than _____% of the size of the adaptor's billing.

["And by arrangement with _____."]

12. The owner will receive a royalty in the amount of _____% of the gross weekly box office receipts. Gross weekly box office receipts will include ticket sales of all kinds and from all sources, less sales taxes and commissions. Said royalties may be calculated on the basis of a royalty pool. Royalties will be due and payable on the same day of the week as the royalties paid to the adaptor.

13. (A) The adaptor may, in his sole discretion, exploit all subsidiary rights in the Play upon such terms as he will deem appropriate without approval or agreement by the underlying rights owner. The underlying rights owner, however, will share in all moneys earned by the adaptor, as provided in paragraph 14 below.

(B) The adaptor will have the unequivocal right to make such arrangements with agents, producers, directors, stars, and other personnel, as the adaptor will deem necessary with respect to the exploitation of all subsidiary rights to the Play, including giving a share of same as appropriate or the payment of sales commissions. Said shares or sales commissions will in turn reduce the owner's earnings therefrom proportionately, as further described in paragraph 14 below.

14. In addition to the weekly royalties as aforesaid, the owner will be entitled to receive _____% of the adaptor's net earnings from the sale or other exploitation of all subsidiary rights. "Net earnings" will be the total adaptor's money remaining after deducting sales commissions, the producer's share, and any other shares the adaptor has granted to other personnel (as described paragraph 13 [B] above). All payments to the owner will be due and payable immediately upon the adaptor's receipt thereof and will be accompanied by a copy of all subsidiary rights statements of earnings.

15. The owner or his representative will have the unequivocal right, during reasonable business hours, to examine all books of the production and the adaptor's books, for the purpose of verifying that correct payments have been made in accordance with paragraphs 12 through 14 above.

16. Copyright to the Play will belong solely to the adaptor and will be taken out solely in his name.

17. The parties expressly deny and disavow any intention to form a partnership or joint venture, and this agreement will not be construed or interpreted to create same.

18. This Agreement is intended to create a mere option on the underlying rights to the work. At such time as the adaptor, in his sole discretion, chooses to commercially exploit the work (prior to the expiration dates set forth herein), the parties intend to negotiate, in good faith, a more formal agreement embodying all of the standard industry terms normally contained in a production agreement for underlying rights in a dramatic play. Until that time, this agreement will remain in effect and be binding on the parties thereto, their successors, heirs, administrators, and assigns.

19. [This agreement may not be assigned by any of the parties without the prior written consent of the other party.] [*Alternative*]

19. [This agreement is to be used if the purchaser of the option is a producer and not the adaptor himself. It is understood that, since the producer will not also be the adaptor, that, upon his acceptance of the Play for production, the producer will assign his rights hereunder to the adaptor, as his sole property, now and forever, and same will be bound hereto.]

20. All notices required hereunder will be in writing and will be directed to the parties at the addresses following their names. Notices will be sent by certified mail, return receipt requested, and will be effective upon mailing.

21. This agreement will be governed by the laws of the State of _____.

22. This is the entire agreement between the parties. No modification thereof will be effective unless entered into in writing and signed by the parties hereto.

23. In the event of a dispute over the terms of this agreement, the parties agree to submit same to a member of the American Association of Arbitrators. The Arbitrator shall require the losing party to pay the reasonable costs and attorney fees of the prevailing party. Any court of competent jurisdiction may enter judgment upon any award given thereby.

24. The parties represent and warrant to each other that they have full authority and power to enter into this agreement and will mutually hold each other harmless and indemnify each other for any judgments, costs, attorney fees, or other expenses incurred by any breach of the covenants hereunder. The owner represents and warrants that he has not previously granted the rights granted herein to any other party and that there are no liens or encumbrances upon said rights.

_____ [Adaptor] [Producer]

_____ Address

_____

_____ Owner

_____ Address

_____

Form 16 Option for Underlying Rights (Musical)

This Agreement entered into this _____ day of _____, 20___, by and between _____ [Adaptors] [Producer] and _____ (Owner) for the adaptation of the owner's copyrighted _____ [Novel] [Play] [Screenplay] [Short story], entitled _____ ("Underlying Work") which the [Adaptors] [Producer] intends to develop into a musical ("Musical") for the live stage.

For the mutual covenants and considerations contained herein, the parties agree as follows:

1. The Owner hereby grants to the _____ [Adaptors] [Producer] the right to adapt the Underlying Work into the Musical. This right is exclusive during the term of this agreement (and any production agreements resulting herefrom). The owner will not grant this right to any other persons or entities. All other rights not expressly granted herein are reserved by the owner.

   (A) The scope of rights the owner hereby grants will consist of _____ _____.

   (B) The materials contained in the Underlying Work will merge with the Musical upon the happening of _____ and will thereafter remain with the Musical forever. After merger occurs as aforesaid, the owner will not be entitled to remove any of the materials contained in the Underlying Work that merged with the Musical. This in no way restricts the owner's right to exploit or otherwise use his Underlying Work in any way he sees fit, and same will continue to exist as a separate work.

2. [The adaptors may adapt the Underlying Work alone or may bring in other collaborators {without further approval by the owner} {subject to the approval of the owner, which approval will not be unreasonably withheld}.] [*Alternate*]

2. [The producer may engage one or more playwrights (book writer), composers, and lyricists (collectively the "Adaptors") to adapt the Underlying Work into a script suitable for the live stage. {The choice of playwright, composer, and lyricist will be in the producer's sole discretion.} {The choice of playwright, composer, and lyricist will be subject to the approval of the owner, which approval will not be unreasonably withheld.}]

3. The adaptors will have until _____ to complete the Musical, which will consist of: a book containing a minimum of _____ manuscript pages and a music score consisting of the music and lyrics for at least _____ songs. The adaptors [producer] will further have until _____ to arrange a staged reading of the Musical. In consideration thereof, the adaptors [producer] will pay to the owner the sum of _____ dollars ($_____), due and payable at the time of the signing of this agreement. This sum will be nonrefundable. However, it will be recoupable against any royalties due to the owner (as described in paragraph 12 below).

4. The [adaptors] [producer] will notify the owner of the date, time, and place of the staged reading and will invite the owner thereto.

5. The owner will have _____ days after the staged reading to signify approval of the Musical. If the owner fails to approve of the Musical or to give timely notice of approval, all of the [adaptors'] [producer's] rights will terminate and revert back to the owner. The owner will then be free to negotiate with and grant the same or different rights to third parties without liability or payment to the [adaptors] [producer]. The [book writer] [producer] will not use any material created from the Underlying Work in any other play, musical, screenplay, novel, or other project whatsoever. Notwithstanding the foregoing, the composer and/or lyricist may use any music and/or lyrics created for the Musical in any other way they see fit, provided same do not specifically refer to or incorporate material contained in the Underlying Work.

6. If the owner approves of the Musical following the staged reading, as aforesaid, the [adaptors] [producer] will have the right (but not the obligation) to extend the option period until _____ months after the owner approves of the Musical, for the purpose of presenting a staged production. In such event, the [adaptors] [producer] will pay to the owner the additional, nonrefundable sum of _____ dollars ($_____), which is recoupable from any royalties due the owner under paragraph 12 herein. This will be known as the Second Option Period.

7. The [adaptors] [producer] will have the right (but not the obligation) to further extend the term of this agreement for a Third Option Period, provided the following conditions are met prior to expiration of the Second Option Period: (A) The [adaptors][producer] pay to the owner the nonrefundable sum of _____ dollars ($_____), which will be recoupable against royalties due the owner under paragraph 12; and at least ____ of the following conditions are met:

   (i) A director of stature agrees to direct the Musical;

   (ii) A star of stature agrees to perform in the Musical;

   (iii) A theater company agrees in writing to present the Musical;

   (iv) [A financially responsible third party agrees in writing to produce the Musical.]

   [*Alternate*]

   (iv) [The producer commits to produce the Musical by entering into a production agreement with the owner.]

   This Third Option Period will commence immediately upon expiration of the Second Option Period and will be for a period of _____ months.

8. The Owner will not have any rights of approval of the cast, director, choreographer, designers, or other personnel necessary to present any readings, and/or staged/full productions of the Musical. Said rights of approval will belong only to the book writer, composer, and lyricist.

9. The Owner represents and warrants that [he] [she] is the legal owner to the Work, and has the full and complete power and authority to convey the rights herein granted; that [he] [she] has not hitherto conveyed, licensed, or otherwise transferred these rights to any other person, or entity; that there are no claims or liens against the title to the Work that would interfere with, restrict, or otherwise limit the use, enjoyment, and commercial exploitation of the [adaptors'] [producer's] rights hereunder.

10. [In the event the adaptors fail to present a staged reading, or a staged production, within the respective time limits aforesaid, their rights hereunder will terminate, without notice, and revert to the owner.]

    [*Alternative*]

10. [In the event the producer fails to present a staged reading or a staged production, or, fails to enter into a production agreement with the owner within the time aforesaid, his rights hereunder will terminate, without notice, and revert to the owner.]

11. The author of the Underlying Work will receive billing credit in all places and at all times in which the adaptors receives credit and will appear in substantially the following form:

    "Based on _____ by _____"

    Said billing will appear immediately following the name of the adaptors and will be in type size no less than _____% of the size of the adaptors' billing.

    ["And by arrangement with _____."]

12. The owner will receive a royalty in the amount of _____% of the gross weekly box office receipts. Gross weekly box office receipts will include ticket sales of all kinds and from all sources, less sales taxes and commissions. Said royalties may be calculated on the basis of a royalty pool. Royalties will be due and payable on the same day of the week as the royalties paid to the adaptors.

13. (A) The adaptors may, in their sole discretion, exploit all subsidiary rights in the Musical upon such terms as they will deem appropriate without approval or agreement by the Underlying Rights owner. The underlying rights owner, however, will share in all money earned by the adaptors, as provided in paragraph 14 below.

    (B) The adaptors will have the unequivocal right to make such arrangements with agents, producers, directors, stars, and other personnel, as the adaptors will deem necessary with respect to the exploitation of all subsidiary rights to the Musical, including giving a share of same as appropriate or the payment of sales commissions. Said shares or sales commissions will in turn reduce the owner's earnings therefrom proportionately, as further described in paragraph 14 below.

14. (A) In addition to the weekly royalties as aforesaid, the owner will be entitled to receive _____% of the adaptors' net earnings from the sale or other exploitation of all subsidiary rights. Net earnings will be the total adaptors' money remaining after deducting sales commissions, the producer's share, and any other shares the adaptors have granted to other personnel (as described paragraph 13[B] above). All payments to the owner will be due and payable immediately upon the adaptors' receipt thereof.

(B) The owner's share of the subsidiary rights will be limited only to earnings from the grand rights to the work. The owner will not receive any earnings from the small performing right, publication, synchronization, mechanical reproduction, or any other rights to the music and lyrics contained within the show.

15. The owner or his representative will have the unequivocal right, during reasonable business hours, to examine all books of the production and the adaptors' books, for the purpose of verifying that correct payments have been made in accordance with paragraphs 12 through 14 above.

16. Copyright to the book of the Musical will belong solely to the book writer and taken out solely in his name. Copyright to any music and lyrics which become part of the Musical will belong, respectively, to the composer and lyricist, or their assignees.

17. The parties expressly deny and disavow any intention to form a partnership or joint venture, and this agreement will not be construed or interpreted to create same.

18. This Agreement is intended to create a mere option on the underlying rights to the work. At such time as the adaptors, in their sole discretion, choose to commercially exploit the Work (prior to the expiration dates set forth herein), the parties intend to negotiate, in good faith, a more formal agreement embodying all of the standard industry terms normally contained in a production agreement for underlying rights in a dramatic musical. Until that time, this agreement will remain in effect and be binding on the parties thereto, their successors, heirs, administrators, and assigns.

[Alternate 19 #1 is used if the playwright herself purchases the underlying rights.]

19. [This agreement may not be assigned by any of the parties without the prior written consent of the other party.]

[Alternative 19 #2 is used if the purchaser of the option is a producer and not the adaptor himself, in which case the producer ultimately assigns the underlying rights to the adaptor.]

19. [This agreement may not be assigned by any of the parties without the prior written consent of the other party, except, however, it is understood that, since the producer will not also be the adaptor, that, upon his acceptance of the Musical for production, the producer will assign his rights hereunder to the adaptors, as their sole property, now and forever, and same will be bound hereto.]

20. All notices required hereunder will be in writing and will be directed to the parties at the addresses following their names. Notices will be sent by certified mail, return receipt requested, and will be effective upon mailing.

21. This agreement will be governed by the laws of the State of _____.

22. This is the entire agreement between the parties. No modification thereof will be effective unless entered into a writing and signed by the parties hereto.

23. In the event of a dispute over the terms of this agreement, the parties agree to submit same to a member of the American Association of Arbitrators. The Arbitrator shall require the losing party to pay the reasonable costs and attorney fees of the prevailing party. Any court of competent jurisdiction may enter judgment upon any award given thereby.

24. The parties represent and warrant to each other that they have full authority and power to enter into this agreement and will mutually hold each other harmless and indemnify each other for any judgments, costs, attorney fees, or other expenses incurred by any breach of the covenants hereunder. The Owner hereby represents and warrants that he has the sole power and authority to grant the rights herein granted; that no one else has any right or interest therein; and that there are no liens or encumbrances upon the rights.

_____ [Adaptors]   _____ Owner
[Producer]

_____ Address   _____ Address

_____   _____

chapter 13 Real Person Release

Many plays, films, and television shows are based on real life incidents that happen to real people, such as court cases, crimes, and political or historical events. Or they purport to be biographies of famous people. Playwrights and producers choose these subjects because, often, the real life happenings are charged with the stuff of high drama, and so they make wonderful subjects for theater. Sometimes, playwrights write docudramas, which name names and are based almost entirely on facts. Or writers use the real life incidents as a basis for a fictitious script. In all such cases, both the playwright and her producer walk a fine line between their rights of freedom of speech and one sweet lawsuit.

Whenever an artist attempts to dramatize real life, she confronts three areas of the law. Any one of them—or all three—could apply to her script, and land her and her producer in court. These areas are:

1. Defamation
2. Right of Privacy
3. Right of Publicity

Defamation, the right of privacy, and the right of publicity are a part of "tort" law. (A tort is a private wrong against another person or entity.) Each of these torts is so complex it would require an entire book by itself. And indeed these subjects have been covered in dozens of books and articles, written by some of the finest legal minds of the twentieth century. These torts are constantly evolving, both through legislature-created law (statutes) and by decisions handed down by judges in the courtrooms (common law). In fact, lawyers and judges are constantly breaking new ground in each of these areas. And each state treats defamation, the right of publicity, and the right of privacy differently, so that it becomes difficult to give blanket guidance. Trust me. Even highly paid entertainment lawyers, employed by the Hollywood film companies, grapple with these issues every day.

So what can a poorly paid playwright and her overworked producer do when they want to present a work based on real life?

Well, in this chapter, I'm going to offer you a potential solution. It won't work in every case, for reasons I'll explain. But, in the instances when you can use it, it will greatly reduce your legal risks.

First, however, let's take a quick, only-scratching-the-surface look at each of these issues.

DEFAMATION

Defamation recognizes that one's reputation and standing in the community are very valuable rights that another may not lightly impugn. You can defame someone by making an oral statement (slander) or by putting it in writing (libel). You can defame a natural person or an entity, such as a multi-billion dollar international corporation. You can even defame a product, like Coca Cola, or a trademarked character, like Mickey Mouse or Barbie.

However, you cannot defame the dead. You can say anything you want about Abraham Lincoln or John Wayne or even your deceased Aunt Gertrude. That's how books get published that allege that Errol Flynn was a Nazi spy, Walt Disney was a puppet of the FBI, Joan Crawford was the Mother from Hell, and the like. Once the subject is dead, his right to uphold his reputation dies with him. (In Agatha Christie's story *Death on the Nile*, an important plot point is based on this very concept.) Even his heirs can't sue you.

The naughty statement must be false. It must hold an identifiable person or entity up to hatred, contempt, or ridicule. Or it injures him in his job, occupation, or business relations. Or the falsehood causes the community to avoid or shun the person or entity.

You have to *publish* the statement. Now, in defamation, publish has a broader meaning than our every day view that publish means to write something in a magazine or book and then distribute it. In defamation, publish simply means you must disseminate the statement, orally or in writing, to a third person. And you only need to communicate to a single third person to publish the statement. If I falsely say, "John, you are a thief," to John's face and no one else hears me, John may take a punch at me, but he can't sue. I have not published my words. But, if I say, "John, you are a thief," and Sue hears me, then I have published—that is, communicated—the falsity to a third person, Sue. Obviously, a theatrical performance constitutes publication, since any statements made within are communicated to the audience. (If I accuse John of theft in a letter to my sister Sue, I've published my words.)

The law has carved out certain defenses in defamation cases. The absolute best defense is the truth. If John really did steal one hundred bucks from me, that's my defense. If I'm just expressing my opinion, well, that's also a defense. (A review is just a statement of the author's opinion; that's one reason it's so tough to sue the critics, though I know more than a few artists and producers, myself included, who wish the law were otherwise.) Sometimes, journalists attempt to couch unverifiable charges against subjects by preceding the accusation with a form of the word "alleged." For instance, "John allegedly stole one hundred dollars from Grippo." In print, this kind of fudging works. But a playwright cannot write a play in which she must precede each accusation against a real life person with the word "alleged." Her dialogue would be unwieldy and even laughable.

GRIPPO: John allegedly stole one hundred dollars from me.

SUE: John allegedly stole one hundred dollars from Paul, too.

MAX: John is allegedly a thief.

If, in fact, the statement does not harm the person's reputation, the speaker or writer is safe. If I tell Sue, "John beats his wife," and the statement is false, I'm in trouble. But if I say, "John took his wife to Hawaii," I'm in the clear, even if the cheapskate only took her to Peoria, Illinois.

Public figures have a tough time suing for defamation. They have to prove the author of the offending communication either knew the statement was false or recklessly disregarded the truth. This is a very high standard to prove. That's why celebrities who sue the tabloids often have a difficult case.

On the other hand, private citizens have a much easier chance of winning when they pursue a claim for defamation. They only have to prove that the playwright acted negligently in publishing the falsity.

However, as with almost everything in the law, the matter is not always quite that black and white. Sometimes private citizens become public figures because they are involved in an incident or a situation that suddenly thrusts them into the limelight. A good example occurs when a hitherto private citizen finds himself in the middle of a newsworthy event. For example, the movie *Dog Day Afternoon* was based on a real life situation in which the customers in a bank were held hostage when a robbery went sour. Another example is the play and the various movie versions of *The Desperate Hours* that were based on the real life case in which criminals held an ordinary family hostage in their home. The event converts a hitherto private individual into a public figure, perhaps even a national celebrity, at least for the moment.

But the playwright attempting to turn one of these events into a theater piece faces a substantial problem: each person involved in the real life incident, in effect, becomes two people. Within the context of the event, John Q. Hostage has admittedly become a public figure. But John Q. still has a private life, within the context of which he remains a private individual. And, at some point, the newsworthiness of the event will die down, and John Q.'s celebrity will diminish. All of this means that John Q. may/may not have a difficult time winning a defamation suit. It means the playwright and her producer may/may not have a good chance of prevailing in John Q.'s lawsuit.

Confusing, isn't it?

Now do you understand the difficulties legal scholars, judges, and entertainment lawyers face when confronted with scripts of this nature?

PRIVACY

Many states recognize that each of us has certain rights of privacy. Each of us has the right:

1. To be free from intrusions into our private lives. (Tell that to the telemarketer who calls you during dinner tonight.)
2. To keep embarrassing facts about ourselves private and not publicly disclosed.
3. Not to be put into a false light.

4. Against having our identities appropriated by third parties, especially for commercial uses. A classic example of the right to privacy occurs when a tabloid publishes photographs secretly taken of a celebrity sunbathing in the nude—Princess Diana's topless photos, Jacqueline Onassis on what she thought was a private beach, or the vindictive ex-boyfriend who posts embarrassing pictures of his former girlfriend on the Web. Like defamation, though, the right of privacy dies with the person.

PUBLICITY

Each person has the right to exploit his own life and image for commercial purposes. Of course, that's what celebrities do all the time.

The right of publicity does not terminate when the person terminates. Thus, the heirs of a deceased celebrity may continue to exploit his identity for up to one hundred years (depending on state law) after his death. That's why the estates of Elvis, Marilyn Monroe, John Wayne, and Bela Lugosi make a lot of money each year licensing their images for product endorsements. Thus, you cannot produce a play depicting the Three Stooges without obtaining the permission of Comedy III Productions, which owns the rights to their personas.

WHO WILL WE SUE?

Who will the owners of all of the above rights sue?

The playwright, her publisher, her producer, and the production company which presents the play, the movie company which adapts the play into a film, the companies which sell and distribute the videocassettes and DVDs of the movie version of the play, the broadcaster who presents a taped, filmed, or audio version of the play, the . . . . Do you get the idea?

And remember also that Mr. Hold Harmless and Ms. Indemnity are lurking about. The playwright represents and warrants in all of her contracts that nothing contained in her play defames any person or entity, or violates any rights or privacy or publicity. Under this legal boilerplate, she could be held responsible for a lot of damages to a lot of people and corporations.

PROTECTING YOURSELF

Here is some general advice that will help protect you:

1. Stick to the facts.
2. Pick public events in the lives of public persons.
3. Disclaim, disclaim, disclaim in all programs, advertising, and press releases. And, when you get through, disclaim some more.
4. Research, research, research until you can verify everything in your script.
5. Retain a specialist in personal rights law to review your script.

Now here comes the almost perfect solution I promised you at the beginning of this chapter: Whenever possible, obtain a legal release from each person named or depicted in your script.

REAL PERSON RELEASE

In Hollywood, it is a matter of routine to seek a release from any real life person named in the script—even if the reference is only in passing. I have personally seen releases signed by the likes of Clark Gable, Joan Crawford, and John Wayne, merely for mentioning their names in certain motion pictures or television shows.

Such a release constitutes the best defense against claims you infringed on the publicity or privacy rights of your real life subject. But the release does have its limitations. Who in his right mind would give you permission to hold him up to ridicule and hatred? So, you won't get a free pass to defame anyone.

For that, you have to wait until your subject bites the dust.

Also many people will not even consider giving you a release unless you provide them with a detailed written description of how you intend to use their name, likeness, etc. Many will insist upon seeing a completed manuscript first. This, then, becomes a tricky proposition, because, it is likely all you can do is provide the subject with a first or second draft. Plays (as well as screenplays) are rewritten and evolve during the production process.

But this in itself creates a problem. By giving the subject your first draft, you are representing that this is how he will be portrayed in your play. And he is giving you his release based on that representation and portrayal. Yet, after the rewrites, your depiction of him may become something else entirely. The subject could argue that you misrepresented your proposed portrayal of him, and therefore his release was obtained under false pretenses. Therefore his release is not binding. He never consented to the new portrayal.

For that reason, it is wise to make clear in all your preliminary conversations and correspondence with the subject the possibility the portrayal may change. If possible, try to avoid making too many changes to his portrayal as the play progresses. Finally, make the release broad enough to cover these possibilities.

I said the idea wasn't perfect. It's just the closest you can get under current law.

Form 17, which follows, takes these factors into account.

NEGOTIATION ESSENTIALS

1. *Title.* Include the title of the piece, even if it is only a working title.
2. *Playwright.* Fill in the Playwright's name.
3. *Producer identification.* If the play is already committed to a production, the name and address of the producer and theater company should be added. In this way, you can have the subject specifically release both you and your producer from any liability, thus making the producer's lawyer extremely happy.
4. *Subject.* Identify the subject by name and address, including any professional names.
5. *Grant of rights.* Try to get the subject to give you the broadest possible grant of rights. It should include his name, even if you intend to depict him under a fictitious name, as well as his personal characteristics, the events in which he was involved which form the basis of your play, biographical information, his likeness, and his voice.
6. *In perpetuity.* The grant must be perpetual. If he puts a limit on the amount of time you can depict him, then the life of your play ceases when the time limit expires.
7. *Irrevocable.* The grant should be irrevocable. You do not want him to revoke his permission; otherwise, again, the life of your play terminates when he revokes his release.
8. *Change rights.* You want the right to change his portrayal in any way you see fit, without first having to go to him for additional permissions. This, together with the following paragraph, covers you during the rewrite process.
9. *Consent to rewrites.* The subject acknowledges that your play is a work in progress and that it may undergo many rewrites, which may change the way

he is depicted in the script. The subject automatically consents to such changes, although unknown at the time of the grant of release.

10. *Sequels, etc.* In your sole discretion as author, you may choose to create (or authorize others to create) motion pictures, television broadcasts and/or series, prequels or sequels, or spinoffs based on or arising out of the present work, any or all of which may continue to depict the subject. You want to do so automatically. You do not have to seek and obtain his subsequent release. Similarly, you do not have to give him additional consideration—that is, money—for any such works.
11. *Publicity and advertising.* You may use his name and likeness in advertising and publicizing the work.
12. *Release of claims.* Most importantly, the subject releases you (the author) and your producer from any claims he may have arising out of the script or the production.
13. *Refrain from suit.* The subject promises he will not sue or file any claims against you or your producers, based on your depiction of him. He also will not allow or authorize others to sue either.
14. *Limited to subject only.* Keep in mind that paragraph 13 applies only to the subject and your depiction of him. If he has a wife, for instance, or children, and you wish to portray them in your project, you must obtain separate releases from each of them. (As related to minor children, refer to "General Contract Preparation Advice" at the beginning of this book.)
15. *Retained rights.* The subject may want to retain the right to exploit his persona in other works—that is, he may not be willing to grant exclusive rights to you, to his story. Or, if he has led a particularly interesting and varied life, he may only be willing to grant you exclusive rights to certain aspects of it. Accordingly, paragraph 4 of the Form Release provides two alternatives, depending upon the arrangement you negotiate.

Form 17 Real Person Release

THIS AGREEMENT entered into this _____ day of 20_____, in the year _____, by and between _____ (the "Playwright") and _____ (the "Undersigned Subject"), both of whom are of legal age and competent mental capacity, for the creation, production, and exploitation of the work presently titled _____ (the "Work").

WHEREAS the Playwright intends to base incidents, characters, and dialogue upon certain events occurring to or involving the Undersigned; to utilize certain of [his] [her] biographical information; and to depict the Undersigned under [his] [her] actual name or personal characteristics, whereby reasonable persons could infer the identification of the Undersigned:

Now, therefore, in consideration of the mutual covenants and agreements made herein, the parties hereby agree as follows:

1. The Undersigned hereby irrevocably and in perpetuity grants to the Playwright, [his] [her] heirs, successors, licensees, and assigns, the absolute right to use [his] [her] name, likeness, biographical data, personal characteristics, and the events occurring to [him] [her], in connection with the Work and exploitation thereof, and to depict [him] [her] therein in any way the Playwright, in [his] [her] sole discretion and artistic judgment will see fit. This will include altering, changing, adding, deleting, fictionalizing and otherwise depicting the Undersigned and said events, as well as depicting the Undersigned by a fictitious name.
2. The Undersigned hereby grants all of the aforesaid rights to the Playwright for use in the Work (including prequels, sequels, and any other subsequent works derived therefrom) including (but not limited to) live theatrical performance, publication, motion pictures, television, radio broadcasts, audio, videotape, or disk recording, Internet, and in all other medium, whether now existing or hereafter devised.
3. This grant of rights shall be effective throughout the world.
4. [This grant of rights is nonexclusive and shall not prevent the Undersigned from otherwise granting or exploiting the rights to {his} {her} persona, on {his} {her} own, or under license to other persons, or entities, including even in competing works.]
   [*Alternative*]
4. [This grant of rights is exclusive. The Undersigned will not otherwise grant, license, or transfer any of the rights enumerated in paragraph 1 to any other person or entity for use in a competing work. A competing work is defined as a work in any media which _____.
   Notwithstanding the foregoing, nothing herein will prevent the Undersigned from otherwise exploiting or licensing _____ {his} {her} persona in a noncompeting work.]
5. The parties understand that this Agreement is only for the rights to depict the Undersigned in the Work. The parties understand and agree that the Undersigned does not have the authority or the power to grant rights to the Playwright to depict any other real life persons or entities who may have been associated with or involved in the events which the Playwright desires to depict in the Work. It shall be the responsibility of the Playwright to obtain any releases, consents, or licenses required from such other persons or entities. The Playwright assumes the full risk, if [he] [she] fails to do so. The Undersigned makes no representations, warranties, or guarantees that such other persons or entities will execute said releases and/or the terms thereof. The Playwright will hold the Undersigned harmless and indemnify him for any claims, actions, costs, attorney fees, judgments, or settlements to or by third parties whom the Playwright depicts in the Work.
6. The Undersigned will not claim or bring suit against the Playwright based on the Work (or any other work derived therefrom) or the depiction of the Undersigned therein, and will not cause or allow others to claim or bring suit on [his] [her] behalf. [He] [She] hereby now and forever releases the Playwright, [his] [her] successors, licensees, or assigns from any and all such claims or actions, now or arising in the future.

7. The Playwright has made no representations, warranties, or guarantees, whether oral or written, as to the manner in which the Undersigned will be portrayed or depicted.

8. The Undersigned understands and agrees that the Playwright is relying upon the covenants, representations, and warranties made herein. [He] [She] further represents, warrants, and agrees that the rights granted herein do not infringe upon the rights of any other persons or entities not a party to this agreement and shall hold the Playwright harmless and indemnify [him] [her] from all claims, judgments, settlements, actions, causes of action, attorney fees, and costs which the Playwright may incur as a result of the breach hereof.

9. The Undersigned hereby enters into these covenants and agreements on behalf of [himself] [herself], [his] [her] heirs, successors, and assigns. All covenants, rights, and agreements hereunder shall inure to the Playwright, [his] [her] successors, licensees, heirs, and assigns.

10. The law of the State of _____ shall govern this Agreement.

11. This constitutes the entire Agreement between the parties. It may not be modified except by a written instrument signed by both parties.

12. Notices required hereunder will be served to the parties at the addresses following their signatures below. Notice will be by certified mail, return receipt requested, and will be effective on the date of the mailing thereof.

13. This Agreement will not be construed as creating a joint venture and/or partnership between the parties.

In Witness Whereof, the parties have hereunto set their hands and seals on the day and date above written.

_____ (Playwright)

_____ (Address)

_____

_____ (Subject)

_____ (Address)

_____

chapter 14 Song Licensing

It is not uncommon for a playwright to require the playing of a popular song inside her play, even if the show is not a musical. A character may put on a CD or turn on a television or radio, and snatches of a song will play. Or a character suddenly sings a tune the audience instantly recognizes. In the Neil Simon play, *Last of the Red Hot Lovers*, the character of Bobbi sings two lines of the Bacharach/David song, "What the World Needs Now Is Love." Regardless of the context, or the playwright's purpose in using a pre-existing composition (rather than having a new song written especially for the show), both the playwright and the theater are interpolating—that is, using—someone else's material in their production.

If the musical composition is in the public domain (such as Beethoven's Sixth Symphony), neither the playwright nor the producer has any problem. The music is there for the using, and Beethoven's estate cannot refuse its use or claim royalties.

However, when the musical materials are still under copyright, then the composer and lyricist enjoy the same protections as the authors of any other copyrighted works (like the playwright herself). The composer and lyricist (as well as the publisher) are entitled to payment of a royalty each time it is performed. They may also grant or refuse the playwright and her producer a license to perform it.

Even in the case of public domain material, such as Beethoven's Sixth, the creator of a particular arrangement of it may also be entitled to a royalty, as well as the right to choose how and when it may be performed. In other words, Beethoven's Sixth, in its original form (as Beethoven himself composed it), is fair game for royalty-free performance. However, if someone creates a new arrangement of it, his work has most likely been copyrighted, and he will enjoy all the rights *to his arrangement* (not Beethoven's Sixth itself), as any other copyright holder.

Many playwrights and producers, especially in the nonprofessional and small theater sector, frequently overlook the legal complications of using other people's material in their productions. Small theaters, in particular, often use curtain-raising music, playing orchestral recordings of copyrighted songs. This music is utilized as the lights go down and just before the curtain rises and the play begins. The music is used to create an atmosphere or set the scene. In other cases, the playwrights simply require their characters to burst into popular song. Permissions are rarely sought. Royalties are almost never paid. Both the playwright and the producer, however, are leaving themselves open to claims of copyright violations, with its attendant legal costs and substantial financial judgments.

On an ethical basis, playwrights should view themselves as comrades with their songwriter colleagues. Both are creating works of art through their talents, sweat, and blood. Both have spent years paying their dues, struggling for recognition, publication, performance, and production. Both hope to earn, at a minimum, a reasonable living out of their material. The playwright should, therefore, sympathize with and support her songwriter brethren, just as she would expect them to do for her.

That being the case, how does one obtain the rights to perform a pre-existing musical composition—we'll call it a "song"—copyrighted by others, in one's play?

THRESHOLD QUESTION

The threshold question is whether the song in question is in the public domain or protected by copyright. The place to start is with the U.S. Copyright Office. For a small fee, the Copyright Office will tell you if the work has been registered for protection in the United States. A private copyright search service will do the same for you. Their fee will be higher, but they will provide you with more extensive information.

Even if a song has been registered for copyright, this does not mean it is still under copyright. Copyright exists for a limited time. When that time expires, the work falls into the public domain. An attorney versed in copyright matters can examine the copyright search and give you an opinion.

For our purposes, however, we need concern ourselves only with material that is still under copyright.

DRAMATIC PERFORMANCES

It is essential to determine whether the contemplated use constitutes a dramatic performance—in which case you are negotiating for what is called the *grand rights*—or a nondramatic performance, in which case you are seeking the *small rights*.

It is often difficult to distinguish between grand and small rights. Indeed, even entertainment attorneys can disagree about a particular use. Sometimes, it is necessary to review each use on a case-by-case basis, carefully considering all of the facts and the context in which the material is to be used.

In general, however, a dramatic performance requires a plot depicted by action and characters. The song must be integral to the telling of a story. As a rule of thumb, any time you use a musical composition as part of a play, you are using it in a dramatic, as opposed to a nondramatic way. Therefore, you are seeking the grand rights. This is true, whether as in the *Last of the Red Hot Lovers* example, a character sings or otherwise performs the song, or whether it is played (as part of the context of the play) on a CD player. Often these are judgment calls. You are usually safest treating the matter as the grand rights.

The difference between grand and small rights is not academic. For the playwright and producer, the difference determines to whom they must look for the licensing rights. It may also affect the fees paid and the scope of license required.

In general, the small rights consist of the rights to perform the song in television or radio broadcasts— for example, Bette Midler sings your song on David Letterman's show. It also includes recordings of the songs outside the show—for instance, Barbra Streisand's recording of "Memory" from *Cats*.

FROM WHOM DO WE LICENSE RIGHTS?

In the case of most popular songs, the music publisher, as part of his contract with the composer and lyricist, obtains the copyright. The publisher, in turn, negoti-ates and licenses the rights to use the song. The publisher typically controls the grand rights. Thus, it is the publisher with whom you must deal if you wish to use the song in your production.

The small performing rights are administered by one of the performing rights societies, such as ASCAP or BMI. Remember that these are the nondramatic rights; it's a license to perform the song on a recording or on the radio in a nondramatic way. Performing a song in a cabaret act may or may not be dramatic and may or may not be small performing rights; each case must be examined individually.

If the publisher and the authors have signed the standard Songwriters Guild contract, the writers must be consulted whenever anyone desires to license the grand rights to the song.

Incidentally, if you license a revue of material by a particular composer—such as Frank Loesser's *Perfectly Frank* or Rodgers and Hammerstein's *It's A Grand Night for Singing*—from their respective licensing agents, your work has already been done for you. The licensing company has already obtained permission from the copyright holders to allow you to perform the revue with your own cast. Your licensing fee to the agents covers the licensing fee to the copyright holders.

On the other hand, if you attempt to put together your own revue of a favorite composer's copyrighted songs, you are now creating your own show, and you damned well better get permission of the copyright holder.

RECORDED MUSIC

There is an added twist if you desire to use a particular recording of a popular song, such as Frank Sinatra's version of "New York, New York." In that case, you must obtain two separate licenses from two different copyright owners:

1. The copyright holder of the musical composition itself.
2. The owner of the sound recording—ordinarily, the record company. However, some major recording artists own the copyrights on their recordings themselves.

To complicate matters further, the copyright holder of the musical composition may be willing to grant you the rights, but the owner of the sound recording may not—or vice versa. In such a case, you either use a different recording, or pick a different song.

In other words, using a copyrighted musical com-position (and a recording thereof) is not as simple as the author typing in the stage direction: "Amy plays Frank Sinatra's recording of 'New York, New York' while packing her luggage."

Are you ready now for another twist?

Even if the musical composition itself is in the public domain (such as Beethoven's Sixth in its original form), the particular recording you want to use may be protected by copyright—such as Leonard Bernstein's recording of Beethoven's Sixth. Thus, even though you may freely use the Beethoven composition, you must, nevertheless, license use of the Bernstein recording from its copyright owner.

Whew!

MUSIC SYNCHRONIZATION

Movie producers frequently use well known recordings of popular songs in the soundtracks of their films—for example: *American Graffiti, National Lampoon's Animal House, Not Another Teen Movie.* The producers have to obtain what are called *music synchronization* licenses from the copyright owners of both the composition itself and the particular recording. Then the producers, through the recording company which issued the recording, must also pay *reuse* fees to the American Federation of Musicians, whose members provided the vocals, instrumentation, arranging, and copying services for the recording. Additional licenses and fees must be paid if the producer of the film wishes to use the recording on a soundtrack album from the film itself. All of these fees can add up to substantial dollars and may require considerable negotiating time by the lawyers for the studios. Incidentally, all of this applies equally to the use of recordings in commercials and television programs.

WHOSE JOB IS IT TO GET RIGHTS?

There are two different schools of thought regarding whether the playwright or the producer should obtain the rights. It may be argued that the playwright should obtain a blanket license for use of the composition inside her script, to cover all productions everywhere. The playwright then charges the producer the licensing fee for the song (in addition to her own royalties), which she forwards to the copyright owner/licensor.

As an attorney, playwright, and producer, I prefer to use a different approach. The producer licenses the composition for his particular production. A blanket license is difficult to administer and can be unfair. As we will see in the next section, music publishers charge different fees depending on the level of production

(among other factors). A successful play will be performed at many different levels of production—from Broadway down to non-Equity professional to community theater to the local high school. The size of the venue in which the play is performed will also vary wildly. How can you create and administer a one size fits all blanket license?

In addition, a particular producer may have a special relationship with the publisher or copyright holder, which might get him some kind of a break on the fee. Or the producer may have a unique situation that might also work to lower (or raise) the fee.

And, finally, the producer must be certain the fee actually reaches the licensor. This is not to imply dishonesty by the playwright. But the only way the producer has of ensuring the fee is properly paid—and he and his production are protected from copyright infringement claims—is to negotiate the license and pay the fee himself. In such a case, the playwright, in turn, should require, as part of her production contract, that the producer hold her harmless for any damages she might suffer if the producer uses the song without first obtaining the appropriate license and paying the fee—that is, against claims of copyright infringement by the owner of the song.

Regardless of which party negotiates the license, the playwright nevertheless should inquire whether the grand rights are even available, before she calls for the use of the song in her script. There may be any number of reasons the rights are not available to her. For instance, they may be under exclusive license to a Broadway show. Or the copyright holder may simply be unwilling to allow the intended use of the song. Perhaps he believes it is not an appropriate context in which he wants his material to be performed. He may not want to license the song at this particular time. (Irving Berlin owned most of his copyrights. Near the end of his life, he even turned down Steven Spielberg, who wanted to use "Always" in a film.) This is the copyright owner's prerogative. You cannot force him to let you use his song.

However, it is both embarrassing and unprofessional for an author to specify use of a particular song, without first knowing that the rights are available. Producers don't want to waste time making inquiries the author could—and should—do.

APPROACH THE PUBLISHER

Usually, in one or two calls to the publisher, you can ascertain whether the dramatic performance rights are available to you for the song you want to use. The publisher will ask you detailed questions about your intended use. Be prepared to provide the following information:

- The level of your intended production—Broadway, off Broadway, stock, community, school, etc.
- The number of performances.
- Contemplated ticket pricing.
- Size of your venue.
- The amount and use of the song.

This last item requires special mention. The amount of the song refers to how much of the song you intend to use. This may be measured in bars or stanzas. Sometimes, it is measured in minutes—the amount of time the song will take to be performed versus the length of your performance. For instance, you may be planning to build an entire dance number around the song, which may run six minutes or more in your two hours performance time. The publisher will consider that factor.

Your use of the song is equally important. Background or incidental music is one thing. But if the song becomes essential to your plot or depiction of a character, the publisher needs to know. The publisher will also ask the context of the show in which you are proposing to use the song.

Be aware also that the popularity of the song will weigh heavily in your negotiations. An obscure, decades old song that incurs hardly any interest is likely to come at a smaller licensing fee than a fairly recent hit. The songwriter's fame and reputation may also play a factor: Even a lesser known Billy Joel song may command a higher fee than one written by Scuttle and Harris, two songwriters whose names are known only to their mothers.

WE CAN'T AFFORD THE SONG

Playwrights owe it to their producers to be flexible when interpolating other people's copyrighted songs into their scripts. Not all songs are available to all producers at all times. Worst of all, not all producers can afford to license songs.

If the producer cannot bear the cost of licensing a particular song for his production, the playwright should offer a fall back, including a public domain composition. In this regard, playwrights and producers should cooperate to meld artistic vision with

budgetary considerations. If a public domain composition simply won't do, then the playwright has two other choices:

1. Either compose an appropriate song herself, if she can, or commission a songwriter to write one.
2. Use her creativity to figure a different way to make her artistic point without using anyone's song.

Of course, if the playwright is unwilling to cooperate and the producer's hands are tied, perhaps the producer should politely return the script with a "Thanks, but no thanks."

ACKNOWLEDGMENTS

Virtually all licensing agreements for interpolated songs require program acknowledgment for the copyright holder and the songwriters. As part of her production agreement with the producer, the playwright should also insist that the producer duly acknowledge any licenses or permissions for use of the copyrighted material of others. This acknowledgment is usually as simple as the following: "The song 'Blubber Belly' by Scuttle and Harris, is used by permission [or under license from] the copyright holder Tummy Tuck Publishers, Inc.," followed by the publisher's address.

SONG LICENSING ESSENTIALS

1. *Use of form 18.* A producer or playwright who wishes to use a musical composition in a single production of a particular play utilizes Form 18.
2. *Royalty alternatives.* Take particular note of the three alternatives to paragraph 3, calling for payment of the royalties. Strike those alternatives that do not apply to your particular situation.
3. *Manner of use.* One must specify exactly the manner in which the song will be used. For instance, you would state: "In Act Two, Scene 3, the character of Carol sings 'Daniel the Cocker Spaniel' to her boyfriend, Phil." The amount of the song to be licensed is strictly limited and must also be particularized: "Carol sings the first stanza." To avoid misunderstandings, I recommend attaching a lead sheet to the agreement, containing the exact music and lyrics to be licensed. Then, in describing the amount of the composition the licensee intends to use, write in "See Lead Sheet attached to and made part of this agreement."

Form 18   Musical Composition License

This Agreement is entered into this _____ day of _____, in the year 20_____, by and between _____ ("Owner") and _____ ("Licensee"), for the musical composition entitled _____ ("Composition") written by _____; and registered in the United States Copyright Office on _____ by the owner.

Whereas, the Licensee desires to use the Composition in a certain live theatrical event entitled _____ (the "Play"), written by _____, in the following manner _____. The amount of the Composition the Licensee intends to use will be limited to _____ _____.

Therefore, in consideration of the mutual covenants and considerations given herein, the parties agree as follows:

1. The Owner hereby grants to Licensee a nonexclusive license to use the Composition in the manner and amount described herein above at the Licensee's primary facility located on or at _____ _____, (the "Facility") beginning on _____ and terminating _____, for _____ performances (including previews and free performances.) In the event the Licensee desires to extend the number of performances, he will promptly notify the Owner and additional fees will be paid on the same terms as hereinafter required. The Licensee represents and warrants that:

   (A) At full capacity, the Facility seats _____ persons.

   (B) Ticket prices for the performances will be not less than _____ dollars ($_____) and not more than _____ dollars ($_____).

   (C) The level of production will be _____.

2. The Owner hereby grants a license for the use of the Composition as herein described solely in the said Play and solely for the Licensee's production as described in paragraph 1 above.

3. The Licensee will pay to the Owner royalties in the following amounts and manner:

   [A flat fee in the amount of _____ dollars ($_____), which will cover all performances of the play as contemplated in paragraph 1 above. Said fee shall be due and payable _____ days prior to the first performance before an audience, whether paid, free, or preview.]

   [*Alternative*]

   [A royalty per performance in the amount of _____ dollars ($_____), based on the ticket prices described in paragraph 1(B) above and the number of performances as described in paragraph 1 above, for a total fee of _____. Said fee will be due and payable _____ days prior to the first performance before an audience, whether paid, free, or preview.]

   [*Alternative*]

   [A royalty in the amount of _____% of the gross weekly box office receipts. Gross weekly box office receipts will consist of all moneys due from ticket sales from all sources whatsoever, less sales commissions and taxes. Said royalties will be due and payable on each Wednesday for the previous performance week and will be accompanied by an itemized box office statement, certified by both the treasurer and the Licensee.]

4. The Owner will have the right to inspect all books of the Licensee for the production during regular business hours.

5. No recordings by film, audio, video, or any other technologies, whether known at this time or hereinafter discovered, will be made of the Play (including recordings "for the archives") wherein the Composition is used.

6. The Owner represents that it owns and controls the rights to the Composition and therefore has full power and authority to enter into this agreement and grant said license hereunder. The Owner will hold the Licensee harmless and indemnify him against any claims that this agreement and the license granted thereunder will infringe upon the rights of any third parties.

7. This license is for utilization of the music and lyrics of the Composition only in the manner stated in paragraph 1 above. The music and lyrics of the Composition may not be printed and distributed to patrons or published in any

publication of the play without additional license from and fees paid to the Owner and codified in a separate agreement therefore.

8. In all programs, credit must be given to the Owner and Writers of the Composition in substantially the following manner:

"_____ (title of musical composition)
Music by _____ (Composer)
Lyrics by _____ (Lyricist)
Copyright _____ by _____ (Owner).
Used under license from _____."

9. This Agreement will be governed by the laws of the State of _____. This Agreement may not be modified, except in a writing signed by both parties. This document contains the entire Agreement of the parties.

In Witness Whereof, the parties have placed their hands and seals on the day above written.

Owner:

By: _____

Licensee:

By: _____

chapter **15**   Archival Recordings

Playwrights should oppose the recording of their productions "for the archives." You will understand the reason I take this position when you read this chapter.

That being said, I know that many theater companies and playwrights will, nevertheless, totally ignore my advice and proceed to tape or film their productions anyway. Both want a record of their show. And, to be fair, recording productions can serve historical and scholarly purposes. I myself can think of a number of shows, whose productions with the original Broadway cast, I would like to have seen. In fact, the New York Public Library for the Performing Arts at the Lincoln Center maintains an onsite library of recordings of various Broadway productions.

Therefore, I am going to show you a reasonably appropriate way to do it legally.

I caution, however, that this method works only in cases of new works by unknown playwrights. Theater companies wishing to record their production of a Rodgers and Hammerstein musical or a comedy they have licensed from Samuel French will find this method totally unworkable. To record your production of a Broadway hit, you need the permission of the copyright owner—which is almost never granted. Any recordings you make otherwise, "for the archives," or for any other purpose, are unlawful. So be forewarned.

Secondly, this method works only for non-Equity theaters. Theaters operating under union agreements must enter into separate, extremely detailed contracts with Actors' Equity Association (as well as the American Federation of Musicians, the Society of Stage Directors and Choreographers, and, possibly, the Dramatists Guild), if they wish to record their productions. Equity, in particular, has special provisions in its collective bargaining agreements for archival recordings.

In addition, if the producer uses any material owned by third parties in the show—such as a snippet of a popular song—the producer must also obtain the third party's consent to include that material in the archival recordings.

Even non-Equity theaters should obtain permission from their talent. See chapter 17 for more information and a form talent contract to use.

The reason this method is more likely to work with an unknown playwright is that the unknown is easier to contact and more likely to want her own recording of her latest opus. (Trust me. The Rodgers and Hammerstein Organization neither wants nor needs a recording of your production of *South Pacific,* as proud of it as you may be.) Bear in mind, however, that you cannot record the work of the unknown playwright without her permission. She does not have to give it to you. However, if both parties want a recording, then the rest of this chapter is for you.

ARCHIVAL NEGOTIATING ESSENTIALS

1. *Purpose.* The purpose of the recording should be clearly stated. Personally I find the term "for the archives" meaningless. (Yes, yes, I know it is the shorthand theater companies use.) It is not easily definable. Just exactly what is meant by "the archives?" And what does the theater intend to do with the video? How will it be used? Will it simply be stored on a shelf somewhere and pretty much forgotten? (In the latter case, then why does the theater want a video in the first place?) Will the video be used to attract funding sources? New subscribers? And if the video is used as a marketing or fund-raising tool, how much of the play will be shown? And where will it be shown? To whom? When tapes are used in this way, ordinarily the playwright does not receive additional royalties.

One purpose playwrights should absolutely forbid—that's right, I said absolutely—is the reproduction and sale of tapes of their plays to patrons, or worse, the general public. In the first place, the playwright would be entitled to royalties for each copy sold. The amount of the royalty must be negotiated. But then the theater must establish a system to furnish the playwright with an appropriate accounting of all of the copies manufactured and sold. Even if the parties can overcome these hurdles, the playwright may be endangering her own chances of a commercial production and/or a movie sale. (Commercial producers and film companies regard such recordings as competitive to their own contemplated productions; moreover, in their contracts, they require the playwright to warrant there are no audio/visual recordings of the material extant.) And there is no theater, Equity or not, that can compete with the money Hollywood will pay for movie rights to a hot play. The purpose, therefore, should be narrow and specific.

2. *Archival location.* Does the theater maintain its own onsite archives? Or does it keep the videotapes off the premises? Some theaters lend or give their production tapes to other cultural institutions, like libraries, museums, or universities for historical, research, or study purposes. Non-Equity companies, which are usually managed by a bare bones staff that has enough to do just putting on its shows, keep very informal records of their productions. I've known cases in which the "archive" is just a dusty old shelf in the artistic director's basement. Tapes remain there until either the company disbands or the artistic director moves on. Maybe one day the artistic director finds he needs a tape to record his favorite TV show. The tapes on the archive shelf are the only ones handy, so . . . .

The playwright needs to ensure that the theater maintains some kind of formal control over its archives. Off-premises archives are often maintained very loosely. And the more remote the archives are to the theater, the less control it has. This is particularly true when the tapes are lent or donated to a third party, such as a museum, a university, or a library.

3. *Artist copies.* In addition to recording the production "for the archives," theaters often give copies of the tape to the actors, the director, and the designers. (Some companies go even further. Everyone, even the business manager, gets one. Don't deny it. I know you freely pass out the tapes.)

Of course, it is natural for the artists to want a souvenir recording of the show in which they were involved. (Amateur and community groups especially want souvenir copies.) Artists want recordings of their performances to showcase themselves to other producers. Directors and choreographers, in particular, have few other ways to display their talents. (The author, after all, has a script she can pass around. And the actors can audition for other roles.)

Although most playwrights can empathize with their fellow artists in this respect, the playwright must remember that with each tape distributed, she loses more and more control over her work. The threshold problem is this: Does the playwright want other persons, not even remotely connected with the production, to view her play? It may be argued that this is a form of networking. The producer who views the tape for the purpose of auditioning the director or choreographer may become so intrigued by the play he wants to produce it. Yes, the tape may open doors in this respect. However, in the case of first and second productions, the play may still be a work in progress. It may not be ready for viewing. In that case, the tape may blow the author's chances forever with that producer who is auditioning the director. Therefore, I would prohibit the theater from passing out tapes to the members of the company.

4. *Tape viewing.* A major issue relates to the identity of persons who may view the tape. Regardless of whether the theater maintains onsite archives or has an off-premises arrangement with another institution, the playwright should insist upon some measure of control over the viewing of the tape. At a minimum, the playwright must require that:

a. Any viewing of the tape must occur onsite. In other words, the tape does not leave the premises.

b. The archival institution must notify the playwright of the date, identity, and purpose when anyone views the tape.

c. The archive itself should also keep a written log.

d. The archival institution first seeks the playwright's permission in advance of any showings of the tape, even by individual persons.

e. The biggest restriction: the theater (and the archive, if it is a separate institution) may not receive any direct or indirect compensation or profits from the tapes or their showings. This does not mean they cannot be reimbursed for normal out-of-pocket expenses. And it does not prohibit the archive, such as a museum, from charging general admission to its facilities as a whole.

None of these are unreasonable restrictions. Form 19 is a simplified consent form that playwrights can use with theaters seeking to make archival recordings of their productions. There is no good reason a theater should refuse to sign it.

If the theater does indeed refuse, then the playwright should withhold permission. And, if the theater proceeds to record the show anyway, it is violating the author's copyright.

Form 19 Author's Limited License to Record Play

THIS AGREEMENT is made this _____ day of _____, 20___, by and between _____ ("Author"), as Author of the play entitled _____ ("Play"), and _____ ("Producer").

In consideration of the mutual promises and covenants herein made, the parties agree as follows:

1. The Author represents and warrants that [he] [she] is the sole creator and copyright owner of the Play and has the full power and authority to enter into this agreement and to grant the license rights herein to the Producer.

2. The Producer [intends to present] [is currently presenting] its production of the Play on the live speaking stage, under separate written license agreement with the Author, dated _____, which is attached hereto as Exhibit A and made a part hereof.

3. The Producer now desires to record its production of the Play by _____ [video-tape, DVD, audio, etc.] for the sole and limited purpose and use of retaining a historical record of its production and for no other purpose whatsoever.

4. The Author hereby grants a limited license to the Producer to record its production of the Play for the sole purposes and uses stated herein and no other purpose whatsoever.

5. The Producer understands and agrees that the recording and/or use of the recording of the Play for any other purpose and/or use, other than those specifically and expressly granted herein, will conclusively constitute a willful violation of the common law and/or statutory copyright of the Play owned by the Author. The Producer understands and agrees that any other recording and/or use of any recordings made thereof may interfere with and/or greatly diminish some or all of the Playwright's rights, interest, ownership, and commercial exploitation of the Play, the value and/or diminishment of which is not possible to quantify at this time. Any violation of this agreement will conclusively constitute a willful material breach of this contract, as well as a material breach of the grant of rights in the attached Exhibit A.

6. The Producer will be permitted to make only one recording of the Play as performed before a live audience of primarily paying ticket holders. For backup purposes only, the Producer may make a single copy of the aforesaid recording. The Producer will make one additional copy, which will be given to the Author, under the terms of paragraph 7 below. All of the expenses of recording and copying the recording, including any fees to performers and other production personnel, will be solely the expense of the Producer.

7. The Producer will give the Author the single additional copy, free of charge, within _____ days after the making of the recording.

8. The Producer may not distribute, offer, sell, donate, or otherwise give away at no charge, or otherwise dispose of its own recording of the Production at any time [except as described in Alternate paragraph 9 below]. Any broadcast of any recording, by audio, television, closed circuit, cable, pay per view, Internet, or any other technologies, whether now known or hereinafter discovered, is expressly and specifically prohibited. In the event the Producer no longer desires to retain its recording of the Play, it will first communicate by written notice its intentions to part with the recording and offer the same, at no charge, to the Author or [his][her] heirs, legal representatives, or assigns. In the event the Author or [his] [her] heirs, legal representative, or assigns, fails to communicate [his][her] acceptance of Producer's offer within twenty-one days of the mailing of the said notice, the Producer will destroy the recording and provide Author with a notarized affidavit of destruction.

9. [Producer will deposit its recording of the Play in an onsite archive, maintained by the Producer and/or persons under his direction and control.]
[*Alternate*]

9. [The Producer does not maintain its own onsite archive. Therefore the Author grants permission to the Producer to {deposit} {donate} its recording of the Play to the following offsite archive _____ _____, ("Depository Archive"), located at _____ _____ and to no other.]

10. The only persons who will be permitted to view and/or listen to the recording of the Play will be the following: [strike any parties whom the Author does not wish to access the tape]

(A) Present and future members of the Producer's production staff and/or company;

(B) Present and future members of the Producer's board of directors [trustees];

(C) Members of the current production of the Play;

(D) Current and/or future subscribers to the Producer's theater company;

(E) Bona fide members of the press;

(F) Current and/or future donors or potential donors [investors] and financial supporters of the producer's company;

(G) Legal and/or accountant representatives of the Producer, in connection with any bona fide legal disputes, claims, and/or causes of action arising out of the Production, and/or duly appointed officers of any court of competent jurisdiction in connection with any legal dispute, claim, and/or cause of action arising out of the Production;

(H) Bona fide researchers and scholars, for educational and study purposes only.

[At least ten days prior to the viewing by any of the aforesaid persons, the Archive must first notify the Author of the request for viewing and obtain the Author's written consent thereto. Absent the Author's consent, the viewing will be expressly and specifically forbidden.]

The archive must notify the Author in writing of the date, time, and identity (including the address) of all persons viewing the recording. In addition to said notice, the archive will maintain, for a period of ten years thereafter, a written log of the foregoing information, for inspection by the Author and/or [his] [her] representative.

Regardless of the location of the Producer's archive [depository archive], viewing may be done only on the site of the archive [depository archive]. The recording may not at any time be removed from the archival site for viewing or any other purpose.

Viewing by the public at large, whether on an individual basis, or by more than one person at a time, is expressly and specifically prohibited. Any advertisement or other materials heralding, publicizing, or promoting the availability for viewing of the recording is expressly and specifically prohibited.

No charge or admission may be made or taken for any viewing, except for a nominal fee to offset the cost of the viewing. Nothing contained herein to the contrary, the archive may charge a general admission fee for access to its facilities as a whole, which fee may be in addition to the aforesaid nominal viewing fee.

[In the event the Producer deposits its recordings with a third-party depository archive, the Producer will, prior to and as a condition of deposit, secure the third party's written acceptance and agreement to all of the terms and restrictions contained herein, including the disposition of the recording in the event either the Producer and/or the third party depository archive no longer desires to keep it, and will furnish a signed original acceptance to the Author.]

11. The Producer may not receive any direct or indirect compensation or profits from its recording of the Play, except reimbursement for reasonable out-of-pocket expenses.

12. The Producer may not, at any time, offer, sell, distribute, or give away copies of any recording of the Play, whether authorized hereunder or not, to members of the general public and/or its patrons, board members, production staff, members of the current or future productions of the Play (whether under the attached or future licenses of the Play from the Author or [his] [her] duly appointed licensor or agent).

13. The Producer may not assign this agreement to any other persons or entities (except successor entities of the theater company) without the Author's written consent.

14. This Agreement will be binding on the parties, their heirs, legal representatives, and assigns.

15. All notices required hereunder will be by certified mail, return receipt requested, and mailed to the parties at the addresses following their respective signatures below.

16. The Producer, at its own expense, will secure all releases, consents, licenses, permissions, and waivers that may be necessary and/or required, from all actors, directors, choreographers, designers, and other persons or entities in connection with its recording of the Play. This will include any third party copyright holders, whose material is included in and part of the Producer's production of the Play, which Producer desires to include in the recording of the Play. The Producer will further hold the Author harmless and indemnify [him] [her] from any claims, disputes, causes of action, judgments, attorney fees, costs and expenses, which the Author may incur or suffer as a result of the Producer's failure to obtain same.

17. The laws of the State of _____ [author's residence] will govern this agreement.

In Witness Whereof, the parties have hereunto affixed their hands and seals, this day and date.

_____ (Author)

_____ (Address)

_____

_____ (Producer)

By: _____ (Title)

_____ (Address)

_____

_____ (Third-party Depository Archive)

By: _____ (Title)

_____ (Address)

_____

part **3** **Performing Artists**

chapter **16** Actors

Alfred Hitchcock has been quoted as saying "Actors are like cattle." In the later years of his life, however, the director attempted to disown that quote. "I never said 'Actors are like cattle,'" he claimed. "I said 'Actors should be *treated* like cattle.'"

I know actors who swear that many producers have taken Hitchcock's advice literally. And I have personally witnessed many incidents that have borne out the actors' complaint. So, in the hope of making the performer's life a bit easier, I humbly offer this chapter.

EQUITY VS. NON-EQUITY PERFORMERS

Actors are classified as either professional or amateurs. Professional actors receive at least some compensation—even a token amount—for their services, while amateurs are never paid. Professionals are further classified by their status as either members of Actors' Equity Association or non-Equity.

Actors' Equity Association acts as the collective bargaining agent for over 40,000 actors and stage managers throughout the country. Currently it administers fourteen national and eighteen regional agreements. It divides itself into regions—Eastern, Central, and Western—and five offices. Its individual agreements are known as *rule books*.

Non-Equity actors are performers who do not belong to the union. While, technically speaking, this encompasses both professional and amateurs, the term, as used in the industry (and as will be used in this book) refers to performers of professional status.

It is a mistake to claim that merely because an actor is non-Equity, it somehow reflects on the performer's skills. (I know of one theater critic for a major newspaper who refuses to review non-Equity shows, because she equates them with amateur or community theater productions. Many of us have repeatedly told her that is not the case. But she refuses to accept it.

That she cannot make the distinction reflects, I think, more on her own professional qualifications than on the performers she snubs.) In fact, many non-Equity actors are extremely talented. Most aspire to union status, but, for one reason or another, have not yet met Equity's rather tough requirements to join. (Bear in mind also that today's stars were, at one time, all non-Equity performers.)

In any case, this chapter is primarily directed toward non-Equity producers and performers. (If you produce or perform under an Equity agreement, you do not need the contract form which follows, since your union has already taken care of you.)

Many non-Equity companies do not use written contracts with their performers. I believe this is a mistake. Just as in every legal relationship, a written contract provides a clear understanding of each party's rights and obligations. If legal action becomes necessary on either side, it provides documentary evidence of what the parties intended their agreement to be.

Therefore the form that follows is for the average non-Equity situation. It is, admittedly, simplistic. But non-Equity companies don't ordinarily need or have the financial resources to provide all the benefits of an Equity agreement; if they did, they would sign an Equity contract.

Remember, also, that non-Equity producers and performers have the same basic concerns and needs as their union counterparts. Usually, however, these expectations are on a smaller scale, commensurate with the particular situation in which the parties find themselves.

As with any arrangement in the theater, contracts should be negotiated in full at the outset. The parties should decide upon the terms of their relationship when the producer first offers to hire the performer.

Even a simple non-Equity agreement can cover the basic issues that both producers and performers should negotiate.

NON-EQUITY ACTOR ESSENTIALS

1. *Start date.* When does the producer expect the performer to actually begin work? The first day of rehearsals? Or does the producer expect the actor to begin work even sooner? For instance, in many summer stock theaters, besides acting, the performers are also expected to build scenery, sell tickets, house manage, etc. Some summer stock companies expect the actors to arrive early and help get the theater in shape for the coming season, well before rehearsals for the first show begin. Or the producer might want the actor available for interviews and other publicity efforts. The parties need to clarify their exact expectations.

2. *End date.* If the show is scheduled to be a limited run, the producer has already established the closing date or the date when the performer's services will terminate. Is the show to be an open end run? In that case, is the performer being hired for the run of the play? Or is the actor merely expected to perform for *x* number of weeks (or months), and then he will be replaced? (For instance, Broadway producers always hope for an open run of many years. They usually sign performers, especially stars, to one-year contracts. If the play runs longer, either the performer signs up for another hitch or the producers hire a replacement.) If the actor is being hired for the season—such as in summer stock— do her services terminate upon the last performance of the last play? Or will she be required to help close up the theater at season's end?

3. *The role.* Which part did I get? Is the contract for one specific show, with the actor playing one specific role? Even if it is one show, will the actor be required to double or understudy other roles? Actors are often selected to be part of a repertory or summer stock company. They may be hired "as cast" for an entire season, in which case they will play a number of roles in different plays.

   This issue comes up either at or prior to auditions, so actors know exactly the kind of company they hope to join. It may be difficult for the producer to specify as early as the contract negotiations which parts the actor will play, because the producer himself may not even know all of the plays he will be presenting in his season. Casting intentions may change as the season progresses and the producer gets to know his actors' abilities better. In such case, the parties can simply craft a clause that allows for such flexibility in casting. However, the producer must be careful to determine whether he wishes to *guarantee* a performer *x* number of roles or performances in a particular season.

4. *Salaries.* The most important question, right? Some theaters pay on a "per performance" basis, while others pay a regular weekly salary. Actors properly want to know whether they get paid for rehearsals or only for performances. Are salaries for rehearsals different from those for performances? Do actors get paid extra for doubling or understudying roles? Is the salary guaranteed? Or is the salary somehow tied to the show's profits? Or do the actors receive a combination of salary and percentage of the profits? How often and when is payday?

   The size of an actor's salary is, obviously, open to negotiation. Some non-Equity companies pay only token amounts—such as $10.00 per performance, with nothing for rehearsals. (This is called "gaining experience." However, the opportunity may also give the actor valuable exposure that may lead to a better paying role, an agent, or any other number of possibilities.) In non-Equity houses, however, there is often very little room for negotiation, since the money just isn't there. Many theaters pay all of their actors the same wages, making no distinction between leads, chorus, or extras. (Equity's contracts make very clear wage distinctions.)

5. *Working hours.* Closely akin to the actor's pay is the issue of weekly working hours. How many performances per week will the actor be expected to work for her salary? Are rehearsals paid on an hourly basis? What constitutes overtime? Does the actor receive extra compensation if rehearsals, performances, or other duties run into overtime? And, if so, how will the overtime be computed? Does the actor receive extra compensation if the producer schedules more than the minimum number of performances per week? Does the actor receive extra compensation for promotional activities— including performing "teaser" bits from the show for radio or television broadcast publicity, or for subscriber previews? Does the actor receive pay for benefit or free performances? Does the producer guarantee the actor at least one day off per week? Does the producer guarantee the actor "rest time" between matinee and evening performances? Does the producer guarantee the actor "rest breaks" during rehearsal days?

6. *Duties.* Under Equity contracts, an actor "acts" and that's the extent of her duties. However, non-Equity companies, which are always chronically short of

help and money (the two go together, don't they?), often require performers to take on double, triple, and even quadruple duties. A typical summer stock actor's day: rehearse one play all day, perform in another in the evening; build scenery during the night; and, if you are lucky, get in a couple of hours' sleep before the next day's rehearsal.

Dinner theaters often require actors to host and serve tables. (And in that employment situation, actors must ask if the producer has computed wages based on the tips he assumes the actor will get as a server. And if, so, what is the basis of his computations? In other words, how much total compensation—wages and tips—may the actor reasonably expect?) And don't even ask what cruise ships expect from their performers. Producers must spell out exactly any additional duties they expect their actors to undertake. And actors should ask: Are the extra duties "volunteer" or "required?" Will I be paid extra for any additional duties? Or are all the duties considered part of my job?

7. *Transportation.* Some theaters provide round trip transportation for actors to come from their residence city to the theater's locale. This may mean an actual airplane ticket or simply reimbursement. Others leave the actor on her own. Once in town, some theaters will transport actors to and from their local place of residence to the theater. In some places, local transportation isn't an issue, because the actors live on the premises.

8. *Housing.* Housing is a major issue. Many theaters do not provide local housing at all. The best they might do is give the actor a list of rental agents in the city and leave her on her own. In other cases, the theater may simply give the out-of-town actor a housing allowance. However, in some cases theaters provide housing either on their premises or nearby.

It is in these situations that both producers and actors have a number of issues to address. Is housing provided on an individual basis for each actor? Or do actors have to share? And, if they do, will they be sharing with members of the opposite sex? How many persons will be living together in the same facilities? Will they have private bedrooms and/or bathrooms? House, apartment, or a dormitory-like facility? Is the housing considered part of the actor's compensation? Is the housing free? Or does the actor have to pay rent? Are the rooms smoking or nonsmoking?

If the roommates cannot get along, are there alternate arrangements? Who will pay for utilities, like gas, heat, water, and electricity? What provisions are there for telephone service? Are local calls free? Are there laundry facilities on the premises? May the actor bring a pet? And, if Fido causes damage, how will the cost of repairs be determined? Will the other persons sharing the rooms be fellow performers? Technical staff? Is the housing within walking distance of the theater and/or rehearsal space? If not, will transportation be provided? Is the area relatively free from crime? Who will be the actor's actual landlord? The theater company? The producer? A board member? How far in advance of the start of the actor's contract may she move in? After her contract ends, how soon thereafter must she vacate? Are there restrictions on the amount and kind of personal belongings she may bring? May she entertain overnight visitors in the rooms?

9. *Worker's compensation.* Actors, especially dancers, occasionally suffer injuries in the course of their employment in a show. Most states require employers to carry some kind of worker's compensation insurance with a recognized carrier. Some large employers self-insure. Many small employers, particularly non-Equity theater companies with limited resources, go bare—that is, don't carry any kind of insurance coverage. They keep their fingers crossed that no one gets hurt. This latter approach is a mistake, both for the company and for their performers.

If a performer/employee is injured while working in a show, non-Equity company or not, the laws in most states may give her the right to collect damages from the producer, if the injuries were caused by the negligence of either the producer or another member of the company. This may include medical and hospitalization costs, as well as lost wages for any time in which she is unable to work while recovering from the injuries. Permanent injuries can sidetrack her career permanently and may result in a recovery of substantial damages against the producer. A performer has a right to know whether she will be covered by worker's compensation while in the producer's employ. And a wise producer will protect both his own assets and his actors by obtaining the appropriate coverage.

10. *Termination of contract.* Under what circumstances and for what causes may the producer terminate the actor's contract early? Poor box office? In that

case, the producer should give the actor at least one week's notice. What if the performer is not working out in the role(s) for which she was cast?

There are two schools of thought on this one. The first school holds that if the producer made a mistake in casting, he remains responsible for the actor's full contract, even if he replaces her. (This is Equity's national position.) The other school holds that the parties bear joint responsibility, and there is, perhaps, some truth to that. In that event, the parties, in a non-Equity situation, must look at the producer's budget and determine (in advance) some kind of fair settlement. And if the producer terminates the actor, he should pay her transportation home.

Another issue arises when it is the actor who wishes to leave the show early. Usually this situation arises because the performer has obtained a better opportunity—a higher paying job, a chance to make Equity, or a movie or TV role. Fairness demands that the actor give the producer sufficient notice for him to obtain a replacement. This is particularly crucial in non-Equity situations, when, very often, there are no understudies to step in and take the actor's place.

11. *Billing.* In non-Equity situations, billing is rarely any kind of an issue. Most non-Equity companies bill all of their actors the same, again making no distinction as to principals or secondary roles. This is especially true in summer stock and repertory companies. Some companies simply bill their actors in alphabetical order, which seems fairest, when no one actor has a greater reputation or following than the others.

Some theaters will follow the tier structure of the play. For instance, in *The Odd Couple*, the actors playing Oscar and Felix will receive top billing, while the Pigeon sisters will be billed together, as will the poker players. In various productions of my play *Sex Marks the Spot*, the producers simply billed the actors in order of their appearance in the show.

12. *Juvenile actors.* Performers who have not yet attained their age of majority in your state require special discussion. In the first instance, reread the contract considerations discussed previously in "General Contract Preparation Advice" for dealing with minors with whom a producer wishes to enter into contractual relations. In addition, most states (as well as the federal government) place limits on the kind of work a juvenile can do. Labor laws in most states prohibit children under a certain specified age (depending on the state) from working at all, though all states make exceptions for child performers. However, even the most liberal laws impose certain restrictions on the number of hours per day juvenile actors may work.

At a minimum, producers usually have to provide adult supervision while children are rehearsing and performing. If the production requires the juveniles to miss regular school attendance, the producer may have to provide *on set* (a motion picture term) tutoring. Either the producer, parent, or the child's agent may have to file certain working papers with the state's department of labor. A producer is well advised to ascertain exactly what his state may require before he hires all those Von Trapp children for his production of *The Sound of Music*.

Are these the only issues that actors and producers should address in their contracts? Well, Equity would say these barely scratch the surface. In fact, some Equity rule books are 170 pages or more, covering virtually every issue that has arisen over the years between actors and directors. The trouble is, in non-Equity houses, the money is not there. Many non-Equity companies are mere storefronts, seating, even at capacity, fewer than one hundred people per performance—and some not even that. Obviously, then, a much more simplified agreement is needed—and that is what follows in Form 20.

Form 20 Non-Equity Actor's Contract

THIS AGREEMENT dated this _____ day of _____, 20_____, by and between _____ ("Producer") and _____ ("Actor").

In consideration of the mutual covenants and conditions contained herein, it is hereby agreed as follows:

1. [The Producer engages the Actor to provide performing services for the role of _____ in the Producer's Production of _____ (the "Play").]
[*Alternate*]

1. [The Producer engages the Actor to provide performing services, "as cast," for the _____ {year} {season} of the _____ ("Theater Company"). The Actor will appear in _____ {number of plays} in roles as yet to be determined by the Producer in his sole judgment. Notwithstanding the foregoing, this shall not constitute a guarantee that the actor shall perform any minimum number of performances or plays. Some of these may be as principal performer, while others may be as secondary and/or chorus roles.]

2. The actor's services shall begin on _____ and terminate on _____, unless otherwise terminated by any of the other provisions contained herein.

3. [During the term hereof, the Producer shall pay the Actor a gross weekly salary of _____, for the actor's services in performance and rehearsals.]
[*Alternate*]

3. [During the term hereof, the Producer shall pay the Actor a gross weekly salary for the Actor's services, as follows:
$_____ during each week in which the Actor performs only;
$_____ during each week in which the Actor rehearses only;
$_____ during each week in which the Actor performs and rehearses.]
[*Alternate*]

3. [During the term hereof, the Producer shall pay the Actor a gross weekly salary for the Actor's services, as follows:
$_____ during each week in which the Actor performs as "Principal"
$_____ during each week in which the Actor performs as "Secondary"
$_____ during each week in which the Actor performs as "Chorus"
$_____ during each week in which the Actor understudies _____ role(s)
$_____ in addition thereto, for each performance in which the Actor performs as understudy.]

4. [During the term hereof, the Actor's duties shall consist of performance and rehearsal only.]
[*Alternate*]

4. [During the term hereof, the Actor's duties shall consist of performance, rehearsal, publicity and promotional efforts for the production, and also the following additional duties: _____
_____.] [*Here the parties should specify any additional duties the Producer may require of the Actor, such as building scenery, working box office, stage managing, serving tables in a dinner theater operation, etc.*] [For these additional duties, the Producer shall not pay the Actor any additional salary.] [For these additional duties, the Producer shall pay to the Actor the additional gross salary of _____.]

5. A normal workday shall consist of _____ hours. On any day in which the Producer schedules more than one performance—such as matinee and evening performances—the Actor shall be entitled to _____ hours rest in between performances.

6. A normal workweek shall consist of _____ days. During each seven days period the Actor shall be given _____ rest day, consisting of twenty-four hours, during which the Producer shall not require [his] [her] services.

7. The Actor shall be entitled to billing in all programs, publicity, promotion, advertising, as follows: _____. [The Actor shall receive billing whenever any other members of the company receive billing, in the same size and style of type as the others.]

8. [During the term hereof, the Producer will not maintain worker's compensation for the Actor.]

[Alternate]

8. [During the term hereof, the Producer, at his own expense, shall cover the Actor for worker's compensation, in the following amounts _____.]

9. [During the term hereof, the Producer will not provide housing for the Actor.]

[Alternate]

9. [During the term hereof, the Producer shall, in addition to the salary payable above, pay to the Actor a per diem for housing at the rate of _____ per day. The Actor shall find and provide {his} {her} own housing.]

[Alternate]

9. [During the term hereof, the Producer shall provide housing to the Actor, as follows:

_____

_____

_____

[Said housing shall be free of charge, except that the Actor shall pay for all _____ {telephone calls, utilities, etc.}.] [The cost of said housing shall be deducted from the Actor's salary at the rate of _____ per day.]

10. [The parties understand and agree that the Actor shall be traveling from _____ {his}{her} out of state residence to the Producer's premises. Therefore, in addition to all other sums hereunder, the Producer shall pay to the Actor the sum of _____ upon the signing of this agreement as round trip transportation.]

[Alternate]

10. [The parties understand and agree that the Actor shall be traveling from _____ {his} {her} out of state residence to the Producer's premises, at the Actor's own expense. The Producer shall have no responsibility for any expenses therefore.]

11. [The Actor represents and warrants that _____ {he} {she} is of legal age for the employment contemplated.]

[Alternate]

11. [The Actor has not yet reached legal age for the employment contemplated. The Actor's {agent} {parent, guardian} shall file the appropriate working papers with any federal or local authorities. {This contract shall be conditioned upon the approval of an appropriate court of competent jurisdiction; the parties will immediately take all action necessary to obtain same.}]]

12. The Producer may terminate this agreement upon one week's notice to the Actor. The Producer will provide return transportation to the Actor's city of residence as follows: _____

_____.

13. The Actor may terminate this agreement upon _____ weeks' notice to the Producer.

In Witness Whereof, the parties have hereunto affixed their hands and seals this day and date.

_____ Producer

_____ Actor

[Add the following if the Actor is a juvenile.]

[_____ Actor's Guardian]

chapter 17 Archive Recordings: Artists

In chapter 15, I discussed recording productions "for the archives," from the playwright's point of view. Now we will turn to the interests of the actors, directors, choreographers, designers, and musicians in archival recordings.

As I indicated in chapter 15, the theater company that wishes to record its productions for historical and scholarly purposes must first obtain the permission of the playwright, as well as the owners of any other copyrighted materials used in the show. However, the producer must also obtain the consent of all of the artists who are participating in the production.

Actors and musicians have a vested interest in their performances. Similarly, directors, choreographers, and designers also have the rights to control the viewing of their work. Obviously, in contracting to perform or otherwise work on a live stage show, these artists give their implied consents to being seen by the audience, as well as the press, since that is the ultimate point of the presentation in the first place. However, these consents do not also automatically include the recording of their respective contributions by videotape, audio, filming, or any other technologies.

Like the playwright, the other artists may not necessarily want their particular participation in this specific production to be preserved for posterity—or at least as long as someone somewhere keeps a copy of the tape. And, in fact, they share similar concerns with the playwright. For one thing, they may not consider the end result to be their best work or appropriately representative of their talents. Secondly, like the playwright, they would be entitled to additional compensation for any commercial exploitation of the recordings. If they are in the early stages of their careers, or still learning their craft, they may not—at some point later in their lives—want early, perhaps, unpolished work to come back and haunt them.

On the way up, artists often participate in projects they don't necessarily regard with pride, either as a way of learning their craft, gaining experience or exposure, or simply paying the bills. Many stars find early appearances, particularly in exploitation or even porno films, embarrassing when these appearances surface later when the performers are at the height of their fame. This is a particular problem if the early work contradicts their present images.

Therefore, before recording any productions, the producer must obtain the consent of his actors, director, choreographer, and designers. The various unions all have their own agreements for these purposes.

Form 21, which follows, addresses this issue for the non-Equity theater company and its artists.

ARTIST ARCHIVE RECORDING ESSENTIALS
Artists may use essentially the same checklist as provided in chapter 15, for author's archival recordings.

Form 21 Artist's Limited Consent to Record Play

THIS AGREEMENT is made this _____ day of _____, 20_____, by and between _____ ("Artist"), and _____ ("Producer").

In consideration of the mutual promises and covenants herein made, the parties agree as follows:

1. The Artist is presently [performing in] [directing] the Play entitled _____, ("Play") under the management and in the employment of the Producer.

2. The Producer now desires to record its production of the Play by _____ [videotape, DVD, audio, etc.] for the sole and limited purpose and use of retaining a historical record of its production and for no other purpose whatsoever.

3. The Artist hereby grants a limited license to the Producer to record [{his} {her} performance in] [{his}{her} direction of] of the Play, as aforesaid, for the sole purposes and uses stated herein and no other purpose whatsoever.

4. The Producer will be permitted to make only one recording of the Play as performed before a live audience of primarily paying ticket holders. For backup purposes only, the Producer may make a single copy of the aforesaid recording. The Producer will make one additional copy, which will be given to the Author. All of the expenses of recording and copying of the recording will be solely the expense of the Producer.

5. The Producer may not distribute, offer, sell, donate or otherwise give away at no charge, or otherwise dispose of its own recording of the Production [*except as described in Alternate paragraph 6 below*]. Any broadcast of any recording, by audio, television, closed circuit, cable, pay per view, Internet, or any other technologies, whether now known or hereinafter discovered, is expressly and specifically prohibited.

6. [Producer will deposit its recording of the Play in an onsite archive, maintained by the Producer and/or persons under his direction and control.]

   [*Alternate*]

6. [The Producer does not maintain its own onsite archive. Therefore the Artist grants permission to the Producer to deposit {donate} its recording of the Play to the following offsite archive _____ (the "Depository Archive"), located at _____ and to no other.]

7. The only persons who will be permitted to view and/or listen to the recording of the Play will be the following:

   (A) Present and future members of the Producer's production staff and/or company;

   (B) Present and future members of the Producer's board of directors [trustees];

   (C) Members of the current production of the Play;

   (D) Current and/or future subscribers to the Producer's theater company;

   (E) Bona fide members of the press;

   (F) Current and/or future donors or potential donors [investors] and financial supporters of the Producer's company;

   (G) Legal and/or accountant representatives of the Producer and/or the Author, in connection with any bona fide legal disputes, claims, and/or causes of action arising out of the Production, and/or duly appointed officers of any court of competent jurisdiction in connection with any legal dispute, claim, and/or cause of action arising out of the Production;

   (H) Bona fide researchers and scholars, for educational and study purposes only.

   Regardless of the location of the Producer's archive [depository archive], viewing may be done only on the site of the archive [depository archive]. The recording may not at any time be removed from the archival site for viewing or any other purpose, other than restoration or preservation.

   Viewing by the public at large, whether on an individual basis, or by more than one person at a time, is expressly and specifically prohibited. Any advertisement or other materials heralding, publicizing, or promoting the availability for viewing of the recording is expressly and specifically prohibited.

   No charge or admission may be made or taken for any viewing, except for a nominal fee to offset the cost of the viewing. Nothing contained herein to the contrary, the archive may charge a general admission fee for access to its facilities as a whole, which fee may be in addition to the aforesaid viewing fee.

[In the event the Producer deposits its recording with a third-party Depository Archive, the Producer will, as a condition of deposit, secure the Third Party's written acceptance and agreement to all of the terms and restrictions contained herein.]

8. The Producer may not receive any direct or indirect compensation or profits from its recording of the Play, except reimbursement for reasonable out-of-pocket expenses. The Artist shall not receive any compensation for any recording of the Play made under this Agreement, provided no other Artist or personnel receive compensation, except the Author.

9. The Producer may not, at any time, offer, sell, distribute, or give away copies of any recording of the Play, whether authorized hereunder or not, to members of the general public and/or its patrons, board members, production staff, members of the current or future productions of the play without negotiating payment thereof and the consent therefore of the Artist.

10. The Producer may not assign this agreement to any other persons or entities (except successor entities of the Producer's company) without the Artist's written consent.

11. This Agreement will be binding on the parties, their heirs, legal representatives, and assigns.

12. All notices required hereunder will be by certified mail, return receipt requested, and mailed to the parties at their addresses below. All notices will be effective on the date of mailing. It will be a relocating party's affirmative duty to notify the other party of any change of address within fifteen days thereof. In the event consents of any kind are required, a request for consent will be mailed by certified mail, return receipt requested, to the last known address of the party whose consent is required. If the post office returns the request as unclaimed, person or address unknown, forwarding address unknown or expired, consent will be conclusively presumed to have been given and the party seeking the consent may rely upon same.

13. The laws of the State of _____ [*Producer's residence*] will govern this agreement.

In Witness Whereof, the parties have hereunto affixed their hands and seals, this day and date.

_____ (Artist)

_____ (Address)

_____

_____ (Producer)

By: _____ (Title)

_____ (Address)

_____

_____ (Third Party Depository Archive)

By: _____ (Title)

_____ (Address)

_____

chapter **18** Nudity

Whenever a producer expects a performer to appear nude in his production, he should obtain her written consent. Actors' Equity Association specifically requires that producers sign a special "Nudity Rider" with members who are to perform nude. Even if the theater company is non-union (non-Equity) it behooves both the producer and the performer to reach a written agreement on the issue.

Performers are vulnerable to unscrupulous producers or directors who seek to exploit their bodies. (I leave it to the reader to imagine the ways.) Quite honest producers with serious artistic intentions may be vulnerable to false claims of sexual harassment, invasion of privacy, rape, or even sexual exploitation of a minor. Both sides should clearly understand the nudity the production requires, the reason it is essential to the show, and the extent to which the performer is expected and willing to undress.

UP-FRONT DISCLOSURE

For that reason, producers should disclose to performers as early in the casting process as possible that nudity is expected. I would clearly state it in any written casting notices, in audition hotlines, and in preliminary phone conversations with performers. The producer should be as specific as possible—topless or full frontal. He should explain the artistic reasons for the nudity. The actress can then decide for herself if she even wishes to audition. It is unfair to both sides to withhold this information until the actress has auditioned, or, worse, has been told she has the part.

In fact, the producer should provide the actress with a full copy of the script (not just her side) before the audition, so that she may better understand the reasons for, and the extent of, the nudity required.

NUDITY RIDER ESSENTIALS

1. *Age.* The actress should warrant she is of legal age to perform as required. In connection therewith, the producer should attach a copy of her driver's license (or other legal proof of age) to the rider. I know that in the theater no one likes to disclose one's true age. But in this case, when there are potential criminal penalties for exploiting underage persons, I believe an exception must be made.

2. *Amount of nudity.* The degree of nudity should be set forth as specifically as possible.

3. *Prohibit photographs.* The producer must prohibit—and use his best efforts to prevent—the taking of photographs or other recordings of the actress while nude, except as noted in the next paragraph.

4. *Publicity.* For publicity purposes, in connection with the production, the actress may consent to being photographed partially or fully nude. However, she should sign an additional consent, which fully discloses the use of any such photographs.

5. *Film/Videotape.* If the producer wishes to film or videotape the production, which would include the actress's appearance in the nude, the actress must sign a separate consent. Again, the uses of the film or videotape must be fully disclosed. In all cases of photographing, filming, or videotaping, Equity must also sign off on the consents, and an Equity representative must be present at the filming or videotaping. The performer also has the right to view the film or videotape before it is shown publicly.

6. *Backstage privacy.* The producer must also use his best efforts to prohibit anyone not connected with the show from the backstage area while the actress is nude.

7. *Auditions/Rehearsals.* Don't even think of auditioning or rehearsing naked performers in your apartment or at the Holiday Inn. Be professional. Auditions and rehearsals should be held in a theater or rehearsal studio.

8. *Trust.* In these matters, there must be a degree of mutual trust. Not every situation can be specifically foreseen and detailed in the contract. For example, for early rehearsals of the show it is usually not necessary to ask the performer to appear nude. Later rehearsals may necessitate nudity. In all situations, the producer and the director should be sensitive to the performer's level of comfort. All parties must behave professionally. There are enough headaches in the production of any show without deliberately looking for more.

9. *Rider.* The consent to perform nude itself may be used by itself or as a rider for the formal actor's contract, which I have described more particularly in Form 20 in chapter 16.

10. *Use consent.* Even if the parties choose to forego a formal contract (not a good idea by itself), I strongly urge producers and performers to at least execute the consent to perform nude. This will avoid potentially explosive misunderstandings about a sensitive subject.

11. *Describe nudity.* In paragraph 1, in the blank lines of the form, the parties should set forth the amount and kind of nudity that will be required and which the performer is willing to do. Some examples might be: "The actress will perform topless in Scenes 1, 5, and 7," or "The actress will perform full frontally nude whenever the script and/or the director requires."

12. *Works in progress.* If the script is a world premiere, second production, or otherwise a work in progress, the parties should acknowledge that changes may occur in the script, while the production is running, and, more or less, nudity may be required. If the project is not a work in progress or changes are not contemplated, paragraph 4 may be stricken.

Form 22 Consent to Perform Nude

THIS AGREEMENT, entered into this _____ day of _____, 20_____, by and between _____ ("Producer") and _____ ("Performer"), in connection with Performer's appearance in the role of _____ in the production entitled _____ ("Play").

For good and valuable mutual considerations, the receipt of which the parties hereby acknowledge, it is agreed by and between the aforesaid Producer and Performer, as follows:

1. It is essential to the artistic concept, vision, and requirements of said Play that the Performer, in conjunction with [his] [her] role as _____ therein, will appear nude in, specifically as follows:
   _____
   _____.

2. Performer hereby consents to appear at all performances of the Play, nude, as set forth in paragraph 1 above.

3. Producer has, prior to entering into this agreement, furnished to Performer a full copy of the script (as it exists at the present time), and Performer has read same to [his] [her] satisfaction and understanding of the nudity required and reasons therefore.

4. The script for this production is a work in progress, and the parties understand that the author may make changes in the script during the contemplated production, in which the Performer is appearing. Said changes may necessitate more, or less, nudity, the extent of which is unknown at this time. Performer hereby consents to appear nude as required by said changes.

5. Producer will prohibit—and use his best efforts to prevent—the photographing, filming, video recording of the Performer, while [he] [she] is nude, unless otherwise agreed to, in a separate writing, signed by the parties.

6. Producer will prohibit—and otherwise use his best efforts to prevent—persons not directly involved with the production from entering the backstage area at all times when the Performer may be partially or fully nude either on stage or in the backstage area.

7. As deemed necessary by the director, Performer will appear nude in the rehearsals of the specific scenes in which [he] [she] will appear nude during actual performances of the production.

8. The Performer hereby represents and warrants that [he] [she] is of legal age to appear nude as required and to enter into this agreement.

In Witness Whereof, the parties have this day and date affixed their hands and seals thereto.

_____ (Theater Company)

By: _____

_____ Performer

chapter 19 — Stage Combat and Stunts

Think of the rape scene in *Extremities*, the fight between Curly and Jud in *Oklahoma!*, or the duel in *Hamlet*. Sword fights, hand-to-hand combat, and other feats of physical derring-do have been staples of theater since ancient times. A well-executed fight scene on the live stage can especially thrill an audience, which knows that unlike the movies there is no camera or computer trickery involved. The actors—even the stars—are really going at it.

However, on the live stage, fight scenes present special challenges for both the actors and the producer. Because the scenes must be replicated at each performance, and the actors do not have special camera angles and stunt doubles to help them fake it, the risk of actual injury is great. No one, especially the actors involved, wants anyone to get hurt. And even the most mercenary producer realizes that an injury occurring to a lead actor can shut down a show.

Unfortunately, some non-Equity producers rely upon the director to stage an effective fight. And, in many cases, even the best directors are not qualified for the task.

I can't emphasize this next point too strongly. Whenever a script calls for sword fights, the use of weapons, stunts, or fight scenes of any kind, the producer must call in a specialist. Some producers skimp on this point for budgetary reasons. And some directors, unwilling to admit they can't cut it, refuse to get help. Big mistake. It is as essential to stage a fight properly as it is to stage a musical number properly. After all, if dancing is part of your show, you would call in a dance choreographer. If fighting or stunts are part of your show, then you spend the money and hire a fight choreographer.

Professional fight directors are as easy to find as dance choreographers. And a good one can contribute immensely to your production. He (or she) will properly train your actors in the essentials and choreograph your fight to be as exciting as a full-blown dance number. Most importantly, the specialist will put the safety of your actors first.

> **True story:** I once produced a show in which the lead character rapes his girlfriend. As a plot point, obviously, it was a major turning point in their relationship. But the playwright called for a very graphic scene of great violence. I called in a specialist who choreographed the rape to be so realistic that, performance after performance, the audience never failed to gasp. Which was, of course, exactly the reaction we wanted. In fact, the local reviewers singled out the rape scene as the highlight of the show. Now the actress could easily have gotten hurt. But she told me she never even got so much as a stray bruise during the entire run. That's what a professional can do for you! Incidentally, the fight director I hired has since gone on to become one of the top fight specialists in Hollywood.

And, make no mistake, the safety of the actors should be the first concern of both the producer and the director.

Now this paragraph is addressed to all you actors. Folks, do I even have to tell you that, as much as you may crave that job, you have to think of your safety first? Is any role worth putting yourself into unnecessary danger? Can you really afford to be laid up for maybe months? I thought you'd say that.

So I herewith propose a "Stage Combat Rider" which you actors should insist—did you hear me? I said *insist*—your producer give you, regardless of whatever other contract terms he is offering. This contract is for your protection.

And, producers, it protects you also, especially in the non-Equity realm. You don't want your actors getting hurt. You don't want the insurance headaches or the possible lawsuits. And, as I mentioned earlier, you don't want the loss of having to shut down your show because your Hamlet is in the hospital. (And, come on, we all know you producers have consciences. Admit it. There now. Don't you feel better?)

So, the next form in this little opus is a simple rider you can add to your actor's contracts. Or, if you aren't using a contract (bad move that, anyway), you can use it as a stand-alone document whenever you present— or perform in—a show that requires stunts, fights, or the use of weapons.

(And, by the way, producers: If you are presenting such a script, it is only fair to disclose any such physical requirements in your casting notices, just as you would disclose nudity. I'd recommend disclosure even if you are presenting *Hamlet* or another work in which the need for combat is well known.)

WHAT THE RIDER DOES

Here's what this form does for both the producer and the actor.

It clearly sets forth the requirement of a fight (or similar physical activity) in the performance. It gives the actor the choice of participating or not, though like nudity, an actor who doesn't want to perform combat will not get the role. Nevertheless, at the very minimum, it particularizes the demands that will be made upon the actor. This disclosure protects the producer from any claim that "I didn't know what I was getting into." At the same time it allows the actor to make a fully informed decision whether to undertake the part.

The producer does not act as a guarantor, however, that the actor will not get hurt. Stunt work, by its nature, carries with it certain hazards that even the most careful planning and preparation cannot eliminate entirely. Hollywood stunts are directed and performed by the best stunt players in the world. Film producers spend a lot of money to minimize risks. Nevertheless, injuries do occur. Because of the limitations of the stage, stunt work is often less dangerous— you can't create a car chase on the stage—yet performers can, and do, get injured. It is unreasonable to ask the producer to completely guarantee no one will be hurt.

By the same token, you will notice I have deliberately omitted the usual Hold Harmless and Indemnity clause. While the actor is assuming certain risks, holding the Producer completely harmless for her injuries is a lot more than a court would allow.

Most of all, however, the form contract obligates the producer to engage a professional fight specialist. This obligation assures the actor that all will be done to protect his safety. And the obligation—which, yes, legally speaking, imposes a duty on the producer— shows that the producer consciously took all steps possible to minimize the danger to his performers. Psychologically, it makes the actor feel the producer really cares about him.

And, Producers, you do, don't you?

STAGE COMBAT RIDER ESSENTIALS

1. *Specific descriptions.* Describe as specifically as possible the kind of stage combat or stunts the Producer expects the Actor to perform—"duel with swords," "fist fight," etc.
2. *Foreseeable risks.* Acknowledge that the producer has disclosed the full nature, seriousness, and foreseeable risks of harm to the actor, through providing the script and consultations with the director. Actor acknowledges that the stunts are necessary to effectively present the play.
3. *Performer acknowledgment.* The actor acknowledges the risk of harm, as well as the possibility that there may be unforeseeable hazards arising out of the stunt work or combat.
4. *Fight choreographer.* The producer agrees to retain a fight choreographer or stunt director to minimize foreseeable risks to the actor.
5. *Insurance.* Nevertheless, the producer will maintain, at his own expense, the appropriate insurance coverage to protect the actor.
6. *No guarantees.* Despite all possible precautions, the producer cannot guarantee that the actor will not be harmed.
7. *Performer agreement.* The actor agrees to participate in the stunt work or combat.

Form 23 Consent to Stage Combat

THIS AGREEMENT made this _____ day of _____, 20_____, by and between _____ ("Producer") and _____ ("Actor") for the Actor's performance in the role of _____ on the live speaking stage in the Producer's presentation of the Play entitled _____, ("Play") for the term beginning _____ and ending _____.

In consideration of the mutual covenants and promises herein given, the parties hereby agree as follows:

1. Producer hereby requires Actor as part of [his] [her] performance in the Play to perform physical stunts approximately as follows: _____.
2. The Actor, prior to accepting the aforesaid role, acknowledges that [he] [she] has been given the opportunity by the Producer to read the script, in the form in which it presently exists, for, among other purposes, disclosure of the aforesaid physical stunts which the Producer requires of the Actor. The Actor also acknowledges that [he] [she] has consulted with, or been given the opportunity, to consult with both the Producer and the Director as to the nature, seriousness, and necessity of the aforesaid physical stunts. The Actor agrees and understands that the same are necessary and appropriate to an effective presentation of the Play and the Actor's performance therein.
3. The Actor acknowledges that the aforesaid physical stunts carry with them the hazard of physical injury to the Actor's person, the extent and nature of which cannot fully be foreseen at this time, regardless of the care and precautions taken to ensure Actor's safety.
4. The Producer, at his own expense, will engage a professional stunt director to arrange and choreograph the physical stunts required; and to train the Actor, all other performers, and all production personnel who are involved in carrying out the stunts, in the appropriate safety precautions, to minimize the risk of foreseeable injury to the Actor.
5. The Producer will maintain the appropriate public liability and/or worker's compensation insurance on behalf of and for the benefit of the Actor.
6. While the Producer and persons under his direction and control will maintain due care to minimize any risks of foreseeable injury to the Actor, nevertheless, the Producer does not guarantee that the Actor will not suffer injury, as a result of participating in the physical stunts.
7. Therefore, the Actor assumes the risk of [his] [her] participation in the physical stunts and hereby consents to engage in same in all presentations of the Play in which [he] [she] performs.

In Witness Whereof, the parties have hereunto set their hands and seals, this date and date.

_____ (Actor)

_____ (Producer)

part **4** **Directors and Choreographers**

chapter **20** Directors and Choreographers

The kind of contract the producer will offer his director depends upon the level of production he is presenting. Many directors and choreographers belong to the Society of Stage Directors and Choreographers.

To simplify our discussion here, we will simply refer to both directors and choreographers under the collective name of "directors," except, of course, when particular contractual terms apply only to one. Many directors are also choreographers—Rob Marshall, Tommy Tune, Susan Stroman—and wear both hats in the same production. In such cases, of course, they receive separate fees and royalties for each artistic duty they undertake.

SOCIETY OF STAGE DIRECTORS AND CHOREOGRAPHERS

The Society of Stage Directors and Choreographers (SSDC) serves as the collective bargaining agent for many professional directors and choreographers throughout the United States and abroad. Prior to its incorporation in 1959, directors and choreographers had no unified voice in negotiating with producers. Essentially they were on their own. They could only hope to strike the best deal they could. Even "name" directors and choreographers had a rough go of it. Both Joshua Logan and Agnes DeMille, for instance, sued Rodgers and Hammerstein on separate occasions to establish certain payments and credits they believed were owed them. In 1962, Bob Fosse established precedent by signing the first SSDC contract to direct and choreograph the original production of the Neil Simon/Cy Coleman/Carolyn Leigh musical *Little Me* for producers Feuer and Martin.

Today the SSDC negotiates and administers collective bargaining agreements in these areas:

- Broadway and national tours
- Off Broadway
- Off-off Broadway (ANTC—Association of Non-Profit Theatre Companies, New York City)
- League of Resident Theatres (LORT)
- Council of Resident Stock Theatres (CORST)
- Council of Stock Theatres (COST)
- American Dinner Theatre Institute (ADTI)
- Outdoor Musical Stock (OMS)
- Non-Equity Tours (Troika)
- Media Choreographers (MCC)
- Non-for-profit Musical Theater (NPMT)

It's quite a long list, but, truthfully, it doesn't cover every theater. Except for the Troika tours, at present the SSDC does not cover non-Equity companies, which, in fact, are more numerous throughout the country than all of the above producers combined.

And it is the non-Equity companies with which we will concern ourselves here. Non-Equity directors and choreographers have much the same concerns as their higher-level colleagues. But they remain at the mercy of the producer.

In truth, of course, non-Equity producers have fewer resources with which to stage their productions and to compensate all of their artists. Since I have produced non-Equity theater, I have first hand knowledge of the issues both producers and directors face. Accordingly, I have crafted Forms 24 and 25, in an effort to address the concerns of both.

Before we plunge into the essential director-choreographer contract terms, however, we must address the single issue that, right now, more than any other, divides directors, choreographers, playwrights, and producers.

Are you ready to enter a hornet's nest?

Okay, here we go.

DIRECTORS' ARTISTIC RIGHTS

Traditionally, playwrights created and owned the copyright to the piece. Directors brought it to life in the physical sense, with the help of the actors, designers, musicians, etc. The producer paid the director for his services, often in the combination of the basic fee and a royalty, based on the gross percentage box office, for each company of the play under the producer's control and management.

Similarly, choreographers created the dance numbers, in consideration of a fee and a royalty. In recent years, the law has recognized that choreographers have the right to copyright their dances. Thus, if you wish to present *Fiddler on the Roof* with the original Jerome Robbins choreography, you must obtain a license from the Robbins estate.

Traditionally, also, as part of the job of bringing a new play to life, directors helped the playwright shape and structure the piece by providing advice and offering suggestions as to the workability of every part of the script. This guidance was simply taken for granted. (For instance, Mike Nichols spent eight months helping Neil Simon shape the original script for *The Odd Couple*.)

However, in recent years, some directors have decided that Tradition isn't enough. Some directors are demanding greater participation in the project. They want either a portion of the author's subsidiary rights income; or the right of first refusal to direct the work in future productions; or the *absolute* right to direct future productions, particularly as the play moves up to additional higher levels. Some directors want all three.

Of course, this position has put them on a collision course with playwrights. Most playwrights oppose these demands.

The Dramatists Guild, which has come out very strongly against the director's requirements, takes the position that one is an *author* only if one can meet all three of the tests the Guild itself uses to define author in its Approved Production Contracts for Dramas and Musicals. These tests are:

1. The person must be involved in the initial stages of the collaborative process. At that point there is merely the germ of an idea, a word processor, and a ream of blank paper. (In fact, this is the way the Copyright law defines a *collaborator*.)
2. The person deserves the billing credit as an author. She is a person who substantially creates the work. Advice and guidance are not enough.
3. The person contributes material that will be an integral part of the script in all future productions. In other words, you can't present the play if you remove the particular person's contribution.

Under these tests, not even Broadway name directors qualify. (Hey, Mr. Producer! Don't stop reading at this point. Trust me. This whole section applies to you, as well as to your playwright.)

THE WRITER'S POSITION

Okay, let's look at the director's function. He is supposed to bring the script from the printed page to the physical stage. Even scripts by the best and most experienced playwrights often contain passages that are unworkable. Sometimes, these scenes are not obvious to anyone until the show gets into the rehearsal phase or actually performs before an audience. It has always been part of the director's basic job function to point out these problems to the playwright. (I know one playwright who takes the position that it is the director's job to solve the problem as well, since the director is the one who must find the way to physicalize the play. And if the director can't solve the problem, he is not doing his job.)

Many playwrights oppose giving the director the right to direct future productions because, quite honestly, he may not turn out to be the right director for the play. Or he may not be all that good. Or, as the work progresses, he may not totally share the playwright's vision. There is often no way to know until late in the production process. (On Broadway, even name directors get replaced once in a while.)

And, okay, suppose you do give the director the right to direct future productions. And, then, in the process of creating the original production, you find you must replace him. Does he still retain rights to the future productions or participation in the author's subsidiary rights income? Or, upon his dismissal, does he relinquish those rights? (Under the SSDC contract, a director who is dismissed for any reason other than breach of contract is still entitled to full payment.) And, if the first director retains any rights, is this fair to his replacement? What if both the original director and his replacement contribute "guidance" to the author? Are they both entitled to the same rights?

And playwrights—myself included—often prefer to work with several different directors as the script progresses through readings, workshops, and productions. We want the benefit of several different viewpoints.

There are pragmatic reasons for not attaching a particular director to a script. If a commercial producer wants to present the play, he may want a different director. Perhaps the first director is not up to the standards required by the higher level of production. Or the producer wants a "name" director. (That is not an unreasonable position for a producer to take.) If the playwright has granted the director first refusal rights—or worse, absolute rights—to direct future productions, then either the playwright or the producer must buy out the director—not a pleasant thought for either of them.

Many playwrights refuse to give refusal rights.

And here is a real author's nightmare. Prior to going into rehearsals, the director says nothing about wanting subsidiary rights participation, rights of first refusal, or absolute rights to direct future productions. But late in the process the director confronts the playwright with his demands. Either the playwright gives the director what he wants or the director walks off the show. Trust me. This scenario is not farfetched. I have seen it happen.

Personally, I believe this conduct is morally and professionally reprehensible. It is extortion, plain and simple. I believe the author should take a stand and simply refuse. If the director walks, he does himself much more harm than the author. He puts himself in breach of contract and damages his reputation. If that is the director's position, I believe it is the best interest of the playwright, the producer, and the production, to let him walk. Period.

THE DIRECTOR'S POSITION

Now that I have outlined the author/producer's reasons for opposing the director on these issues, fairness demands I give equal time to the directors.

Directors argue that often their visual contribution to a first or second production launches the play on its way to success. In addition, the director's advice and guidance help the author create a workable script that can have a long and profitable life.

Some directors introduce the play to theaters with which they are working, therefore acting as de facto agents. Occasionally, a director comes along very early in the progress of the script and spends substantial time helping the author nurture it.

A few directors claim they even rewrite portions of the script themselves.

I leave it to the reader to decide whether, in her particular case, the director is entitled to anything beside the basic fee and possibly a percentage of the box office of the production he directs. However, I will offer my responses to the director's arguments.

In most cases, the director's visual contribution to the piece, even in a dazzling production, does not entitle the director to anything more than the basic fee and his royalty of the box office of that production. A dazzling production may call attention to the play, but it will call equal attention to the director. (And if, because of that production, the director receives a career-making opportunity to direct another play or a movie, is the playwright then entitled to a part of the director's earnings for life? After all, without the author's play, the director would not have had the material with which to dazzle the industry.) And if the director is only directing a staged reading or workshop, there is little visual contribution to make.

And when the director brings a play to a theater, he is really saying to the theater: "Please hire me. I'd like to do this play, but if you have something else for me to do, that's just as well." Directors want a job, folks, not necessarily a production for someone else's play.

I advise producers and playwrights at non-Equity theaters to consider these issues carefully, because they are likely to come up. You need to be prepared with your response, so no one can put a gun to your head.

Form 24 and 25 do not give the director and choreographer any subsidiary rights participation. They do offer guarantees of future employment in brackets, which may be retained or stricken as the parties choose. They also give the director and choreographer rights to copyright their work, provided their copyrights do not interfere with the author's copyright of her play. Remember, however, that these clauses are negotiable; I include them for those parties who wish to use them, while other readers may simply strike them from the forms. (A further warning: by its very nature, choreography is easier to separate from the author's work than direction and easier to copyright. It is often difficult to separate the work of the director from the author's work. I advise readers to consider these problems very carefully before they retain or strike these clauses in the director's contract.)

Remember also that, as I indicated above, if a single person directs and choreographs the show, she is entitled to a separate contract for each function.

DIRECTOR AND CHOREOGRAPHER ESSENTIALS

(Unless otherwise noted, references to "director" also apply to "choreographer.")

1. *Services*. Director provides normal services in connection with the show.
2. *Fees*. Director and choreographer fees are negotiable. At the upper levels, directors and choreographers are entitled both to a basic fee and a royalty based on the gross weekly box office take. When a director also choreographs the show, he receives a separate fee and a separate royalty for each function. At the lower levels, the budget does not always allow for both fees and royalties. A director may have to take a lower fee and no royalties. Or the producer cannot guarantee a fee; he may compensate the director only with a royalty off the box office take, thereby requiring the director to take on part of the risk. A director-choreographer may be paid only one fee for doing both jobs.

   In some respects, this may not seem fair. On the other hand, entry and mid-level directors need opportunities to practice their craft and showcase their work, so a trade-off may be the only satisfactory solution. The producer will pay the advance fee to the director in two installments. The first installment is due before the director starts work, while the second occurs no later than the official press opening of the show. This advance is nonrefundable.
3. *House Seats*. The director has the right to purchase house seats, the number of which is negotiable between the parties.
4. *Transportation/Housing*. If the producer requires the director to render services outside of the director's city of residence, the producer will pay his reasonable transportation and housing costs.
5. *Billing*. A director is always entitled to billing in all programs, advertising, houseboards, and flyers. The director is entitled to a separate credit line, which he does not share with anyone else. The size and type are negotiable. Some directors may negotiate a box around their name, signifying their importance. A major director may also negotiate billing on a separate line on the marquee. In rare instances (mostly in the Broadway theater) a star director may even get his name above the title, although this is more often true in Hollywood than in the live theater.
6. *Length of employment*. The Producer guarantees the director employment for a minimum and maximum number of weeks. The director will be required to attend auditions and casting sessions. (If the company is repertory or stock, it will simply cast out of its available pool of actors.) The amount of time involved depends upon the level of production and the production schedule. (The SSDC has specific requirements for employment weeks, depending upon the contract used.) A small production may only be able to afford one or two weeks work.
7. *Post-opening supervision*. In the Broadway theater the director is required to visit the show at least once every eight weeks (unless other work projects interfere), to supervise the quality of the production. In the case of long runs, in particular, maintaining the quality of the show is often a very difficult task. Actors may become bored with their roles and either slack off or ad lib new things. Although it is the stage manager's job to keep the show running as the director intended on opening night, often even the best stage manager encounters resistance. Actors, especially stars, are notorious for refusing to obey the stage manager. Sometimes, the director must appear to enforce discipline. Therefore, directors must oversee their productions, calling *brush-up* rehearsals when necessary.

   Even at lower levels of production, actors performing in a long run tend to get stale, and the director and choreographer may have to "crack the whip." Regardless of the level of production, directors and choreographers should visit their shows at least once each month and call brush-up rehearsals, as appropriate, to maintain quality. Directors and choreographers do not get paid for brush-up rehearsals or post-opening supervision. However, if they fail to see the show periodically or hold brush-up rehearsals, their royalties may be reduced.
8. *Additional companies*. If the producer intends to present additional companies of the play under his management, he must give directors and choreographers notice of his intentions. The director and choreographer have ten days to decide whether to direct the additional company. Each is entitled to additional fees and royalties for each additional company he directs or choreographs. If the director or choreographer declines the employment, he is, nevertheless, still entitled to a royalty based on the gross weekly box office for that company, albeit at a reduced rate.

   At lower levels of production, this rarely comes up. Non-Equity theater companies have all they can do to manage one production. Moreover, few non-Equity productions attract such a level of interest as to warrant more than one company. If the show achieves that level of success, it is likely a commercial producer will take it over. Because the original director has shepherded the show to success, the commercial producer may decide to employ him for his own production; on the other hand, success or not, the commercial producer may prefer a name director. No one can predict the outcome.

9. *Playwright ownership*. As I have discussed above, the playwright owns any suggestions or advice the director contributes, since this guidance is part of the director's normal duties. Both the director and choreographer may copyright their respective work, as long as their copyrights do not interfere with the playwright's own copyright.

10. *No assignment*. The producer hires the director because of his unique talents, abilities, and—in some cases—box office name. Therefore the director cannot assign his contract to another director.

11. *Termination*. If the producer terminates the director for any reason, except breach of contract, he must still pay him in full.

12. *Recordings*. The producer may not record the show by any means without the director's consent.

13. *Choreographer assistants*. Choreographers pick their own dance captains and assistants. In the commercial theater they also pick the rehearsal pianist subject to the approval of the composer, providing the producer does not maintain a staff pianist for the season. At the lower levels, the pianist may be a member of the company or on regular salary to the producer, and therefore the choice is not the choreographer's.

Form 24 Director Agreement

THIS AGREEMENT made this _____ day of _____, 20___, by and between _____ ("Producer") and _____ ("Director").

In consideration of the mutual covenants, promises, terms, and conditions herein granted, the parties agree as follows:

1. The Producer engages the Director to direct and the Director agrees to direct the Producer's production of the play presently entitled _____ by _____ ("Play").

2. The Play will begin paid public performances on _____.

3. The Director will provide the normal services associated with the direction of a play of the nature and kind as the Play, including supervising and conducting auditions; casting actors for the various roles contained in the Play (in consultation with the Playwright and the Producer); participating in such production meetings as may be necessary and appropriate; consulting with the author; consulting with and supervising designers, stage crew, and the other personnel as will be necessary for the effective presentation of the Play; conducting rehearsals; advising the actors in their performances; and promoting and publicizing the Play through interviews and other appropriate interactions with members of the press. If the Producer will require any other duties or services of the Director, the parties agree to negotiate compensation for same in good faith.

4. The Producer will compensate the Director for the aforesaid services as follows: a nonrefundable fee of _____ dollars ($_____), which will be payable as follows:

   _____% no later than _____ days prior to the beginning of principal services by the Director;

   _____% not later than the official press opening of the Play.

   [In addition to the foregoing fee, the Producer will also pay the Director a royalty in the amount of _____% of the gross weekly box office sales of each company of the Play under the Producer's management. The Producer will first deduct all fees hitherto paid to the Director before the payment of percentage royalties. The gross weekly box office sales are defined as ticket sales from all sources, including box office, mail order, ticket brokers, group sales, internet sales, subscriptions, telephone sales, Ticketmaster, and discount ticket services.]

5. The Director will be entitled to purchase _____ pairs of house seats at the full box office price for each performance of each company under the Producer's management. The seats will be in the section of the theater commonly and traditionally reserved for house seats in that particular theater. The seats will be held in reserve from general sale for the Director's purchase until _____ P.M. for each matinee performance and until _____ P.M. for each evening performance. Any seats not purchased by that time will be offered for sale to the general public at the full box office price. Director will not resell the house seats at a premium over the box office price. Director further agrees to comply with all laws, rules, and regulations governing the use and disposition of house seats promulgated by the appropriate governmental authorities having jurisdiction thereof.

6. The Producer will pay the reasonable cost of transportation for the Director from [his] [her] city of residence to all cities in which the Producer requires the Director to render services.

7. The Producer will pay the reasonable costs of housing accommodations for the Director in all localities in which the Producer requires the Director to render services, except in the Director's city of residence. All housing accommodations will be at least the equivalent of those enjoyed by the Producer.

8. The Producer will employ the Director for a minimum of _____ weeks beginning on _____ and terminating on _____.

9. The Director will receive billing credits in all programs, flyers, publishing, advertising, and promotional materials, [including theater marquees] under the Producer's control, in which the Playwright's name also appears. Said billing will be on a separate line in which no other credits appear and will be in a size and style of typeface as follows: _____.

10. (A) After the press opening of the Play, the Director will be responsible for supervising and maintaining the quality of the production. At least once in every _____ weeks' period, the Director will attend one public performance of

the Play. When appropriate, the Director will conduct brush-up rehearsals with the actors and other personnel, in order to sustain the quality of the production. In the event the Director fails or refuses to comply with the foregoing, [his] [her] weekly royalty will be reduced by one-half until [he] [she] completes the work.

(B) Provided the Producer consents, the Director may be excused from the foregoing post-opening supervision whenever [his] [her] other professional obligations prevent [him] [her] from doing so. However, the Producer's consent under this paragraph on an occasional basis will not operate as a waiver of the Director's responsibilities as set forth in paragraph 10(A) above.

11. The Director will have the option to direct all future companies of the Play, under the Producer's management within the United States. The Producer will give the Director written notice of his intent to present each additional company. The Director will have ten days after receipt of the notice to notify Producer of [his] [her] intent to exercise this option. In the event the Director fails to notify Producer within ten days of [his] [her] affirmative intent to direct said future company, the Director's option (as to that company only) will lapse, and the Producer may engage another director of his choosing. In such case, the Director's royalty for said company will be reduced to _____% of that company's gross weekly box office sales for a nonmusical or _____% of the gross weekly box office sales for a musical. For each company of the Play which the Director elects to direct, [his] [her] royalty will be _____% of the gross weekly box office sales for that company in the case of a nonmusical; or _____% of the gross weekly box office sales for a musical.

12. (A) As part of the Director's normal services in connection with the production of the Play, [he] [she] may offer suggestions, guidance, advice, bits of business, lines of dialogue, or other material to the Playwright. The Playwright will be free to accept or reject any such contributions. The Director understands and agrees that, as part of the Producer's contract with the Playwright, all such material contributed or offered by the Director to the Playwright will become the Playwright's sole property, copyrightable by [him] [her], and, at the Playwright's sole discretion, used in all future productions and publications of the Play, without compensation, claim, right, title, credit, ownership, or copyright by and to the Director. However, if the Playwright and the Director agree that the Director will contribute rewriting services to the Play, the Director will negotiate in good faith a separate contract for the same with the Playwright.

(B) Notwithstanding the foregoing, the Producer agrees and understands that the direction of the Play will remain the sole property of the Director and may not be used or reproduced in any additional companies or productions of the show without the Director's consent. The Director may submit said Direction to the U.S. Copyright Office for copyright thereto in the Director's sole name, provided same does not interfere with the copyright of the Play.

13. This is a personal services contract and may be not be assigned by the Director without the Producer's written consent.

14. In the event the Producer terminates the Director for any reason, other than breach of contract, the Producer will pay the Director in full under this contract.

15. No recordings, whether by audio, video, film, or other means, whether now known or hereinafter devised, will be made of the Play without the Director's consent. Notwithstanding the foregoing, however, the Director hereby consents to the recording and/or performance of excerpts from the Play not to exceed 300 seconds for radio and/or television broadcast, for the purpose of publicizing and promoting the Production, provided the Producer receives no compensation or profits therefrom, except the nominal costs of production.

16. The laws of the State of _____ will govern this Agreement.

17. This Agreement is binding on the parties, their heirs, successors, and assigns.

18. In the event a claim or a dispute arises out of this contract, which the parties cannot resolve in face-to-face discussions, either party may bring the matter before a member of, and under the commercial rules of, the American Arbitration Association. The arbitration will be binding on both parties. The arbitrator may require the losing party to pay the costs and reasonable attorney fees of the prevailing party. Judgment upon such arbitration award may be entered by any court of competent jurisdiction.

19. Notices required hereunder may be mailed to the parties at the addresses following their names below. Notices will be by certified mail, return receipt requested, and will be effective on the date of mailing.

In Witness Whereof, the parties have hereunto set their hands and seals this day and date above written.

_____ (Producer)

_____ (Address)

_____

_____ (Director)

_____ (Address)

_____

Form 25 Choreographer Agreement

THIS AGREEMENT made this _____ day of _____, 20___, by and between _____
("Producer") and _____ ("Choreographer").

In consideration of the mutual covenants, promises, terms, and conditions herein granted, the parties agree as follows:

1. The Producer engages the Choreographer and the Choreographer agrees to stage the musical numbers for the Producer's production of the Musical presently entitled
   _____ ("Musical) by
   _____ ("Bookwriter")
   _____ ("Composer")
   _____ ("Lyricist")
   (Collectively the "Authors")

2. The Musical will begin paid public performances on _____.

3. (A) The Choreographer will provide the normal services associated with the staging of the musical numbers of a show of the nature and kind as the Musical, including supervising and conducting auditions; casting dancers for the dancing chorus contained in the Musical (in consultation with the Authors, Director, and the Producer); participating in such production meetings as may be necessary and appropriate; consulting with the Authors and Director and Producer; consulting with and supervising designers, stage crew, and the other personnel as will be necessary for the effective presentation of the Play; conducting rehearsals; creating dance numbers as appropriate; advising the dancers in their performances; and promoting and publicizing the Musical through interviews and other appropriate interactions with members of the press. If the Producer will require any other duties or services of the Choreographer, the parties agree to negotiate compensation for same in good faith.

   (B) The Choreographer shall be entitled to select assistants and dance captains, whose compensation will be the expense of the Producer.

   (C) [The Choreographer shall be entitled to select the rehearsal pianist, in consultation with the composer and the music director, whose compensation will be the expense of the Producer.]

   [*Alternate to C*]

   (C) [The rehearsal pianist will be selected by the Producer.]

4. The Producer will compensate the Choreographer for the aforesaid services as follows: a nonrefundable fee of _____ dollars ($_____), which will be payable as follows:

   _____% no later than _____ days prior to the beginning of principal services by the Choreographer;

   _____% not later than the official press opening of the Play.

   [In addition to the foregoing fee, the Producer will also pay the Choreographer a royalty in the amount of _____% of the gross weekly box office sales of each company of the Play under the Producer's management. The Producer will first deduct all fees hitherto paid to the Choreographer before the payment of percentage royalties. The gross weekly box office sales are defined as ticket sales from all sources, including box office, mail order, ticket brokers, group sales, internet sales, subscriptions, telephone sales, Ticketmaster, and discount ticket services.]

5. The Choreographer will be entitled to purchase _____ pairs of house seats at the full box office price for each performance of each company under the Producer's management. The seats will be in the section of the theater commonly and traditionally reserved for house seats in that particular theater. The seats will be held in reserve from general sale for the Choreographer's purchase until _____ P.M. for each matinee performance and until _____ P.M. for each evening performance. Any seats not purchased by that time will be offered for sale to the general public at the full box office price. Choreographer will not resell the house seats at a premium over the box office price. Choreographer further agrees to comply with all laws, rules, and regulations governing the use and disposition of house seats promulgated by the appropriate governmental authorities having jurisdiction thereof.

6. The Producer will pay the reasonable cost of transportation for the Choreographer from [his] [her] city of residence to all cities in which the Producer requires the Choreographer to render services.

7. The Producer will pay the reasonable costs of housing accommodations for the Choreographer in all localities in which the Producer requires the Choreographer to render services, except in the Choreographer's city of residence. All housing accommodations will be at least the equivalent of those enjoyed by the Producer.

8. The Producer will employ the Choreographer for a minimum of _____ weeks beginning on _____ and terminating on _____.

9. The Choreographer will receive billing credits in all programs, flyers, publishing, advertising, and promotional materials [including theater marquees] under the Producer's control, in which the Playwright's name also appears. Said billing will be on a separate line in which no other credits appear and will be in a size and style of typeface as follows: _____.

10. (A) After the press opening of the play, the Choreographer will be responsible for supervising and maintaining the quality of the production. At least once in every _____ weeks' period, the Choreographer will attend one public performance of the Play. When appropriate, the Choreographer will conduct brush-up rehearsals with the actors and other personnel, in order to sustain the quality of the production. In the event the Choreographer fails or refuses to comply with the foregoing, [his] [her] weekly royalty will be reduced by one-half until [he] [she] completes the work. (B) Provided the Producer consents, the Choreographer may be excused from the foregoing post-opening supervision whenever [his] [her] other professional obligations prevent [him] [her] from doing so. However, the Producer's consent under this paragraph on an occasional basis will not operate as a waiver of the Choreographer's responsibilities as set forth in paragraph (A) above.

11. The Choreographer will have the option to choreograph all future companies of the Play, under the Producer's management within the United States. The Producer will give the Choreographer written notice of his intent to present each additional company. The Choreographer will have ten days after receipt of the notice to notify Producer of [his] [her] intent to exercise this option. In the event the Choreographer fails to notify Producer within ten days of [his] [her] affirmative intent to choreograph said future company, the Choreographer's option (as to that company only) will lapse, and the Producer may engage another Choreographer of his choosing. In such case, the Choreographer's royalty for said company will be reduced to _____% of the gross weekly box office sales. For each company of the Musical which the Choreographer elects to choreograph, [his] [her] royalty will be _____% of the _____% of the gross weekly box office sales.

12. As part of the Choreographer's normal services in connection with the production of the Musical [he] [she] may offer suggestions, guidance, advice, bits of business, lines of dialogue, or other material to the Authors, individually or collectively. The Authors will be free to accept or reject any such contributions. The Choreographer understands and agrees that, as part of the Producer's contract with the Authors, all such material contributed or offered by the Choreographer to the Authors will become the Authors' sole property, copyrightable by the Authors, and, at the Authors' sole discretion, used in all future productions and publications of the Musical, without compensation, claim, right, title, credit, ownership, or copyright by and to the Choreographer. However, if the Authors and the Choreographer agree that the Choreographer will contribute rewriting services to the Musical, the Choreographer will negotiate in good faith a separate contract for the same with the Authors.

13. This is a personal services contract and may be not be assigned by the Choreographer without the Producer's written consent.

14. In the event the Producer terminates the Choreographer for any reason, other than breach of contract, the Producer will pay the Choreographer in full under this contract.

15. No recordings, whether by audio, video, film, or other means, whether now known or hereinafter devised, will be made of the Play without the Choreographer's consent. Notwithstanding the foregoing, however, the Choreographer hereby consents to the recording and/or performance of excerpts from the Musical not to exceed 300 seconds for radio and/or television broadcast, for the purpose of publicizing and promoting the Production, provided the Producer receives no compensation or profits therefrom, except the nominal costs of production.

16. The laws of the State of _____ will govern this Agreement.

17. This Agreement is binding on the parties, their heirs, successors, and assigns.

18. In the event a claim or a dispute arises out of this contract, which the parties cannot resolve in face-to-face discussions, either party may bring the matter before a member of, and under the commercial rules of, the American

Arbitration Association. The arbitration will be binding on both parties. The arbitrator may require the losing party to pay the costs and reasonable attorney fees of the prevailing party. Judgment upon such arbitration award may be entered by any court of competent jurisdiction.

19. Notices required hereunder may be mailed to the parties at the addresses following their names below. Notices will be by certified mail, return receipt requested, and will be effective on the date of mailing.

In Witness Whereof, the parties have hereunto set their hands and seals this day and date above written

_____ (Producer)

_____ (Address)

_____

_____ (Choreographer)

_____ (Address)

_____

Trade publications offer a wealth of useful information to anyone in the performing arts. Frequently, this material focuses on the business of presenting live theater. The following trade publications occasionally print business or legal advice, and a subscription to them is money well spent.

American Theatre

Theatre Communications Group
520 Eighth Avenue, 24th Floor
New York, New York 10018-4156
(212) 609-5900
www.tcg.org

Backstage

770 Broadway, 4th Floor
New York, New York 10003
(800) 745-8922
www.backstage.com

The Dramatist

The Dramatists Guild Of America
1501 Broadway, Suite 701
New York, New York 10036
(212) 398-9366
www.dramaguild.com

Performink

3223 N. Sheffield Avenue
Chicago, Illinois 60657
(773) 296-6600
www.performink.com

Weekly Variety

360 Park Avenue
New York, New York 10010
(800) 323-4345
www.variety.com

appendix B   Performing Arts Attorneys

As I indicated in the preface, no book can take the place of an attorney's judgment and experience. Although the material contained both in this book and *The Stage Producer's Business and Legal Guide* will save you a lot of time and legal fees, you may still, at times, need to consult a lawyer.

Regardless of whether you are an independent producer, an officer of a theater company, or an artist, you should make sure the attorney with whom you are consulting is qualified to handle your needs. Within the legal field, there are numerous specializations. Many lawyers who are extremely capable and skilled in one area of law may not, necessarily, be able to help you. Theater law is an extremely specialized field, and you should look for counsel experienced and knowledgeable in its practices.

Here is a checklist of questions you should ask a prospective attorney before you engage her services:

SELECTION CHECKLIST

1. How much of her practice is devoted to entertainment law?
2. How much of her practice is devoted to theater law?
3. Does she represent individual artists?
4. Does she represent theater companies and/or producers?
5. Is she also an agent or personal manager?
6. What professional courses has she taken in the last three years?
7. Has she taken any professional courses in performing arts law?
8. Does she belong to any bar associations? If so, which ones?
9. Is she active in these associations?
10. Is she a member of any entertainment law committees of the bar associations? Which ones?

11. Is she on the board of any nonprofit performing arts companies? Which ones?
12. Has she ever been employed by a performing arts organization of any kind? Which one?
13. Has she ever published professional articles in the area of theater law? Which periodicals published them?
14. What else in her background qualifies her to practice theater law?
15. Can she give you at least three persons who can serve as professional recommendations for her services?
16. How often can you expect communications from her regarding your matter? An attorney rarely can give you an exact timetable, regardless of the type of case you have brought her. But she may be able to give you an estimate of the length of time it will take to complete each step.

USING YOUR ATTORNEY EFFECTIVELY

1. Prepare a written list of your questions in advance of your office appointment or telephone consultations.
2. Gather all correspondence, checks, contracts, memorandums, e-mails, and other documentation regarding any legal matter that you may possess.
3. Organize all of the materials into some kind of order.
4. Bring all documentation to your meeting with counsel.
5. If you are in doubt whether a writing pertains to your problem, bring it with you anyway. Let your attorney decide its relevance.
6. If you are served with legal summons—meaning someone is suing you—do not procrastinate. Every summons has a deadline by which you must

answer the complaint—that is, the allegations against you. If you miss the deadline, you could be responsible for the financial damages the party who is suing you is seeking, even if you are completely in the right. Call your attorney right away.

7. If you are sued for any reason, do not stroke out. Anyone can file a lawsuit, for just the minimal fees the court charges for filing. Winning the suit is another matter. Your attorney can best advise you of your chances of winning or losing.

8. Have confidence in your attorney. Do not—I repeat, *do not*—listen to your friends, colleagues, or your Great Aunt Martha, all of whom will offer you unsolicited—and usually wrong—advice. (And, whatever you do, don't compare their experiences in "similar" matters to your own. Every case is different.) Trust only in your own attorney's advice.

9. Be patient. Legal matters can drag on for a long time. Even contract negotiations take time. And lawsuits can go on for years before they are resolved.

10. Don't pepper your attorney with questions every ten minutes. This prevents her from working on your matter, as well as the other files on her desk. Trust that she is giving your problem due attention.

11. On the other hand, don't simply sit back and forget your case. If you do not hear from your attorney periodically—or within a reasonable time, depending on the matter—it is all right—and even desirable—to ask for an update.

12. Finally, obey your attorney. It doesn't do any good if you listen to her advice and then promptly go off and do things your way. In fact, that's the surest way to come out of any legal matter as the loser.

INDEX

Books from Allworth Press

Allworth Press is an imprint of Allworth Communications, Inc. Selected titles are listed below.

THE STAGE PRODUCER'S BUSINESS AND LEGAL GUIDE
by Charles Grippo (paperback, 6 × 9, 256 pages, $19.95)

THE BUSINESS OF THEATRICAL DESIGN
by James L. Moody (paperback, 6 × 9, 288 pages, $19.95)

BOOKING & TOUR MANAGEMENT FOR THE PERFORMING ARTS, THIRD EDITION
by Rena Shagan (paperback, 6 × 9, 288 pages, $19.95)

BUILDING THE SUCCESSFUL THEATER COMPANY
by Lisa Mulcahy (paperback, 6 × 9, 240 pages, $19.95)

PRODUCING YOUR OWN SHOWCASE
by Paul Harris (paperback, 6 × 9, 240 pages, $18.95)

CAREER SOLUTIONS FOR CREATIVE PEOPLE: HOW TO BALANCE ARTISTIC GOALS WITH CAREER SECURITY
by Dr. Ronda Ormont (paperback, 6 × 9, 320 pages, $19.95)

TECHNICAL THEATER FOR NONTECHNICAL PEOPLE
by Drew Campbell (paperback, 6 × 9, 256 pages, 38 b&w illus., $19.95)

CASTING DIRECTOR'S SECRECTS: INSIDE TIPS FOR SUCCESSFUL AUDITIONS
by Ginger Howard (paperback, 6 × 9, 208 pages, $16.95)

IMPROV FOR ACTORS
by Dan Diggles (paperback, 6 × 9, 224 pages, $19.95)

MASTERING SHAKESPEARE: AN ACTING CLASS IN SEVEN SCENES
by Scott Kaiser (paperback, 6 × 9, 256 pages, $19.95)

THE PERFECT STAGE CREW: THE COMPLEAT TECHNICAL GUIDE FOR HIGH SCHOOL, COLLEGE, AND COMMUNITY THEATER
by John Kaluta (paperback, 6 × 9, 256 pages, $19.95)

Please write to request our free catalog. To order by credit card, call 1-800-491-2808 or send a check or money order to Allworth Press, 10 East 23rd Street, Suite 510, New York, NY 10010. Include $5 for shipping and handling for the first book ordered and $1 for each additional book. Ten dollars plus $1 for each additional book if ordering from Canada. New York State residents must add sales tax.

To see our complete catalog on the World Wide Web, or to order online, you can find us at
www.allworth.com.